CW00808731

The Kogod Library of Judaic Stu
9

Disempowered King

Monarchy in
Classical Jewish literature

Yair Lorberbaum

מכון שלום הרטמן
SHALOM HARTMAN INSTITUTE

continuum

Published by Continuum International Publishing Group
The Tower Building, 11 York Road, London SE1 7NX
80 Maiden Lane, Suite 704, New York, NY 10038

www.continuumbooks.com

British Library Cataloguing-in-Publication Data
A catalogue record for this book is available from the British Library

ISBN: 978-1-4411-5429-3 (hardback)
ISBN: 978-1-4411-4088-3 (paperback)

Typeset by Free Range Book Design & Production
Printed and bound in Great Britain by
CPI Antony Rowe, Chippenham, Wiltshire

To my parents Zafrirah and Ya'akov

Contents

Introduction

This book deals with the understanding of the king, his stature, and his prerogatives in early rabbinic literature, and particularly in Tannaitic literature. The Talmudic approach to monarchy that I will suggest is contrasted with the different approaches to monarchy found in the Bible. An additional and complementary context to be taken into account is the royal rule with which the tannaim were familiar in their own day – namely, the Roman Empire. Our discussion will focus upon *Mishnah Sanhedrin* (Chapter 2), the halakhic midrashim, and passages in the Babylonian and Palestinian Talmud that revolve around this mishnah.

Three different approaches to the monarchy emerge from the Bible: direct theocracy, which rejects monarchy entirely as it rejects all other forms of human rule; royal theology; and limited monarchy. I shall describe these three approaches extensively in the first chapter of this book. From our analysis of *Tractate Sanhedrin* in the Mishnah and from the halakhic midrashim in *Sifrei Devarim*, it becomes clear that the tannaim adopted a specific biblical model of monarchy – namely, that of a limited monarchy – which they reworked and fashioned in their own way. The primary institution that limits the king and oversees his activities, according to this model, is the Sanhedrin, the High Court.

In the second and third chapters of this book, I shall describe the sages' understanding of monarchy as it follows from the Talmudic sources. The second chapter deals with various aspects of "the Law of the King" – that is, the royal powers and limitations. The third chapter, which is a direct continuation of that which precedes it, focuses on the relationship between the institution of kingship and the law. The main focus of discussion in both these chapters concerns those laws pertaining to the King. However, we also discuss aggadic sources that bear a close relationship to them. As the detailed discussion of the halakhic and aggadic sources will show, the other approaches toward monarchy found in the Bible – i.e. direct theocracy, and especially royal theology – are present in the background of these sources. As in both the halakhic and aggadic sayings of the tannaim, there is a discussion and debate, at times implicit and at times explicit, in these approaches. In other words, the competing understandings of the monarchy are "actors" in the Talmudic sources, at least as "significant alternatives," from which the importance of their detailed presentation in the first chapter follows.

The fourth chapter will deal with the political outlook that emerges from the tannaitic halakhah and will provide us with the contexts and reasons for the sages' choice of the approach of limited monarchy and the manner in which they formulated it. In this chapter, we shall also bring sources from the Talmudic literature, which contain or imply reasons for rejecting the other two approaches.

As mentioned, the tannaim explicitly or implicitly rejected the other two biblical models, royal theology and direct theocracy. Nevertheless, one may find echoes and remnants of these two biblical approaches in Talmudic sources: they appear in several minority opinions regarding halakhic matters, in the approach of midrash and exegesis and – in the clearest and most explicit manner – in the later aggadah. In the fifth chapter of this book I will present these sources and note the tension between them and the dominant approach toward monarchy in the tannaitic sources, particularly in their halakhic portions.

The sixth chapter will discuss the political approach of the sages – as follows from the *sugyot* (passages) concerning the monarchy – in light of their political status in the Jewish society in Palestine of their days. The underlying assumption of this discussion is that the sages were not merely passive spectators of the sociopolitical arena but rather functioned therein as active "actors," struggling for their own status. The Talmudic sources themselves seemingly testify to this. If we assume that in the Mishnah the king corresponds to the *nasi* ("prince") and his household, while the Sanhedrin represents the status of the sages, we may infer the political attitude of the sages from their discussion of the issue of monarchy and the manner in which they related to various social groups and political institutions of their time. In the course of doing so, we will attempt to trace the nature of the innate political ideal in the world of the sages, and primarily their political goal or ideals.

Unlike matters relating to the king in the Bible, which have been studied in dozens of articles and books from every possible side and aspect, the subject of the king in rabbinic literature has only been discussed in a very limited manner.[1] During the 1990s a number of books were devoted to political thought in early rabbinic literature (or Talmudic

---

1   I cannot present here a survey of the research regarding the subject of the king in the Bible. The bibliography at the end of the book, which represents only a small part of what has been published on the subject, will provide the reader with a suitable impression of both the quantity and scope of research on this subject.

literature) but, rather surprisingly, they hardly discussed the issue of the monarchy in its different aspects.[2] The uniqueness of the present study is thus not only that it discusses for the first time several aspects of the issue of monarchy in Talmudic literature that have not yet been discussed in research but primarily in the conceptual framework it proposes, within which these matters will be clarified. I do not pretend to fully encompass all aspects of this complex issue. However, the framework that I propose is likely to shed new light both upon the details and the overall picture.

2   For discussion of various aspects of the political approach in Talmudic literature, see G. M. Freeman, *The Heavenly Kingdom: Aspects of Political Thought in Talmud and Midrash* (Lanham, Md., 1986); S. Roth, *Halakhah and Politics: The Jewish Idea of the State* (New York, 1988); M. Sicker, *The Judaic State: A Study in Rabbinic Political Theory* (New York, 1988); J. Neusner, *Rabbinic Political Theory* (Chicago, Ill., 1991). See also the book by J. Berman, *A King in Israel: Rulership over the Generations in Light of the Halakhah and the Status of Knesset Laws in the World of Halakhah* (in Hebrew) (B'nei Barak, 2003). This latter rich work deals with the subject of the king throughout halakhic literature, including Talmudic literature, but is lacking in any critical historical dimension. Other works, more relevant to this study, will be discussed or cited in the footnotes in the body of the book.

Acknowledgments

It is my pleasant duty to thank my colleagues at the Shalom Hartman Institute in Jerusalem and at the Faculty of Law of Bar-Ilan University, who assisted me with comments and advice, both in conversation and in reactions to the manuscript. I wish to thank particularly Michael Walzer, Noam Zohar, Menahem Lorberbaum, Shlomo Naeh, Vered Noam, Ariel Picard, Israel Knohl, Amihai Radzyner, Haim Shapira and Adiel Schremer. Thanks to the heads of the Shalom Hartman Institute, Professor David Hartman and Dr. Donniel Hartman, for their help and support throughout the course of my work on this project. My gratitude to the Law Faculty at Bar-Ilan University, to its head, and to the academic and administrative staff, for the intellectual and material support during the course of writing this book. Thanks also to Rabbi Jonathan Chipman, who prepared the English translation of this book with both accuracy and elegance of expression. To my wife Orli and to my children – Hilla, Micha, Yotam, Yoel, and Rotem – for their warmth, love, and patience.

ONE

Three Approaches to Kingship in Israel

Ignoring for the moment what scholars refer to as "direct theocracy," we find that the only form of government recognized by the Bible is monarchy. In the Bible, we do not find oligarchy or plutocracy in the Greek sense of these terms, and certainly not democracy. Nor can possibilities of political organization other than monarchy be found, also in rabbinic literature. Nevertheless, as we shall see below, monarchy in the Bible is not a cohesive idea; as a form of government, monarchy includes various different, competing possibilities.

Examination of the different books of the Bible reveals three different approaches to monarchy or, rather, three understandings of that political system whose focus is the king. Two of these are versions of monarchic rule that elaborate or imply the status of the king and his prerogatives, while the third relates to monarchy by way of negation. The first approach is a version of royal theology, according to which the king is a (demi-)god; the second is limited monarchy, in which the king is not a god; and the third approach is that of direct theocracy, which rejects monarchy and negates the political authority of human beings, God Himself being the king.[1] In what follows, we shall survey these three biblical approaches, beginning with the third approach, which is hostile to monarchy, and thereafter present those two approaches that affirm it and that, as mentioned, also compete with one another.

1.1 Direct Theocracy: God Is the King

One approach found in the Bible negates the institution of monarchy and is in practice opposed to the very idea of human political sovereignty. According to this approach, political authority belongs to God alone, and the bestowal of the function of the king upon a mortal human being is a kind of deification of him, tantamount to idolatry. This approach therefore proclaims God as king.

The opposition between God's kingship and human kingship emerges most clearly and explicitly in the Bible in the words of Gideon in the Book of Judges, when he addresses "the men of Israel" who have

---

1   This threefold distinction is familiar to research literature. I borrowed this incisive definition from M. Halbertal, "God's Kingship," in M. Walzer et al. (eds.), *The Jewish Political Tradition, Vol. 1: Authority* (New Haven, Conn., 2000), pp. 128–132.

asked him to rule over them (i.e. to serve as king) and even to establish a dynasty. To their request – "Rule over us, you and your son and your grandson also; for you have delivered us out of the hand of Midian" – Gideon answers, "I will not rule over you, and my son will not rule over you; the Lord will rule over you" (Judges 8:22–23).[2] A similar approach is implied by God's words to Samuel in the "Law of the Monarchy" (*mishpat ha-melukha*). In the Book of Samuel, all the "elders of Israel" demand: "appoint for us a king to govern us like all the nations." After Samuel has presented the request to God, God responds that:

> they have not rejected you, but they have rejected me from being king over them. According to all the deeds which they have done to me, from the day I brought them up out of Egypt even to this day, forsaking me and serving other gods, so they are also doing to you.
>
> (1 Samuel 8:5–8)[3]

The view that God is king appears in the Bible in the Book of Judges. This book, at least in its first portion, teaches what Martin Buber refers to as "direct theocracy." Unlike their neighbors, the Israelites, according to Judges, live in a situation of unmediated theocratic rule. They are not led by kings or princes, nor by priests (i.e. the theocracy is not a hierocracy) but by judges.[4] The "primitive period in Israel," to use Buber's

---

2   While the term "king" does not explicitly appear in this chapter, this is clearly the intention. See Y. Amit, "The 'Men of Israel' and Gideon's Refusal to Reign" (in Hebrew), *Shenaton: An Annual for Biblical and Ancient Near Eastern Studies,* 11 (1997): 25–31; at p. 25 n. 1. Amit thinks that the refusal to reign as king, placed in Gideon's mouth, is not based upon a theological consideration but upon reservations from basing the monarchy upon military power. According to her, this story expresses the view that, in the absence of general consensus, it is impossible to establish a kingship.

3   Further expression of this principled reservation from the royal rule is found in the parable of Jotham, Judges 9:5–17. See Martin Buber, *The Kingship of God,* trans. R. Scheimann (New York, 1967), p. 75; D. Daube, *Ancient Hebrew Fables* (Oxford, 1973), pp. 3–9; and cf. Y. Kaufmann, *The Book of Judges* (in Hebrew) (Jerusalem, 1962), p. 201.

4   As is well known, the origin of the term "theocracy" is in Josephus, *Contra Apion,* II.164–165. However, in Josephus, God's rule is not direct but is mediated by the priests, headed by the high priest. See Josephus, *Contra Apion,* II.184–187. As noted by D. Goodblatt, *The Monarchic Principle: Studies in Jewish Self-Government in Antiquity* (Tübingen, 1994), pp. 33–34, Josephus' "theocracy" is really a hierocracy.

language (that is, the period between their taking possession of the land and the coronation of the first king) is characterized by a minimum of governmental institutions and "the complete absence of any assurance of continuity." The office of judge is not understood as a fixed office but rather as a mission or charge for a limited period. It is a charismatic office (in the sense used by Weber), whose termination is part of its essence. Buber continues, arguing that the king is fixed in his office, the completion of his wish being the continuation of his dynasty, whereas the judge has nothing but his immediate task.[5] And, indeed, in the period of the judges there was no demand for continuity; during this age there was no form of sovereignty recognized other than unmediated spiritual activity. The anti-monarchical Book of Judges does not recognize the intermediacy of priests; the judges, as Buber notes, do not direct queries to the priest as the people were accustomed to doing (Judges 20:18, 27) or as the kings did (1 Samuel 23:2).[6]

The only circumstances under which it is possible, according to the Book of Judges, to have a mortal human leader are temporary crises, when a judge or "deliverer" is appointed to resolve these crises, primarily by means of a heroic battle that frees the people from the yoke of an oppressor or foreign conqueror.[7] And, indeed, many of the accounts of battles and deliverance appearing in the Book of Judges emphasize that the deeds of the judge are none other than God's long hand. Thus, for example, in the case of Barak's battle with Sisera, the prophetess Deborah says to him, "I will surely go with you; nevertheless, the road on which you are going will not lead to your glory, for the Lord will sell Sisera into the hands of a woman" (Judges 4:9). These words are intended, of course, to emphasize that it is not the commander's heroism (nor the woman's wisdom) that is relevant but rather the long and devious hand of God. In Israel's wars with the Midianites, God takes exception to the number of combatants who were assembled to make battle under the leadership of Gideon (32,000; Judges 7:3) and tells Gideon: "The people with you are too many for me to give the Midianites into their hand, lest Israel vaunt themselves against me, saying, 'my own hand has delivered me'" (Judges 7:2). Through a somewhat bizarre process of selection, the force is reduced to a total of 300 men, who battle successfully against Midian,

5   Buber, *Kingship of God*, pp. 76–77. On Buber's political approach, see Z. Harvey, "Anarchy and Theocracy in Martin Buber's Philosophy" (in Hebrew), in A. Kasher and M. Halamish (eds.), *Israelite Philosophy* (Tel Aviv, 1983), pp. 9–19.

6   Buber, *Kingship of God*, pp. 158–159.

7   On the term *moshi'a* ("savior"), see Z. Weisman, *Saviours and Prophets: Two Aspects of Biblical Charisma* (in Hebrew) (Tel Aviv, 2003), pp. 23–45.

Amalek, and all the people of the East; these are, according to the biblical account, "like locusts for multitude; and their camels were without number, as the sand which is upon the seashore for multitude" (Judges 7:12). These descriptions were, of course, intended to emphasize that it is God's hand that wages war and delivers the people from its oppressors, the judge a mere instrument for their defeat.[8]

In this context, it should be noted that the judge is the ultimate charismatic "Office" – because, among other reasons, it is connected with victory in war and the redemption of the people from their enemies. Charismatic leadership, as Weber writes, "is primarily leadership that takes care of the violent confrontation of one human community against another one ... In a place where there is no war or hunting of animals, there is also absent there a charismatic leader – the 'goat of war,' as we like to call it."[9]

The limitations imposed upon the judges' activity by God are intended to moderate the structured charisma of this office. The tendency of the Book of Judges to challenge the charisma of the judge – which is not always successful, as may be seen in the case of Gideon – indicates that the realization of direct theocracy by means of "rule of the judges" is difficult but not impossible. The difficulty is not so much rooted in

8   Buber, *The Kingship of God,* pp. 68–69, 76–77. According to Buber, the Book of Judges is composed of two documents: the first, Chapters 2–12, is theocratic and anti-monarchic and calls for the "kingdom of heaven"; the second, Chapters 17–21, criticizes the anarchic theocracy and praises royal rule. The two documents are separated by the legend of Samson, which resembles neither one nor the other. The second document is a "political declaration" intended to demonstrate how many abominations and improprieties came about due to the absence of a king. Its slogan is the repeated verse, "In those days there was no king in Israel, each man did that which was right in his eyes." See B. Uffenheimer, *Ancient Prophecy in Israel* (in Hebrew) (Jerusalem, 1984), pp. 121–137, in which he analyzes the differences between Buber's approach and that of Kaufmann (pp. 123–127). On the Book of Judges see Y. Amit, *The Book of Judges: The Art of Editing* (Leiden, 1999). For an up-to-date commentary and further bibliography, see Amit, *The Book of Judges,* pp. 96–99, 260–262. Amit thinks that "The Book of Judges as a whole, as a crystallized historiographic work, that deals with the people of Israel as a unified body is a tendentious work, began to take shape in connection with the period following the destruction of Samaria." See Amit, "The Men of Israel," p. 25.
9   See M. Weber, *On Charisma and Institution Building: Selected Papers,* ed. S. N. Eisenstadt (Chicago, Ill., 1968). Weber's models for analyzing charismatic leadership were taken from the Bible, and particularly from the Book of Judges. On charisma in the Bible and on the charisma of the judges, see, recently, Weisman, *Saviors and Prophets,* pp. 12–90.

the lack of efficacy of this "system" of rule as it is in the contradiction between direct theocracy – whose concern is with the negation of the deification of human beings – and the "rule" of the judges and its inbuilt charisma. This tension seems to run like a thread throughout the Book of Judges.[10]

Direct theocracy, which, as stated, appears in the Bible primarily in the Book of Judges, is a kind of anarchism.[11] This approach is based upon the assumption of God's involvement, not only in the great dramatic events of history but also in local, everyday providence: the people need to walk in the path of the Torah, and God will worry about the rest.[12] We must again emphasize that "direct theocracy" (including its inbuilt anarchic component), more than being a positive approach to the nature of "effective" or "just" rule, is in essence a protest against and rejection of established political leadership. Leadership by human beings is tantamount to rejection of the kingdom of heaven and thus tantamount to idolatry.

Another expression of the conception that God is the political ruler is found in the words of the prophet Hosea:

> I am the Lord your God from the land of Egypt; you know no God but me, and besides me there is no savior. It was I who knew you in the wilderness, in the land of drought; but when they had fed to the full, they were filled, and their heart was lifted up; therefore they forgot me. . . . I will destroy you, O Israel, who can help you? Where now is your king, to save you; where are all your princes, to defend you – those of whom you said, "Give me a king and princes"? I have given you kings in my anger, and I have taken them away in my wrath.
>
> (Hosea 13:4–11).[13]

---

10   Compare with Weisman, *Saviors and Prophets*, pp. 43–45.

11   Within the Bible, this approach would appear to be unique to the Book of Judges. Apart from the words of Hosea, to be cited below, it is difficult to find in the Bible any principled objection to the king. See M. Elat, *Samuel and the Foundation of Kingship in Ancient Israel* (in Hebrew) (Jerusalem, 1998), pp. 63–65.

12   See J. Licht, s.v. "The Kingdom of God" (in Hebrew), *Encyclopaedia Biblica*, IV.1121. According to Licht, Gideon's words express the outlook "that God is the king of Israel, and that He literally rules over them; he comes and goes before then, just as kings of flesh and blood come and go before other peoples." Compare with Amit, "The Men of Israel," pp. 25–26.

13   See M. Garsiel, "The Dispute between Samuel and the People" (in Hebrew), *Beit Miqra*, 87 (1981): 324–343, and the references there, n. 4.

It would appear that, similar to the words of Gideon in the Book of Judges and like Samuel's response to the request of the elders, Hosea also portrays the ideal form of rulership as God's direct rule over the people. It is God Himself who saves the people, not any king of flesh and blood. Like Samuel, Hosea also characterizes the request for a king as forgetting God – that is, as idolatry.

There are those who suggest that this approach also existed in Second Temple literature.[14] Thus, for example, Josephus portrays the theological-political ideology of the group of Zealots as follows:

> As for the fourth philosophy, Judas the Galilean set himself up as leader of it. This school agrees in all other respects with the opinions of the Pharisees, except that they have a passion for liberty that is almost unconquerable, since they are convinced that God alone is their leader and master. They think little of submitting to death in unusual forms and permitting vengeance to fall on kinsmen and friends, if only they may avoid calling any man master.[15]

This group of zealots rebelled against the Romans in the Second Temple period. Josephus describes their views after describing the three other "philosophies": i.e. that of the Pharisees, the Sadducees, and the Essenes. For our purposes, this sect represents, among other things, that approach which negates human rule. Its "philosophy," according to Josephus, is not only of liberation from the yoke of foreign conquest that suppresses the people and imposes paganism but also the replacement of its yoke by the direct rule of God: "they are convinced that God alone is their leader and master." In other words, the Zealots' political-theological approach requires direct theocracy.

To use the terminology of Isaiah Berlin, the "fourth philosophy" does not seek liberty in the negative sense; for its members, freedom is not merely the removal of foreign and external political oppression. Rather, according to the Zealots, liberty bears an explicitly positive significance: it involves direct "subjugation" to God and His commandments; "subjugation" to God, and to Him alone, gives man freedom.[16] The rule

---

14   See A. Rofé, "Qumran Paraphrases, the Greek Deuteronomy and the Late History of the Biblical *Nasi*," *Textus*, 14 (1988): 169–173.

15   Josephus, *Antiquities*, 18.23.

16   I. Berlin, "Two Concepts of Liberty," in his *Four Essays on Liberty* (Oxford, 1969), pp. 118–172.

of flesh and blood, be it foreign rule or that of an ally, is subjugation, and therefore a kind of idolatry.[17]

1.2 Royal Theology: The King Is God

Another approach to monarchy found in the Bible asserts (often in somewhat moderated form) a royal theology. Various versions of this understanding of monarchy were prevalent in the ancient world: in Mesopotamia, in Egypt, and to a large extent also in Canaan.[18] This approach also appeared in Late Antiquity: among the Hellenistic kings, in the Roman Empire (from the time of Augustus), and even in the Middle Ages.[19] According to this approach, the king is a kind of extension of God upon earth. The widespread view in Mesopotamia (Assyria, Babylonia, Akkad, and Sumer) was that the king is the "image of God," while in ancient Egypt the king himself was understood as a God. The Hellenistic

---

17   A similar approach to that of Gideon appears in the story of the delegation to Pompeius (in 63 BCE), brought by Josephus in *Antiquities* XIV.41–45. The story also appears in Deodorus of Sicily, at 2.40; cf. M. Stern, *Greek and Latin Authors on Jews and Judaism* (Jerusalem, 1974), vol. I, pp. 184–185. Josephus relates there that both Hyrcanus II and Aristobolus II claimed the kingship of Judaea and sought the support of the Roman commander. They were opposed by the dignitaries of the Jews – "the nation," in Josephus' language – who sought not to be under the rule of a king because their ancestral tradition was to obey the priests, while the two brothers (whose origin was admittedly priestly) sought to change the form of rule to a monarchy and to turn them into slaves. The argument of the dignitaries was that the traditional rule among the Jews had been of the priests and not of the king. According to them, one ruled by a king was a slave. The dignitaries thus objected in principle to royal rule (and with their opposition support is also reflected for the rule of the high priest). See Goodblatt, *The Monarchic Principle*, p. 23. As we shall see below, ideas regarding God's direct rule over Israel are also found in rabbinic aggadah.

18   See S. Mowinckel, *The Psalms in Israel's Worship*, trans. D. R. Ap-Thomas (Oxford, 1967), pp. 50–55; and cf. H. Frankfort, *Kingship and the Gods: A Study of Ancient Near Eastern Religion as the Integration of Society and Nature* (Chicago, Ill., 1971). In the notes below I shall also relate to the differences between them.

19   On royal theology among the Hellenistic kings, see S. F. R. Price, *Rituals and Power: The Roman Imperial Cult in Asia Minor* (Cambridge, 1984), Chapter 2. The basic work on the cult of the Roman emperors is still L. R. Taylor, *The Divinity of the Roman Emperor* (Middletown, Conn., 1931). See also P. Zanker, *The Power of Images in the Age of Augustus* (Ann Arbor, Mich., 1990); on the Middle Ages, see E. H. Kantarowicz, *The King's Two Bodies: A Study in Mediaeval Political Theology* (Princeton, NJ, 1957).

king had a special relationship to God, and in Rome Augustus referred to himself as "the son of God" (*divi filius*), as did many of the Roman emperors who followed in his wake.

Underlying this approach is the recognition that the king's authority and political power are based upon his "Divinity" or the fact that he is the representative of God: the king is called to the throne, is crowned by God, and acts as His long arm. This approach carries deep implications for the sociopolitical authority of the king. As alluded to above, one cannot speak of a single, homogeneous approach to royal theology throughout the ancient Near East. There are differences between the royal theology predominant in Egypt and the view of the king in Mesopotamia.[20] In Egypt, the king was the incarnation of God: he was born from the gods; his metaphysical status was as one of them, and upon his death he united with the God Osiris. In contrast, in Mesopotamia and Asia Minor the king was a human being transformed into a god by means of various ceremonies and rituals. At times he was chosen while still in his mother's womb, and at times already from the primordial times, the very "beginning of time." Kingship was imposed upon him from on high; he was filled with the divine "aura" (*hilah*) and "glory" (*kavod*), and in certain ceremonies he was referred to as the "son of God" or "the image of God" (*zelem elohim*).[21] At times, the plenum devolved upon him by the act of anointing and the ritual of periodical coronation at the New Year festival. At that time he was united with the Godhead by means of a ritual marriage – a ritual that served as part of the fertility ritual of every new year (*hieros gamos*). The king in Mesopotamia, and even more so in Egypt, was thus the representative of the gods upon earth, and it was through him that they activated their power and their dominion. He was a kind of channel through whom blessing and fertility flowed from the gods to human beings.

In the ancient Near East, and particularly in Mesopotamia, the king was also the representative of human beings before the gods; he embodied the entire people in his own self and in his personality. This dual status of the king – divine but at the same time representing the people before the gods – was expressed among other things in the religious ritual.[22] The king was the high priest (in Egypt he was the only priest), and in cultic worship he represented the gods to human beings on the one

---

20 See Frankfort, *Kingship and the Gods,* pp. 231–242.
21 On the divine "halo" and "glory" of the Mesopotamian king and on him being in the image of God, see M. Weinfeld, "God the Creator in Gen. I and in the Prophecy of Second Isaiah" (in Hebrew), *Tarbiz,* 37 (1967): 105–132.
22 Mowinckel, *The Psalms in Israel's Worship,* p. 51.

hand and, on the other, the people before God (in Egypt the emphasis was on the former function while in Mesopotamia it was on the latter). For this reason, the king was the central figure in the drama of the cult, a figure who embodies the struggle and victory of the forces of life and rebirth over the forces of chaos and evil. Not only does the king, as high priest, execute the ritual, but the ritual itself is focused upon him. As representative of the people, the king is the one directly atoned for, the one who must be purified and redeemed in the name of the community and on its behalf; as the representative of God, he channels blessing and abundance from the upper realms to the people and the land.[23]

This widespread understanding of the king was essentially similar throughout the ancient Near East. At a certain stage, the Israelites evidently inherited this approach toward monarchy from the peoples of Canaan, who were in turn influenced by Egypt on the one hand and by Mesopotamian culture on the other.[24] Indeed, several of the characteristics of royal theology briefly surveyed above are found in the biblical approach toward monarchy. This approach is particularly widespread in the royal hymns in the Book of Psalms.[25] This has been noted by bible scholars and even by several of the classical commentators, yet the fullest and most detailed picture of the biblical version of royal

23   The function of the king as channeling blessing and abundance from the upper worlds stands out particularly when he is chosen by the goddess as her consort in ritual marriage. Through his mystical union with the goddess, the king becomes filled with powers of fertility and vitality (he participates in the revivification of fertility: Tammuz). See Mowinckel, *The Psalms in Israel's Worship*, p. 51.

24   Biblical scholars disagree regarding the question of when this approach entered Israel. See T. N. D. Mettinger, *King and Messiah: The Civil and Sacral Legitimation of the Israelite Kings* (Lund, 1976); and compare with R. S. Hendel, "The Social Origins of the Aniconic Tradition in Early Israel," *The Catholic Biblical Quarterly*, 50 (1988): 365–382. Royal theology in the Bible is characterized by the tension between the approach of desert leadership (the leader as *sheikh*), which was evidently widespread in Israel prior to the Babylonian and Egyptian influence, and that of kingship in the ancient Near East (in its Canaanite version), as having divine powers. Nevertheless, the overall approach of royal theology is always present in the background of these sources (see below) and explains many characteristics of the biblical version of royal theology. See Hendel, "The Social Origins of the Aniconic Tradition."

25   The following may be included among the royal hymns in the Psalter: Psalms 2, 18, 20, 21, 45, 60, 72, 89, 110, 132, 144:1–11, and evidently also Psalm 75 (and cf. Psalms 28, 61, 63, 84, 99, and 101). See Mowinckel, *The Psalms in Israel's Worship*; Y. Kaufmann, *The Religion of Israel: From Its Beginnings to the Babylonian Exile* (in Hebrew) (Jerusalem, 1960), vol. II, Book 2, p. 695.

theology is articulated by bible scholars from the School of Myth and Ritual, whose most prominent spokesmen were Hermann Gunkel and, especially, Sigmund Mowinckel.[26] Even though certain of their theses are controversial (as I shall note below), it is impossible to disagree with many of their findings.

While some of the above-described characteristics of royal theology were modified in Israelite religion, the king's relationship to God also remained a basic concept in the Israelite approach. Numerous biblical verses describe the king (or specific kings) as the son of God. Thus, for example, the Psalmist calls his "anointed" "my king": "The Lord said to me, 'You are my son, today I have begotten you'" (Psalms 2:7).[27] In the prophecy of Isaiah, the future king of Judah is described as follows: "For to us a child is born, to us a son is given; and the government shall be upon his shoulder. And his name shall be called: 'Wonderful Counselor, Mighty God, Everlasting Father, Prince of Peace'" (Isaiah 9:5). Some scholars think that this prophecy is based upon an Egyptian coronation ritual, in which the speakers are angels, members of the heavenly entourage, who declare the birth of a son to whom they attribute the title, "Mighty God."[28] There are researchers and commentators who read these verses in a literal sense, while others read them metaphorically, and still others think that the title "son of God," attributed in the Bible to the king, is a kind of legal formula of adoption, similar to those formulae that were widespread in the royal ideology in Mesopotamia.[29] We do *not* need to decide among these suggestions, as in all of these readings it is impossible to deny the special relationship of the king to God. I shall return to this point further on.

Because of his special relationship to God, the king was attributed in the Bible with additional special titles and characteristics. At times he is described as the servant of God, who enjoys His closeness and affection. In a number of verses the king is attributed with eternal life ("He asked life of you; you gave it to him, length of days for ever and ever," Psalms 21:5)

---

26   On this school, see s.v. "Myth and Ritual," in M. Eliade (ed.), *Encyclopedia of Religion*, vol. X (1987): 282–285; and cf. R. A. Segal (ed.), *The Myth and Ritual Theory: An Anthology* (Oxford 1998).

27   Cf. Psalms 110:3; 2 Samuel 7:14; 1 Chronicles 17:13; and see below.

28   See I. Knohl, *The Divine Symphony: The Bible's Many Voices* (Philadelphia, Pa., 2003), p. 89 and n. 7.

29   On adoption in Mesopotamia, see s.v. "Adoption" (in Hebrew), *Encyclopedia Biblica*, vol. I, pp. 432–433; and see J. Liver, s.v. "King, Kingship" (in Hebrew), *Encyclopedia Biblica*, vol. IV, p. 1084; and Hendel, "The Social Origins"; see especially Mettinger, *King and Messiah*, pp. 265–267, and the references there.

and with superhuman powers.[30] Anointment with holy oil transforms him into "another person." Coronation gives him a "new heart," and, because of the holiness that God radiates upon him, it is a grave sin to harm him (1 Samuel 10:6, 9; 24:7; 31:4; 2 Samuel 1:14). The king is "the anointed of the Lord"; he is "filled with the spirit of the Lord"; and he is chosen by God, adopted by Him, and sustained by Him (1 Samuel 10:6, 9; 11:6; 16:13).[31] The king is the source of the people's power and, in several places, is described as "the spirit of his nostrils" and even as "the candle of Israel."[32] Among the king's attributes are: fear of God, justice, and wisdom. As the son of God (like the Mesopotamian kings), the king deserves to rule over the entire world: "Ask of me, and I will make the nations your heritage, and the ends of the earth your possession"; "May he have dominion from sea to sea, and from the river to the ends of the earth."[33] This political ambition is not realistic; it is a religious postulate based upon the view that God is the Lord of the world and the king is His long arm.[34] It is not for naught that the throne of the king in Jerusalem symbolizes the mountain of the world. Even the horns and the crown attributed to him in Scripture, which are widespread symbols for gods and kings in the ancient Near East, lend him a divine dimension.[35]

It is difficult to determine whether the royal theology implied by the Bible is rooted in a "metaphysical" connection between the king and God and upon mythical elements similar to Mesopotamian (or Egyptian)

---

30 Cf. Psalms 72:5; 1 Kings 1:31; see, for example, Psalms 89:22; Micah 5:3; Numbers 24:17.

31 See, for example, 1 Samuel 10:24, 16:1; see, for example, Psalms 2:2, 18:25, 89:27.

32 On the king as the "breath" of the people, see Lamentations 4:20. This motif is widespread in Canaan and Egypt, appearing, for example, in the El-Amarna Letters. Regarding the term "the candle of Israel," see 2 Samuel 21:7. The king is also perceived as the source of the people's vitality; see Hosea 3:4.

33 Psalms 2:8; 72:8 (correspondingly), and see also the continuation of the second passage, Psalms 72: 9–11; cf. Psalms 89:26.

34 The roots of this motif are found in Egypt and in Mesopotamia and belong to the fundamental core of royal theology. Pharaoh is portrayed as the ruler of the cosmos, as king of the four corners of the world. The language used in Psalms 72:8–11, quoted above, "and he shall rule from sea to sea and from the river," is similar to a formula which is found in a Babylonian text: "He shall rule from the upper sea [the Mediterranean] until the lower sea [the Persian Gulf]." See Liver, "King, Kingship," p. 1083.

35 See 1 Samuel 2:10; Psalms 89:18; and cf. Psalms 132:17; Deuteronomy 33:17 (horns); 2 Samuel 1:10; 2 Kings 11:12; Psalms 110:2, 45:7, 2:9; Micah 7:14 (crown). See also Mowinckel, *The Psalms in Israel's Worship,* pp. 53 ff.

patterns of thought or whether the Bible modified this relationship.[36] I shall return to this question below. But whatever the answer to this question, it is clear that the king's unique relationship to God – as expressed in the biblical passages mentioned above – is not simply "royal court rhetoric"; this relationship is a concrete component of Israelite faith and ritual, at least according to the approach to kingship that follows from Psalms and other chapters in the Bible.[37]

According to this biblical approach, the king is also the representative of the people before God. As in Mesopotamia, he is a channel through which abundance flows from the upper world or realms into the lower ones.[38] This status is embodied, among other things, in the king's priestly functions. And, indeed, according to these sources, the king serves in the priesthood; in practice, he is the Priest – the high priest.[39] The king

---

36   It should be noted that there is a dispute among scholars of the ancient Near East regarding the proper manner of reading texts that speak about king-gods, and we cannot elaborate here. Many biblical scholars negated the existence of royal theology in the Bible or have ignored it. See, for example, Kaufmann, *The Religion of Israel*, vol. II, Book 1, pp. 95–97 and 115 ff. On Kaufmann, see below; and see also Liver, "King, Kingship," p. 1094. Even Mowinckel argues that the metaphysical connection between the king and God is modified in the biblical approach, as opposed to the royal theology of Mesopotamia and Egypt. See Mowinckel, *The Psalms in Israel's Worship*, pp. 58–59. Frankfurt, by contrast, in the epilogue to his major work (in which he summarizes the approach to kingship in Israel), completely ignores the biblical version of royal theology, adhering to the approach of limited kingship found in Deuteronomy – as if that represented the view of the Bible as a whole. See Frankfort, *Kingship and the Gods*, p. 343.

37   Thus, S. E. Loewenstamm, "Man as Image and Son of God" (in Hebrew), *Tarbiz*, 27 (1957): 1–2. See, however, the insightful words of Mettinger, *King and Messiah*, p. 14.

38   The king's righteousness brings benefit to the people (Psalms 72), while his sins are the sins of the people (2 Samuel 21:24). The day of the king's coronation (the day of anointing) is a festival day that lays the foundations for the future of the people. This day is celebrated every year, not only in Egypt and Mesopotamia but also in Israel (scholars who have examined this matter referred to the following sources: Psalms 132, 84:10, 63:12). It is clear, therefore, that the king plays a role in the important moments of the annual-cyclical cult. Thus does David behave when the sanctuary is transferred to Jerusalem and Solomon in the building of the Temple. The Book of Kings was written in light of the assumption that the king's relationship with God determines the situation of the people.

39   A number of biblical scholars think thus. See, for example, S. Japhet, *The Ideology of the Book of Chronicles and its Place in Biblical Theology* (Frankfurt, 1969) (in Hebrew, Jerusalem, 1977), pp. 441–442, n. 130. On the modification of this approach in the Book of Chronicles, see pp. 443–444.

thus conducts the ritual; he stands at the center of the festival, offering sacrifices and prayers on behalf of the people observing. For example, regarding what is stated in Genesis concerning the Canaanite king Melchizedek ("Melchizedek king of Shalem ... and he was priest to God Most High," Genesis 14:18), the Psalmist declares: "A Psalm of David. The Lord said to my lord: Sit at my right hand, till I make your enemies your footstool ... The Lord has sworn and will not change His mind, you shall be my priest for ever after the manner of Melchizedek" (Psalms 110:1–4). This verse – under the inspiration of the kings of Canaan and Mesopotamia – combines priesthood with monarchy.[40]

According to Mowinckel, several of the royal hymns in Psalms relate to a coronation festival. Following him, a number of scholars have asserted that the *sitz im leben* of several of these psalms is the annual festival of coronation and anointment of the king, observed in Israel as it was in Mesopotamia. According to Mowinckel, the coronation festival was celebrated periodically and had two foci: the anointing of the Temple and the crowning of the king in his palace.[41] It follows from these psalms that, just as in Babylonia, the festival of coronation bore the character of purification and forgiveness, and the king had to render an accounting of his deeds. Mowinckel, as mentioned, thinks that these hymns are associated with the coronation festival conducted on the New Year, reflecting the influence of the Babylonian feast of coronation, also celebrated on the New Year. He interprets Psalm 110 ("A Psalm of David. The Lord said to my lord, sit at my right hand") as a response to the ethical demands of the king; God's answer is found in Psalm 72 ("God, give your justice to the king, O God") as well as in Psalm 20 ("Now I know that the Lord will save His anointed, He will answer him from His holy heavens"; Psalms 20:7); 21, 89 and 18 ("Great triumphs He gives to His king, and He shows steadfast love to His anointed, to David and his descendants for ever"; Psalms 18:50).[42]

---

40 See D. Goodblatt, "The Union of Priesthood and Kingship in Second Temple Judea" (in Hebrew), *Cathedra*, 102 (2001): 7–28; p. 16. The approach of Psalms to the unity of priesthood and kingship in the framework of Mesopotamian royal theology is opposed to what follows from Deuteronomy, namely, that there is a clear separation between the two; see below. This separation, not explicitly formulated in the Bible, follows from precedents of structural separation of realms in the Bible between the political leadership and the priesthood: thus, Moses and Aaron, Joshua and Eleazar, David and Zaddok and Eviatar, Joshua and Jehoiada, Josiah and Hezekiah, Zerubavel and Joshua. See Goodblatt, "The Union of Priesthood," pp. 7–28.

41 See 1 Kings 1:33; 2 Kings 11:10–13.

42 Mowinckel identifies Psalm 45 as a hymn for a royal wedding and notes its parallels in Egyptian royal hymns.

Interestingly, Yehezkel Kaufmann – who drew a categorical distinction between "pagan myth" and biblical monotheism, by implication criticizing those biblical scholars who wrote under the inspiration of the Myth and Ritual School – is not unequivocal regarding Mowinckel's thesis. Initially, Kaufmann strongly attacks the claim that the royal hymns in the Book of Psalms are connected with the cult of the king on New Year's Day and completely rejects the existence of a magical-mythical ceremony of this type in Israel.[43] Further on in the discussion, however, he tends to accept the claim that these hymns pertain to (folk) festival and ritual, whose concern is the coronation of the king on the New Year. In the final analysis, Kaufmann also agrees that "there is contact here between the culture of Israel and the culture of Babylonia."[44]

An explicit expression of the relationship between the destiny of the king and that of the people follows from the dirge of the author of Lamentations on the destiny of Zedekiah, the last king of Judah: "The breath of our nostrils, the Lord's anointed, was taken in their nets, he of whom it was said, 'In his shadow we shall live among the nations'" (Lamentations 4:20).[45] Moreover, according to this understanding of kingship, the king of Israel has direct access to God and, like the kings-priests in the ancient Near East, also has prophetic abilities.[46]

The royal hymns of the Psalter do not describe any specific historical king but rather are concerned with the royal ideal.[47] They make no distinction between the personal and the public. The royal hymns are thus hymns of the community. The heading, "for David," does not mean that David was the one who composed the psalm but rather that it relates to David as the paradigmatic figure of king.[48]

---

43   Kaufmann, *The Religion of Israel*, vol. I, Book 1, pp. 178–181; and especially his discussion of the Book of Psalms, *The Religion of Israel*, vol. II, Book 2, pp. 649–653.

44   Kaufmann, *The Religion of Israel*, vol. II, Book 2, pp. 496–498.

45   See Liver, "King, Kingship," p. 1088.

46   The apprehension of David as a prophet is found, evidently, in the Book of Chronicles. See the references and discussion in Japhet, *Ideology of Chronicles*, p. 468, n. 61.

47   Most of the psalms relate to God and, in doing so, to the king who stands before him. The Psalmist focuses particularly on the relationship between God and the king and on what God gives him (power, abundance, wisdom, etc.); God is at the center and the king is secondary to Him. It is no coincidence that these psalms later acquired messianic significance, in the Jewish tradition, and particularly in the Christian tradition. See Mowinckel, *The Psalms in Israel's Worship*, pp. 75–76.

48   At a later stage a democratization of religion or of the religious feeling occurred: God became personal, and the Psalms were interpreted as personal prayer

One of the essential functions of the king, according to the royal theology, is to administer justice. In this area too, the king acts with divine inspiration, so that even in his function as judge he is a kind of long arm of God. Moreover, because of his relationship with God, the king not only executes judgment but is at times considered the source of the law. It was thus in Mesopotamia and Egypt and thus also (in a more moderate way) in the biblical version of royal theology.[49] The function of the king as judge and as responsible for the legal system, acting under divine inspiration, follows from the royal hymns in the Psalms. For example, "A Psalm of Solomon. Give the king your justice, O God, and your righteousness to the royal son. May he judge the people with righteousness, and the poor with justice" (Psalms 72:1–2); concerning David, we are told in the Book of Samuel, "So David reigned over all Israel; and David administered justice and equity to all his people" (2 Samuel 8:15); while regarding Solomon it is stated that God appointed him as king so that "he might execute justice and righteousness" (1 Kings 10:9); Jeremiah calls to the kings of Judah to do "justice and righteousness" (Jeremiah 22:15), and he prophesies, "I will raise up for David a righteous branch ... and he will do justice and righteousness in the land" (Jeremiah 22:5).[50] Moshe Weinfeld claims that the social

(Mowinckel, *The Psalms in Israel's Worship*, pp. 78–79). However, according to their original meaning, it was the king who had a connection with God, and everyone else related to God through him. The change in the reading of these Psalms occurred slowly. The personal prayer of the prophets made a significant contribution to this, laying the foundations for a relationship between God and the individual without the intermediacy of the king. This change evidently took place after the Destruction of the First Temple; the community and the Temple were restored, while the king, as a key figure, disappeared, replaced by the high priest. The Temple was transformed into a place of pilgrimage (for individuals), and the individual became a real member of the community. The ritual in Jerusalem, originally intended for purification of the king and of his court, became, in the priestly law of Leviticus, relevant to every individual. But see Japhet, *The Ideology of Chronicles*, who shows how, already in the Book of Chronicles (one of the later biblical books), the view prevails that the people have an independent political standing.

49 M. Weinfeld, *Social Justice in Ancient Israel and in the Ancient Near East* (Jerusalem, 1995), pp. 45–65. On the ruler as judge in the ancient Near East, cf. the references in Elat, *Samuel and the Foundation*, p. 50, n. 72. On the relation between ruler and law and judging in Israel, see Elat, *Samuel and the Foundation*, p. 58.

50 See also 1 Chronicles 18:14; Psalms 99:4. On the meaning of the word pair מִשְׁפָּט וּצְדָקָה ("justice and righteousness"), see Weinfeld, *Justice and Righteousness in Israel and the Nations: Equality and Freedom in Israel in the Light of Ancient Near Eastern Concepts of Justice* (Jerusalem: Magnes Press, 1985), pp. 25–44.

enactments attributed to David in the Second Book of Samuel upon his ascent to the royal throne ("and David did justice and righteousness to all his people") are rooted in the Mesopotamian tradition of *mišarim* (introduction of social arrangements by the king).[51] In addition to these functions, the king is also the commander of the army, and, as in the economic realm, military success is to a large extent dependent upon his position in relation to God.

The most explicit example of royal theology in the Bible is found in the descriptions of King Solomon. A number of verses in the Book of Chronicles describe Solomon as sitting upon the divine throne: "Then Solomon sat upon the throne of the Lord as king instead of David his father" (1 Chronicles 29:23).[52] Other verses identify his kingship with the kingship of God: "He has chosen Solomon my son to sit on the throne of the kingdom of the Lord over Israel" (1 Chronicles 28:5); "But I will confirm him in my house and in my kingdom for ever, and his throne shall be established for ever" (1 Chronicles 17:14).[53] Sarah Japhet claims that these verses identify the kingship of Israel with the kingdom of the Lord, clearly implying that the king of Israel, in sitting upon his throne, is essentially sitting upon the throne of God, and that itself is the kingship of God.[54] "Israel's monarchy," writes Japhet, "and the kingdom of God are identical" and "the king acts in YHWH's capacity in his kingdom."[55] Japhet further emphasizes that this characterization is not unique to the kingship of Solomon or to that of the Davidic dynasty; according to the Book of Chronicles, it pertains to the institution of monarchy in Israel per se: every legitimate king in Israel (from the moment he is anointed in accordance with God's

---

51   See Weinfeld, *Justice and Righteousness,* p. 47 on the Mesopotamian *misaru* (uprightness). On the king's relation to justice, see also R. de Vaux, *Ancient Israel: Its Life and Institutions* (London, 1961), vol. I, pp. 150–152. In contrast to the Mesopotamian approach, according to which the king is the source of justice, in the biblical approach (even in its royal theological version), God is always the source of the law. See B. M. Levinson, *Deuteronomy and the Hermeneutics of Legal Innovation* (Oxford, 1998), p. 138.

52   On other verses, see below.

53   Cf. 2 Chronicles 9:8: "May the Lord your God be blessed, Who has wanted you to place you upon His throne as a king to the Lord your God"; 2 Chronicles 13:8: "and now you say strengthen yourselves before the kingship of God by the hand of the sons of David."

54   Japhet, *Ideology of Chronicles,* the chapter on the king, pp. 396–398. And compare I. L. Seeligmann, "From Historical Reality to a Historiosophic Approach in the Bible" (in Hebrew), *Peraqim* (Jerusalem, 1971), p. 304 n. 66.

55   Japhet *Ideology of Chronicles,* p. 398.

will) embodies the kingship of God.[56] This explicit identification of the institution of monarchy with the kingship of God is indeed unique to the Book of Chronicles. However, as noted above, the motifs of royal theology in relation to Solomon also appear in other biblical books.

Japhet rightly contrasts this approach to that attributed to Gideon in the Book of Judges: "I will not rule over you, and my son will not rule over you; the Lord will rule over you" (Judges 8:23). Unlike the Book of Chronicles, in which the kingship of God is embodied in the rule of flesh and blood, in the case of Gideon God's kingship entirely negates any form of human rule. According to Gideon, a human king is the antithesis of the kingship of Heaven. The identification of the king of Israel with the kingship of Heaven stands in stark opposition to the words of Samuel who, as we remember, describes the people's desire for a king as indicating rejection of God (1 Samuel 8:7). According to Samuel, a kingship of flesh and blood substitutes the kingship of God, and the two cannot exist together.[57]

The kingship of God through means of the king is thus a sort of theocracy. The direct theocracy of the Book of Judges is, in practice, a kind of anarchy (with the exception of crisis situations where a charismatic judge is sent to save the people, and then, after working for their deliverance, ceases to lead them). In contrast, in the understanding of monarchy in the Book of Chronicles, a ruler of flesh and blood concentrates extensive authority or powers in his own hands. Moreover, precisely because of the heavenly origin of the king's authority (his throne is the throne of God, his kingdom is the kingdom of heaven), this authority extends to all matters of the kingship, and its extent is almost unlimited. Indeed, according to the Book of Chronicles and other biblical books, which describe the king in terms of royal theology, the king's powers extend to all aspects of life: political, religious-ritual, legal, economic, military, and administrative.[58]

56   Japhet, *Ideology of Chronicles*, p. 406.
57   Japhet, *Ideology of Chronicles*, pp. 400–2. Japhet comments there that this opposition is implied as well in Samuel's speech prior to his death, where he promises that "the Lord will not abandon His people" (1 Samuel 12:22) – even though with the appointment of the king the kingdom of Heaven ceased.
58   For these reasons, they did not wish to refer to this form of rule as a "theocracy." Compare Japhet, *Ideology of Chronicles*, p. 402. For a description of the function and authorities of the king in these areas according to the Book of Chronicles, see Japhet, *Ideology of Chronicles*, p. 404.

In many biblical passages, Solomon is depicted as the son of God. In addition to the verse in Chronicles mentioned earlier, this motif also appears in the Book of Samuel in the prophecy of Nathan:

> When your days are fulfilled, and you lie down with your fathers, I will raise up your offspring after you, who shall come forth from your body, and I will establish his kingdom. He shall build a house for my name, and I will establish the throne of his kingdom for ever. I will be his father, and he shall be My son.
>
> (2 Samuel 7:12–14)

The motif of the son also appears in the parallel passage in Chronicles:

> When your days are fulfilled to be with your fathers, I will raise up your offspring after you, one of your own sons, and I will establish his kingdom. He shall build a house for Me, and I will establish his throne for ever. I will be his father, and he shall be My son; I will not take My steadfast love from him, as My grace will not move from him, as it was before.
>
> (1 Chronicles 17:11–13)[59]

It is possible that the status of "son of God," which we have already encountered in various passages in the Book of Psalms ("the Lord said to me, you are My son. I have given birth to you this day," Psalms 2:7), is a formula of legal adoption, or it may merely be a metaphor expressing a relationship of intimacy and dependence between the king and God.[60] As noted earlier, this status is common with regard to kings of the ancient Near East, both in Mesopotamia and in Egypt (where it assumed an almost literal meaning).[61]

---

59   cf. 1 Chronicles 22:10; 28:6.
60   See Hendel, "The Social Origins," p. 379.
61   See the discussion in Frankfort, *Kingship and the Gods,* pp. 299–301. Loewenstamm writes that the declaration of Hammurabi – that he is "the seed of the kingship that [the god] Sin has procreated" – is courtly language, and he removes from it almost all theological significance: "Man as Image," pp. 1–2. However, most researchers think that this declaration and other similar ones reflect a substantive approach to the unique stance of the king and his special relationship to God. Thus, for example, Seeligmann writes concerning Nathan's words in Samuel (and in Chronicles): "Within this view of the eternity of the dynasty there are included certain elements of deification of the king that were accepted, in various forms, in the ancient Near East. In Nathan's prophecy, it states ... 'I will be his father and he

Does the description of the king of Israel as sitting upon the throne of God (in whom the "kingdom of Heaven" is realized) include the notion of the deification of the king? The various schools within biblical scholarship are divided on this question. Scholars from the Myth and Ritual School – a leading spokesman of which is Mowinckel – think that the biblical king possesses a divine dimension.[62] This school's point of departure is the parallelism between the Scriptures and the extra-biblical sources, primarily Mesopotamian, both in the sociological-ritual context and in terms of motifs and linguistic idioms. Of particular interest are the parallels between the Mesopotamian sources and the royal hymns in the Book of Psalms, some of which I have noted above. Critics of this school focus primarily on the image of monarchy that emerges from the biblical historiography; according to them, this kingship lacks the divine component.[63] However, it is a mistake to think that elements or motifs of royal theology are absent from the biblical historiography (including the Deuteronomistic history). Thus, for example, the Book of Chronicles, which has a historiographic genre, is filled with such motifs, and, as noted by Japhet, the question of the deification of the king arises therein in all its strictness.[64]

will be my son.' … This idea of the adoption of David and his household by God, comes in place of the usual view outside of Israel, in which the god or goddess gives birth to the king." See Seeligmann, "From Historical Reality" and compare Weinfeld, who thinks that this is not mythology but a purely legal metaphor; M. Weinfeld, "The Covenant of Grant in the OT," *Journal of the American Oriental Society*, 90 (1970): 184–203, at p. 192; and cf. Japhet, *Ideology of Chronicles*, p. 413 and n. 47. Regarding our matter, the question as to the mythic element in royal theology in the Bible is of secondary importance. In any event, we have here a version of royal theology (possibly diluted from the theological viewpoint but not necessarily from the political one).

62 Concerning this school, see the references in n. 26 above. On Mowinckel's stance, see *The Psalms in Israel's Worship*.

63 The most important critic of the School of Myth and Ritual is Martin Noth. See Noth, "God, King and Nation," in his *The Laws in the Pentateuch and other Essays*, trans. D. R. Ap-Thomas (Edinburgh, 1966), pp. 156–175. It should be noted that criticism of this school relates also to the manner in which it describes the status of the king in Mesopotamia. Thus, for example, Frankfort (*Kingship and the Gods*) modifies the divine-mythic status of the Mesopotamian king in comparison to that of the king in Egypt. This moderating tendency has implications as well on all the qualities of the king and even affects the interpretation given by Frankfurt as to the king's role in the cult. For a survey of the scholarly critique of the Myth and Ritual School and the answers given by the school in relation to royal theology, see H. S. Versnel, *Transition and Reversal in Myth and Ritual* (Leiden, 1993), pp. 1–48.

64 See Japhet, *Ideology of Chronicles*.

On this point I should comment that the discussion of this issue among the scholars is not without an apologetic aspect. As in other matters pertaining to the relationship between the Bible and myth, magic and theurgy, so too in the issue of royal theology, connected by its very essence to these matters, scholars have adopted a variety of research strategies – beginning with ignoring it, through metaphorical and allegorical readings – all in order to preserve biblical "monotheism," which distances God from the world and from man.[65] Yet none of these techniques can completely obscure the motifs of royal theology in the Bible. An explicit example of this is Yehezkel Kaufmann's "hesitant" discussion of this subject.[66]

For our purposes, the precise nature of royal theology in the Bible is of secondary importance. Even if we assume that the mythic component of the deification of the king and the accompanying motifs were diluted in the Bible, it is still difficult to ignore the fact that numerous biblical passages present a picture of a monarchy bearing a sacral character. Even if the king is not literally the "son of God" or the "image of God" in the Bible (in a manner distinct from other human beings), it is difficult to reject the large number and wide variety of verses describing his unique relation to God. There is evidently a difference between the status of the king in the cult according to the biblical sources and his status and function in the cultures of the ancient Near East. The Bible may assign a function in the cyclical ritual of the New Year to the king (particularly in the Book of Psalms); however, the ritual marriage of the king with the goddess (*hieros gamos*) that brings about the revival of the dead god is lacking therein.[67] Also missing from the Bible is the cult of statues of the king in the temples and their relation to the cult of statues of the gods.[68]

65   See Y. Liebes, "De Natura Dei," in his *Studies in Jewish Myth and Jewish Messianism* (Albany, NY, 1993), pp. 55–61; Y. Lorberbaum, "The Doctrine of Corporeality of God Did Not Occur Even for a Single Day to the Sages, May Their Memory Be Blessed" (*The Guide of the Perplexed*, vol. I, p. 46); "Anthropomorphism in Early Rabbinic Literature: A Critical Review of Scholarly Research" (in Hebrew), *Jewish Studies*, 40 (2000): 3–54.

66   See Kaufmann, *The Religion of Israel*.

67   On this ritual, see s.v. K. W. Bolle, "*Hieros Gamos*," in M. Eliade (ed.), *Encyclopedia of Religion* (New York, 1987), vol. VI, pp. 317–321; especially p. 321. See also Frankfort, *Kingship and the Gods*, pp. 295–299.

68   On the cult of images and statues of the kings in the ancient Near East, see Frankfort, *Kingship and the Gods*, pp. 301–306; and see I. J. Winter, "Idols of the King: Royal Images as Recipient of Ritual Action in Ancient Mesopotamia," *Journal of Ritual Studies*, 6 (1992): 13–42.

It is nevertheless impossible to simply dismiss those scriptures describing the divine status of the king as empty rhetoric and metaphor.

On this point it is worth adopting the distinction, already alluded to above, between divine kingship and sacral kingship. Divine kingship identifies the king with God and sees the king as *deus incarnatus*. Hence, not only does he fulfill a central role in the temple but he himself becomes an object of ritual worship.[69] In contrast, the approach that sees the king in sacral terms does not view him as a god but attributes to him a special relationship to God.[70] According to this approach, the king is liable to have ritual functions, but he himself does not become a cultic object.

As we have noted, in the Bible the sacral king fulfills a central function in the cult: he embodies the entire public in his personality and represents them before God; he enjoys divine inspiration; he is responsible for the legal system, serving as the source of justice; he determines policy in matters of war, foreign affairs, and security; and he is responsible for the administrative area. In many respects – apart from him being an object of cult – the status and authorities of the sacral king are similar to those of those kings in the ancient Near East to whom a divine dimension is attributed.[71]

An explicit expression of the sacral status of the king in the Bible is found in numerous descriptions, according to which he is appointed by being anointed with oil. According to these sources, the ritual of anointing is a means of appointing the king and is a substantive element in determining his status. Anointing with oil as a ceremonial vehicle (as opposed to rubbing the body with oil for medicinal or aesthetic purposes) played a variety of different functions in the ancient Near East: it served in ceremonies to indicate change in legal status of acquiring property or in personal status; it served to sanctify ritual articles – for example, the anointing of monuments, of the temple, and of statues of the gods in Mesopotamia, and also to initiate individuals into sacral functions

---

69 In this respect, the functions fulfilled by the king in the cult are derived from the fact that he himself serves as an object of worship. Thus, for example, the ritual marriage with the goddess; see the references in note 67 above, and see below.

70 See Mettinger, *King and Messiah*, p. 14.

71 But see Japhet, *The Ideology of Chronicles*, pp. 422–431. She draws a distinction between the Book of Chronicles, which in her opinion brought about a "democratization" (the Book of Chronicles tends to see the people as an active factor and negates the exclusive representative nature of the king), and the Book of Kings (and other biblical books), which see the king as the only active factor, to whom the people are secondary.

– priests and perhaps even prophets.[72] In the Bible, the anointing of kings belongs to the third category as we shall see below.

Students of the Bible and of the ancient Near East distinguished between two kinds of ritual anointing: that with the purpose of purification, in which there is an element of liberation, and that concerned with strengthening and intensification.[73] Anointment purifies and liberates, for example, in the case of maidservants and manservants, whose purpose is to signify a change in their legal status and their being freed from the rule of their masters. Such anointing evidently does not involve any sacral aspect. Some researchers think that the anointing of the priests also bears the character of purification and liberation, as it was intended to separate the priest from his family and to release him from his social obligations so that he might be available to worship God and be subject to Him alone.[74]

Unlike anointment that is purifying and liberating, the anointment concerned with strengthening or intensification is to transfer power and authority and to convey honor and glory. Those findings from the ancient Near East that testify to the anointing of high officials in Egypt and Mesopotamia belong to this category.[75] In the Bible, the anointing of

72 See J. Liver, "Anointing" (in Hebrew), *Encyclopaedia Biblica,* vol. V, pp. 526–531; and Mettinger, *King and Messiah,* pp. 208–223. Thus, for example, in the findings from Uggarit, according to which a handmaiden was freed from her slavery in a ceremony of anointing with oil. See Liver, "Anointing," p. 528; Mettinger, *King and Messiah.* On the anointing of monuments, see Genesis 28:18 (Jacob and the pillar in Beth-el); 31:13; 35:14. On the anointing of the Sanctuary, mentioned in several places in the Torah, see, for example, Exodus 29:1–30; 30:22–33. In Mesopotamia there was a special class of priests known as *pashihu* (the anointers), whose function was to anoint cultic artifacts with oil. See Liver, "Anointing," p. 528. Concerning the anointing of priests, see Exodus 28:41; on the anointing of prophets, see 1 Kings 19:16, which states that Elijah was commanded to anoint Elisha as his successor. But later, in the story of the actual sanctification, anointing is not mentioned. Rather, the act by which the spirit was conveyed upon Elisha involved placing Elijah's mantle upon him. It is possible that this is a purely borrowed use of the term. See Liver, "Anointing," p. 530.

73 See the extensive survey of research in Mettinger, *King and Messiah,* pp. 185–187; and his comprehensive discussion there, pp. 188–232.

74 E. Kutsch thinks that anointing as purification and liberation characterized the anointing of priests in Jewish sources from the period of the Babylonian Exile and the Second Temple. In his opinion, the anointing of the high priest is not to be understood as copying or borrowing from the anointing of the king. Cf. Mettinger, *King and Messiah,* p. 186; and compare Liver, "Anointing," p. 529.

75 While kings of Egypt and Mesopotamia were not anointed, they were anointed in the Hittite kingdom and, as mentioned, in Israel. Like the anointing of the king

the king belongs to the strengthening type of anointing, which doubtless bears a sacral character.[76] In the ordinary course of events, the king is anointed by the priests with the holy oil which was in the Temple.[77] In the case of David and Jehu, who were anointed clandestinely, the prophet fulfilled the role of the priest.[78] As we have stated, the priest or prophet were messengers of God, and from this point on the anointed king is known as "the anointed of the Lord." This term, which appears numerous times in the Bible, indicates that, according to the biblical view, all of the Kings were anointed – including the king who inherited his father's throne and not only the king who began a new dynasty.[79]

in the Bible, the anointing of vassal kings and princes in Egypt by the pharaoh involved conveying the authority and glory of the pharaoh upon the one anointed. See Liver, "Anointing," p. 530.

76　Kutsch distinguishes between two types of anointing of kings in Israel in the Bible: political anointing – by the people – intended to establish a set of relations between the king and the people, in which the people convey authority upon the king; and sacral anointing – by God, through means of a prophet or priest. In contrast, de Vaux thinks that anointing was a ritual intended to establish master–vassal relations between God and the king. See De Vaux, *Ancient Israel,* p. 152. Mettinger (*King and Messiah,* pp. 185–232, especially p. 188) summarizes three positions in the research regarding anointing: (1) the sacral interpretation – i.e. anointing creates a special connection between God and the king; (2) the sacral–political interpretation – anointing conveys authority upon the king by the people; (3) an intermediate position – these two kinds of anointing were originally intertwined and were only later separated. Mettinger (*King and Messiah,* and see especially his summary on pp. 230–232) thinks it possible to identify a development within the Bible regarding anointing. The early form of the ritual carried a political character – for example, in David's anointing over Judah and Israel by the people. The turning point occurred with Solomon, who was anointed by Zaddok the priest; there the anointing becomes a religious ritual: he is imbued with the "spirit" and a relationship is created between the king and God. The (anointing) priest is understood as acting in the name of God. Later, this anointing was applied retrospectively to kings from the past: first to David, and thereafter to Saul, and the term "the anointed of the Lord" became a key concept in the connection between the king and God.

77　See 1 Kings 1:39, where Zaddok the priest anoints Solomon in the presence of Nathan the prophet. And cf. 2 Chronicles 23:11; Psalms 89:21.

78　Liver, "King, Kingship," p. 1101.

79　See Liver, "King, Kingship"; J. Liver, *The House of David: From the Fall of the Kingdom of Judah to the Fall of the Second Commonwealth and After* (in Hebrew) (Jerusalem, 1959), p. 52; and cf. M. Cogan and H. Tadmor, *II Kings* (New York, 1988), p. 106. But compare also *Sifra, Mekhilta de-Milu'im* (ed. Weiss); and *Tosefta Sanhedrin* 4.11 (ed. Zuckermandel), 421; *Babylonian Keritut* 5*b* and numerous parallels; and

The anointing of the king involves both a change in status and his sanctification to the position by God. As mentioned, the biblical sources teach us that the anointing conveys upon the king some of the divine glory, because of which he is granted special qualities. It is said of Saul, immediately after he was anointed by Samuel, that "God gave him another heart ... and the Spirit of God came mightily on him, and he prophesied" (1 Samuel 10:9–10). Immediately after David's anointing it is said that "the spirit of the Lord came mightily on David from that day forward" (1 Samuel 16:13). The ceremony of anointing is thus explicitly connected to the spirit of God resting upon the king, to the halo and splendor that surround him or, in other words, to a divine status or at very least to his sacral stature.[80]

see below, Chapter 2, pp. 84–95. According to the *Sifra* and the *bereitot* in the *Babylonian,* and on the basis of various biblical sources, Joseph Naveh thinks that in the Bible too kings were only anointed in cases of controversy. Naveh claims that wherever the people refers to המלכה, making someone king, it also refers to anointing, and that all cases of anointing–coronation described in the Bible occur "only when the king ascending the throne is not the legal heir or at the conclusion of a process of competition between various contenders to the throne." See J. Naveh, "Marginalia on the Inscriptions From Dan and Ekron" (in Hebrew), *Eretz-Israel: Archaeological, Historical and Geographical Studies,* 26 (1999): 119–122; and, more recently, J. Naveh, "Epigraphic Miscellanea," *Israel Exploration Journal,* 52 (2002): 240–253. Naveh's proofs and arguments are not convincing, due to, among other reasons, the formula commonly used in the Bible (which he himself cites): "and so-and-so lay with his fathers, and such-and-such reigned after him": according to this the term "coronation" ("and he reigned"), which (according to Naveh) also includes anointing, refers to one who inherits the kingship from his father, peacefully and without rivals.

80   On the relationship between the anointing of kings and that of priests in the Bible, see Liver, "Anointing," pp. 529–530; and cf. Mettinger, *King and Messiah.* Another explicit expression of the sacral (if not divine) character of the king is reflected in the prohibition that appears in the Bible against cursing the king, which is always in close conjunction to the prohibition against cursing God. Thus, for example, in the testimony of the two "evildoers" against Naboth ("you have cursed God and the king"), because of which "they stoned him with stones and he died" (1 Kings 21:10–13). Likewise, the one who curses the anointed of the Lord in 2 Samuel, where cursing the king is understood as cursing the anointed of the Lord (2 Samuel 19:22). One can similarly understand the language in Exodus 22:27, which combines the two together: "You shall not curse God, nor revile a prince in your people." See Liver, "King, Kingship," p. 1088, who writes that cursing the king, according to the verse in Exodus and other sources, is considered as "reviling Heaven."

According to the approach of royal theology, both in its strict formulation (divine king) and in its more moderate formulation (sacral king), there is a clear relation between theology and politics. Thus it was in the ancient world and also in the Bible. The political standing of the king and his authority are based upon his relation to God and his ceremonial functions. In most forms of government in the ancient world, it was impossible to draw a distinction between politics and theology: political authority and religious authority were inseparably intertwined.

The "metaphysics" or myth that lie at the basis of royal theology are likely to seem alien and hostile to speculative philosophical thinking. Upon second thought, however, a certain structural similarity can be discerned between this political approach and the Platonic idea of the philosopher-king. As in many other matters pertaining to the relationship between philosophy and metaphysical speculation and myth, here too one may view the Platonic political approach – inseparable from Plato's metaphysics – as the conceptualization (not necessarily conscious or even half-conscious) of royal theology.[81] Just as in royal theology, so too the philosopher-king is an exclusive ruler around whom the entire kingdom revolves; like the divine king, who has a special relation to God, so too the philosopher-king has a special relation to the "heavenly" world, the world of ideas; like the divine king, who serves as a channel for the divine plentitude, so too the philosopher-king mediates between the "divine" wisdom, which resides in the world of ideas, and the earthly state; and, as in the case of the divine king, so too the success of the philosopher-king is a condition of the success of the state.[82] As noted earlier, this approach did not cease to exist in the ancient world; it found its way into the Hellenistic world, the Roman world, the medieval world, and there are even manifestations of it in the modern period.[83]

81 On the understanding of philosophy, specifically Platonic philosophy, as a conceptualization of ancient myths, see Eliade, *The Myth of the Eternal Return*, trans. W. R. Trask (New York, 1954), pp. 31–33. On pp. 34–35, Eliade writes, "And in that case, Plato could be regarded as the outstanding philosopher of 'primitive mentality'; that is, as the thinker who succeeded in giving philosophical currency and validity to the modes of life and behavior of archaic humanity. Obviously, this in no way lessens the originality of his philosophical genius; for his great title to our admiration remains his effort to justify this vision of archaic mankind theoretically, through the dialectic which the spirituality of his age made available to him."

82 On the status of the philosopher-king, see Plato, *Republic*, VI.485 ff., VII.515.

83 This is so, even if Maimonides' understanding of royalty-leadership may be seen as a neo-Aristotelian philosophical conceptualization of royal theology. According

The relationship between theology and politics underlies the two biblical approaches to kingship surveyed thus far. The former approach – that of direct theocracy – recognizes this close relationship, thus entirely negating the rule of flesh and blood. The second approach – royal theology – strengthens it and bases political rule upon it. The third biblical approach to monarchy, which we shall discuss in the next section, differs from both of these.

1.3 Limited Monarchy: The King Is Not God

The third approach to monarchy found in the Bible states that the king is not God. The underlying theology of this approach is that the political realm is not exclusive to God; the direct rule over human beings and the authority to conduct their everyday affairs are not necessarily an inseparable part of His substantive attributes or activities. Unlike direct theocracy, this approach argues that granting of political authority to human beings does not entail sacrilege since not every human rule necessarily leads to the deification of the ruler. Unlike royal theology, this political view rejects the ahistorical myth of the "divine" king or of the king who is alone "the image of God." It argues that the king is not the long arm of God, that his rule has nothing to do with the cycles of nature, that

to Maimonides in *The Guide for the Perplexed,* the ability to lead and to rule is explicitly connected with "the divine overflow coming toward us." In the chapters on prophecy in Book II of the *Guide,* pp. 373–374, Maimonides distinguishes between the sages (who receive the intellectual overflow "only toward the rational faculty") and the prophets (upon whom the overflow "reaches both faculties – both the rational and the imaginative"), and between them and "those who govern cities … the legislators, the soothsayers, the augurs, and the dreamers of veridical dreams," among whom "the overflow only reaches the imaginative faculty, [there being] defect of the rational faculty." Because of the "divine abundance," which is a kind of a divine "glory" (in Weber's term "charisma"), the king-leaders rule over peoples and states and succeed in gathering together the human race, among whom "there are many differences between the individuals belonging to it, so that you can hardly find two individuals people who are in any accord with respect to … moral habits" (Maimonides, *The Guide for the Perplexed,* Chapter 40). Leadership, according to Maimonides, is not merely an earthly matter. He also identifies among the leaders – that is, the kings of ancient times and in his own day (and certainly among prophet-leaders) – divine powers (which according to his approach are of course "natural"); we cannot elaborate on this topic here. On the relationship between Kabbalah and Hasidism and the royal ideology, see M. Idel, *Messianic Mystics* (New Haven, Conn., 1998), pp. 21–23, 112, 264, 314; see also M. Idel, *Kabbalah: New Perspectives* (New Haven, Conn., 1988), pp. 196–197.

it is not on his account that the rivers rise or the harvests are abundant. Nevertheless, this understanding of monarchy does not replace the king by the direct, unmediated rule of God. At least in its biblical version, this approach argues for a monarchy with limited authority in which the king does not cross the boundary separating the human from the divine. Preservation of the exclusive status of God is reflected in the struggle against the transformation of the political realm into the cosmological and the historical to the mythic.[84]

This approach underlines the Chapter of the King (*parashat ha-melekh*) in Deuteronomy 17.[85] This chapter is the only source in the Torah in which the institution of monarchy is established in a normative-formal manner.[86] A clear separation is made there between the political and the religious and theological.[87] One may perceive there an effort to subjugate the king to other authorities: first and foremost to the Torah but also to other institutions: the Sanhedrin, the local courts, the priests, the Levites, and the prophets. Comparison between the status and function of the king in Deuteronomy 17 and the conception of the king in the royal hymns in the Book of Psalms (and in other biblical documents, such as the books of Samuel, Kings, Chronicles and the prophetic books) reveals the profound difference between them. According to the Book

84   See Halbertal, "God's Kingship."

85   Deuteronomy 17:14–20. The phrase, "the Chapter of the King" (פרשת המלך) is also quite common in Talmudic literature. See *Tosefta Sanhedrin* 4.5 (ed. Zuckermandel, 421); *Mishnah Sotah* 7.2, 8; and cf. Lieberman, *Tosefta kifeshuta,* Sotah, 684. At times, and in certain contexts, I shall designate this chapter by the term "the Commandment of the King" – notwithstanding that it is clear from the language of the verses that they are not commanded concerning his appointment (see below). Likewise, at times I refer to 1 Samuel 8 as the "Chapter of the King" and at times as "the Codex [or Charter] of the King" – all according to the subject matter.

86   Kingship in Israel is mentioned in the Torah in a number of additional places: see Genesis 17:6, 16; 35:11; 36:31; Deuteronomy 28:36; and possibly also Deuteronomy 33:5.

87   The fundaments of this approach may also be found in the "Codex of the King" in the Book of Samuel. See A. Silver, "Kingship and Political Agency," in M. Walzer et al. (eds.), *The Jewish Political Tradition* (New Haven, Conn., 2000), pp. 122–126. Silver thinks that the people's request is not to replace God but reflects their desire for secular politics. In his opinion, this chapter signifies the birth of secular political authority in the Bible. On the relationship between the Chapter of the King in Deuteronomy and the "Codex of the King" in Samuel, see Levinson, *Deuteronomy and the Hermeneutics,* pp. 138–143, and his article, "The Reconceptualization of Kingship in Deuteronomy and the Deuteronomistic History's Transformation of Torah," *Vetus Testamentum,* 61 (2001): 511–534.

of Deuteronomy, the king has nothing to do with the cult in the Temple (or in the Sanctuary); the cult is given over entirely to the priests. Even though this is not explicitly mentioned in the section, a separation between the priesthood and the monarchy would seem to follow: the king is not a priest and is certainly not allowed to be the high priest.[88] In the Book of Deuteronomy, therefore, the king has no direct relationship to God and certainly does not enjoy divine status. As we mentioned, the king does not relate to God as his son in an exclusive manner; on the contrary, the title "son" refers in Deuteronomy to Israel as a whole ("you are the sons of the Lord your God," Deuteronomy 14:1). The Chapter of the King repeatedly emphasizes that the basic status of the king is like that of his brethren and therefore he is warned "that his heart may not be lifted up above his brethren" (Deuteronomy 17:20).

The language of the Chapter of the King in Deuteronomy shows that the appointment of a king is not an "absolute commandment" (to quote the language of R. Naftali Zvi Yehudah Berlin, the *Natziv*): "When you come to the land ... and you shall possess it ... and then say, 'I will set a king over me, like all the nations that are round about me ... You may indeed set as king over you him whom the Lord your God will choose'" (Deuteronomy 17:14–15). Despite the seeming opposition between the conditional language of the opening phrase: "When you come ... and then say, 'I will set upon me'" and the definitive language of the subsequent phrase: "you shall surely place," it would appear that the legal category found here is one of permission or authorization.[89] In terms of a widely used jurisprudential distinction, the norm applied in Deuteronomy 17 regarding the king does not impose an obligation but rather conveys authority: God (from the mouth of Moses) tells Israel, "If you wish to establish royal rule, I allow (or authorize) you to do so, against My will." This reading is reinforced by the wording: "like all the nations round about," indicating that the request for a king is understood by God as expressing the desire of the people to resemble the nations, from whom He wishes to separate them. And, indeed, the chapter continues with a series of conditions and exigencies distinguishing the Israelite

88   Compare D. R. Schwartz, "On Pharisaic Opposition to the Hasmonean Monarchy," in his *Studies in the Jewish Background of Christianity* (Tübingen, 1992), pp. 44–56; Goodblatt, "The Union of Priesthood and Kingship," p. 13.

89   This tension also exists in verse 15 itself: initially Moses states, emphatically, "you shall surely place" but thereafter comes the qualification, "whom the Lord your God shall choose" and immediately returns to the people: "from among your brethren you shall place." The final phrase is superfluous, for God appoints the king.

king from those of the nations. It is in this manner that one ought to understand the first "exigency": "whom the Lord your God will choose." The "choosing" by God does not convey upon the king any divine or sacral status. This follows, as mentioned, from the entire complex of personal and political limitations detailed immediately thereafter.[90] And, indeed, Scripture repeatedly emphasizes the substantive equality between the king and his brethren-subjects: "from among your brethren you shall set as king over you … that his heart may not be lifted up above his brethren" (Deuteronomy 17:16, 20).

Not only does the Chapter of the King in Deuteronomy remove any divine element from the king, be it cosmic, mythic or sacral, but it also repeatedly emphasizes the limitations of his authority: it is forbidden for him to have many wives or to have an excess of silver or gold.[91] He is also not allowed to have too many horses – that is to say, his army also needs to be limited. The Chapter of the King repeatedly emphasizes the king's subjugation to the Torah:

> And when he sits on the throne of his kingdom, he shall write for himself in a book a copy of this law, from that which is in charge of the Levitical priests; and it shall be with him, and he shall read in it all the days of his life, that he may learn to fear the Lord his God, by keeping all the words of this law and these statutes, and doing them … that he will not turn aside from the commandment, either to the right or to the left.
>
> (Deuteronomy 17:18–20)

The emphasis upon "before the priests and the Levites" implies the king's subjugation to the authorized interpreters of the Torah. According to the adjoining section, "the priests and the Levites" (and "the judge who shall be in those days") constitute the High Court authorized to interpret the Torah and to teach its commandments.[92] The clear impression is that

---

90 In this respect, the choice of the king is different from the choice of "the place" where the High Court will sit, mentioned a few short verses earlier (Deuteronomy 17:8, 10).

91 The limitation placed upon accumulation of property by the king stands out in light of the conjecture that one of the meanings of the root מלך (alongside that of rule, advice, and regret) is "to own property," which is one of the central aspects of the power and rule of the king. See G. Biton, "On the Meaning of the Root מלך" (in Hebrew), *Beit Miqra*, 96 (1984): 85–87.

92 The term "high court" (בית דין גדול) is not mentioned in Deuteronomy 17 nor, certainly, is the term "Sanhedrin": these terms are anachronistic with regard to

the Chapter of the King in Deuteronomy, more than determining the authority of the king, emphasizes his limitations.

The limited authority of the king becomes clear, not only from the limitations imposed upon him by the Chapter of the King but also from the context of this chapter in the Book of Deuteronomy – appearing immediately after a statement fixing the authority of the local courts (Deuteronomy 16:18–21; 17:2–7) and that of the High Court (Deuteronomy 17:8–13). The people are commanded to behave "according to the word which you shall be told" by the judges who sit in the High Court. The passage emphasizes, "according to the instruction which they give you, and according to the decision which they pronounce to you, you shall do; you shall not turn aside from the verdict which they declare to you, either to the right hand or the left" (Deuteronomy 17:11). In the absence of an explicit commandment to obey the king, the obligation to obey the court acquires further weight. Moreover, the adjacency of these two chapters and the emphasis, "before the priests and the Levites," likewise imply that the king is also subject to the court.

Following the Chapter of the King, the Torah establishes additional institutions among which, as already mentioned, is the priesthood.[93] It would seem that within this system is embedded the idea of separation or scattering of authorities, at the heart of which lies the view that one may not concentrate excessive political power within a single social institution.[94] Whether or not the idea of separation of authority is implicit in these chapters of Deuteronomy, it is clear that the editorial framework of the Book of Deuteronomy – which places the chapter of the king alongside those of the local courts, the High Court, the priesthood, and prophecy – indicates the relatively low position of the king, whose authority, as we have seen, is in any event limited.

Moreover, the silence of the Chapter of the King and its proximity to the chapter of the High Court teach that, according to the Book of Deuteronomy, the king does not have any judicial authorities. While

---

the Bible. However, a kind of supreme judicial-legislative institution does seem to be described there (Deuteronomy 17:8–13); cf. below.

93   Another institution is that of the prophet: see Deuteronomy 18:15–22; and cf. Levinson, *Deuteronomy and the Hermeneutics*. Levinson comments that the order of things there is not necessarily either ascending or descending. See his discussion there, pp. 142–143.

94   See S. R. Driver, *Deuteronomy* (Edinburgh, 1901), p. 210. This point was also noted by S. A. Cohen, *The Three Crowns: Structures of Communal Politics in Early Rabbinic Jewry* (Cambridge, 1990), p. 10; and cf. Levinson, *Deuteronomy and the Hermeneutics*.

the Chapter of the King does not explicitly deny him this authority, it is impossible to ignore the fact that there is no mention whatsoever in this chapter of him performing justice and righteousness. As mentioned, according to royal theology (in all its versions), performing justice and conducting a judicial system are among the explicit functions of the monarchy. This claim may seem surprising and, in the absence of cogent proof, even unlikely. On the other hand, one may claim that it is possible to conclude, from the silence of the Torah, that it does not deny the king this function; whatever is not explicitly denied is part of his function. In the final analysis, the performance of justice is among those prerogatives that belong to the king in a "typical" and "natural" fashion. However, as Bernard Levinson noted, the conclusion that the king has no judicial or legislative authority seems to follow, both from an analysis of the contents and language of the Chapter of the King, as well as from the editorial framework of the Book of Deuteronomy.[95]

This conclusion – that the king enjoys no authority in the legal realm – likewise follows from a comparison of the Chapter of the King in Deuteronomy to the Law of the Monarchy in the Book of Samuel. The biblical author mentions two reasons why the elders of Israel addressed Samuel with the request that he appoint over them a king: the first was that his sons, whom he had appointed as "judges over Israel," did not walk in his ways and "they turned aside after gain; they took bribes and perverted justice" (1 Samuel 8:1–4). The elders, who demand "appoint for us a king to govern us like all the nations" (1 Samuel 8:5), referring to rule and leadership in the broad sense, certainly included within this judging and doing justice in the narrow sense.[96] In contrast, the Chapter of the King in Deuteronomy makes no mention whatsoever of judicial authority or of doing justice. The Torah's silence on this matter is thunderous, particularly against the background of presenting the judicial authorities of the local courts and of the High Court in the adjacent chapter. The obvious conclusion is that the Chapter of the King does not intend for the king to have any real function in the legal system and that the Book of Deuteronomy removed from his power the performance of justice.[97]

95 Levinson, *Deuteronomy and the Hermeneutics*.
96 See also further on: "And this matter was evil in the eyes of Samuel, that they said, 'Give us a king to judge us'" (1 Samuel 8:6). But thereafter a distinction is drawn: "and the people refused to listen to the voice of Samuel and said, 'No, for we will have a king over us, and we will be like all the nations. And our king will judge us and go out before us and fight our battles'" (1 Samuel 8:19–20).
97 See Levinson, *Deuteronomy and the Hermeneutics*. On the opposition between the Chapter of the King in Deuteronomy and the Deuteronomistic history,

The difference between the status of king as judge according to the royal theology and his status in this regard according to the Book of Deuteronomy is even more apparent in light of the emphasis placed in this book (and in other books of the Torah) on God's presence in the court.[98] To recall, one of the characteristics of royal theology (even in its modified version of sacral monarchy) is the close connection of the king to God. This relationship is also reflected in the function of the king as judge: because of the relation of the king to God (or the presence of God within him), the judgment of the king is a sort of judgment of God. In the Book of Deuteronomy as well is a relationship between judgment and God – not, however, between the king and God but between God and the (high) court. In the chapter adjacent to the Chapter of the King, in which the powers of the Great Court are determined, it states, "If any case arises ... which is too difficult for you ... then you shall arise and go up to the place which the Lord your God will choose" (Deuteronomy 17:8). That is to say: the High Court is located in the Temple, and God, who is present in the Temple, is also present among the members of the Court, who are "the priests and Levites" and "the judge who shall be there in those days" (Deuteronomy 17:9). The presence of God among them assures that no error will fall in their decisions. It is not for naught that the Book of Deuteronomy emphasizes:

> Then you shall do according to what they declare to you *from that place which the Lord will choose,* and you shall be careful to do according to all that they direct you; according to the instruction which they give you, and according to the decision which they pronounce to you, you shall do; you shall not turn aside from the verdict which they declare to you, either to the right or to the left.
>
> (Deuteronomy 17:10–11)

see Levinson, "The Reconceptualization of Kingship," pp. 530–533. The Deuteronomistic history is the first detailed, systematic description of the history of Israel, and it includes Deuteronomy to 2 Kings. This work has been given the designation, "the Deuteronomistic history," because of the great similarity between it and the Book of Deuteronomy. On the Deuteronomistic history, see N. Na'aman, *The Past That Shapes the Present: The Creation of Biblical Historiography in the Late First Temple Period and After the Downfall* (in Hebrew) (Jerusalem, 2002), p. 128.

98   My comments on this point are based upon H. Shapira, "For the Judgment is God's: On the Relation between God and Human Judgment in Jewish Legal Tradition," *Bar-Ilan Law Review,* 26 (2009): 51–89.

Scripture's emphasis upon it being "from that place" indicates the connection between God who is present in that "place" and the instructions and decisions of the Court, which are like the decisions of God; deviation from them is tantamount to rebellion, not only against those who are authorized by Him to decide in halakhic matters but also against the instructions of God himself.[99]

The view that God is present in the judicial process appears elsewhere in the Torah. For example, the chapter concerning conspiring witnesses, further along in the Book of Deuteronomy, uses language similar to that found in the section about the High Court: "Then both parties to the dispute shall appear before the Lord, before the priests and the judges who are in office in those days" (Deuteronomy 19:17); "before the Lord" here means "before the priests and the judges." R. Moses Nahmanides was referring to this concept when he wrote:

> God will not allow the righteous judges who stand before Him to spill innocent blood, for judgment belongs to God and He judges among the judges. And all this is a great merit of the judges of Israel, and the promise that the Holy One blessed be He will agree by them and with them in the matter of judgment. And this is the reason [why it writes] "both parties to the dispute shall appear before the Lord" (v. 17), for it is before the Lord that they stand when they come before the priests and judges, and He will guide them in the path of truth.[100]

---

99 It is not for naught that the Torah goes on to state emphatically: "And the man who shall act deliberately, in not hearkening to the priest who stands there to serve before the Lord his God." The prohibition against straying from the instructions of the court either to the right or the left gives the court a status of infallibility, based on the belief that the court is guided by God.

100 Nahmanides (Ramban), *Torah Commentary,* on Deuteronomy 19:19, trans. Charles B. Chavel (New York: Shilo, 1976), vol. II, p. 434, and cf. Exodus 21:6 "and his master shall bring him before the judges (*elohim*)"; and further on (Exodus 22:8): "the matter of the two of them shall go up to the judges (*'ad ha-elohim*); he whom the judges find guilty shall pay double to his neighbor." Nahmanides explains there: "And in my opinion, Scripture says, 'and his master shall bring him before the judges (*elohim*)' and 'the matter of the two of them shall go up to the judges (*'ad ha-elohim*),' to allude that God will be with them in matters of judgment, He will find innocent and He will find guilty. Hence it is said, 'he whom the judges (*elohim*) will find guilty'; and Moses also said, 'for judgment is God's' (Deuteronomy 1:17). And Jehoshaphat also said, 'For it is not for man to judge, for God is with you in the matter of judgment' (2 Chronicles 19:6). And Scripture also says: '*Elohim* stand in the congregation of God, among *elohim* they judge'

Against the background of God's presence in the court according to the Book of Deuteronomy (and according to the Torah in general), the absence of connection between God and the king in the Chapter of the King stands out all the more strikingly. This difference reinforces our conclusion regarding the separation of the king from matters of judgment, and even emphasizes it. If we examine Deuteronomy 16:18–18:22 as the founding document of the various governing bodies in Israel, which has as one of its fundamental principles the separation among the various branches, we find that this document stresses that God is found specifically in the court in the Temple – and not with the king in his palace. In practice, this is another aspect of the separation between king and priesthood, noted earlier, in which the Temple, the priesthood, and the law are a single organic unity distinct and separate from the king. This finding particularly emphasizes the great distance between the limited approach to the monarchy found in the Book of Deuteronomy and the royal theology found in the Book of Psalms and other chapters of the Bible.

Another no less explicit expression that the king, according to the Chapter of the King in the Book of Deuteronomy, does not have divine status and is even lacking in sacral status is rooted in the complete absence of the topic of anointment in this chapter. As noted, anointment is the ceremonial means of establishing and setting up the divine king, or at least the sacral king, which appears repeatedly in the Bible in those places where the understanding of kingship is divine or sacral.[101] The language used in this chapter is: "you shall place upon yourself a king" (Deuteronomy 17:14–15), without any hint that the appointment takes place through a ceremony of a sacral nature. While it is stated that the king will be he whom "the Lord your God shall choose" (Deuteronomy 17:15), one cannot conclude from this that this choice conveys upon the king greater wisdom, the divine spirit, prophecy, or any other special qualities or powers.[102] On the contrary: as we emphasized above, this chapter specifically emphasizes the closeness

(Psalms 82:1) – that is: within the congregation of *elohim* he judges, for *elohim* [God] *is the judge.* And it also says, 'the two people who have the dispute shall stand before the Lord' (Deuteronomy 19:17)": Nahmanides, *Torah Commentary,* Exodus 21:6 (ed. Chavell, vol. I, p. 416).

101 See above, Section 1.2 (near n. 77) and the bibliography there.

102 Compare Liver, "King, Kingship," p. 1088, who for some reason describes the king according to the Book of Deuteronomy as "the chosen of the Lord and His anointed one, and he is sanctified by virtue of this status with special holiness." It seems to me that these elements are entirely lacking from the Chapter of the King in Deuteronomy, one clear expression of which is the total absence of any mention of the subject of anointing.

between the king and his "subjects" ("that he not lift up his heart above his brethren") and his subjugation to the priestly-Levite "wisdom." As stated, this chapter does not at all mention that the anointment of the king takes place through anointing with oil. It unreasonable to assume that the absence of the topic of anointing in the Chapter of the King in the Book of Deuteronomy – which also lacks all the other signs of a king having such a status – is accidental.

The three biblical approaches to the subject of monarchy surveyed in this chapter may be described as three mutually exclusive models. Admittedly, there is always a certain gap between any pure model and its concrete realization, in the sense that in concrete states of matters components belonging to pure models that are generally different from one another are mingled together. However, the models surveyed regarding monarchy hardly "mingle" with one another in their historical realizations; such is the case at least insofar as we are discussing the realization of these models in the history of ideas. Regarding the relationship between direct theocracy (in which the king is God) and royal theology (in which God is king) and limited monarchy (the king is not God), this fact is hardly surprising. Indeed, it is difficult to see how one could combine an approach (or model) that negates the legitimacy of human rule – and, as such, the rule of flesh and blood – with political models that affirm it. However, even those components of rule based upon royal theology, or at very least sacral monarchy, and the components of a rule based upon a limited understanding of monarchy exclude one another. Even though there is necessarily a great deal of overlap between the authorities of a sacral (or divine) king and those of a limited, earthly king, a great gap in the scope of their authorities nevertheless remains, also in relation to the attitude toward cult, and, to a large extent, the legal system. This claim also holds true regarding the nature of the authority in the case of overlap or similarities. It is thus with regard to the limitations on the earthly king regarding foreign and military matters, and administration, as opposed to the unlimited authority enjoyed by the sacral king in these areas.

The approaches or models proposed above are particularly useful in terms of studying the approach to monarchy in rabbinic literature. As is well known, this literature is extremely fragmentary and refrains, evidently deliberately, from providing the student with broad, predetermined intellectual structures. However, this does not mean that this literature is limited to a random collection of laws, brief homilies, and interpretations of verses, proverbs, and similar unconnected material. Zunz was correct when he wrote that "the aggadah is frequently subject to misinterpretation when studied in a fragmentary way."[103] This statement is likewise true of the halakhah, as well as of the connection between it and the aggadah.[104] One of the great difficulties facing anyone attempting to study rabbinic literature is reconstructing the broad structures of thought that underlie the "fragmented" sayings found therein. This problem, which presents difficulties in studying any topic, likewise arises regarding monarchy. The benefit of the models proposed above lies in their organizing and explanatory power. As I shall attempt to demonstrate below, these approaches or models are extremely useful for organizing the "fragmented" Talmudic material relating to the issue of the king, and they are also advantageous for clarifying the relationship in this subject between rabbinic literature and the Bible, upon which this literature is based.

103 L. Zunz, *Sermons in Judaism* (in Hebrew), edited and completed by H. Albeck (Jerusalem, 1974), p. 124.

104 See Y. Lorberbaum, *The Image of God: Halakhah and Aggadah* (in Hebrew) (Jerusalem, 2004), pp. 149–155.

TWO

Rabbinic Literature: The Law of the King

In the Talmudic sources, one finds echoes of all of the three approaches discussed in the first chapter of this book: namely, royal theology, limited monarchy, and direct theocracy. Nevertheless, there is no doubt that the dominant approach of the Mishnah, of the halakhic midrashim, and of the Talmudic discussions (particularly those of the Babylonian Talmud) is that the king is not God – the approach of limited monarchy. This approach is particularly striking in the halakhic sources. In contrast, in the non-halakhic, or aggadic, sources – found primarily in the words of the amoraim of Palestine, and possibly even later – echoes can be found both of the God-is-king approach (i.e. direct theocracy) and of the various versions of royal theology.

The halakhah, as it emerges from the Mishnah, from the halakhic midrashim, and from the Talmudic discussions, in practice adopts the Chapter of the King in Deuteronomy. The status of the king, his powers, and primarily the limitations on his authority, are fashioned in tannaitic halakhah, and in its wake also among the Babylonian amoraim, in line with the model of the biblical chapter. Within the realm of the halakhah, the sages reject, at times explicitly and at times by implication, the two other models of monarchy. In the course of its development and refashioning, they adopt the third approach, which argues that monarchy "is not in the heavens."

While most of the tannaim maintain that there is an obligation to appoint or name a king, they also hold that the king is subject to the Torah and to its authorized interpreters: namely, the Sanhedrin.[1] The sages (both tannaim and amoraim) repeatedly emphasize that the king must impose fear, but, in the wake of the Chapter of the King in Deuteronomy, rabbinic law places greater emphasis upon the limitations on the king's power than on his authority. According to tannaitic halakhah, the king is separated from the Temple and from its cult, and even from the judicial system – that is to say, from the execution of justice and righteousness – and even his initiative in foreign affairs and military matters is limited.

---

1   On the mitzvah to appoint a king in tannaitic halakhah, see G. J. Blidstein, "The Monarchic Imperative in Rabbinic Perspective," *AJS Review,* 7–8 (1982–1983): 15–39; p. 16.

The limitations upon the king may also be seen in the edited form of the Mishnah, which bears a clear resemblance to the editing of Chapters 16–18 of Deuteronomy. As I shall demonstrate below, the tannaim limit the king with regard to the number of women he is allowed to marry, the amount of gold and silver that he may accumulate, and the number of horses he may have in his stable. On this point they deviate considerably from biblical law as stated in Deuteronomy.

This chapter and the next will deal with the status and authority of the king in the Talmudic halakhic literature. The first and second sections below deal with various aspects of the commandment to appoint a king; the third, fourth and fifth concern the powers of the king and his realms of authority; while the last two sections of this chapter deal with various aspects of the separation between monarchy and priesthood. The third chapter, which is a direct sequel to the present chapter, focuses upon the relationship between the king and the law.

2.1 The Commandment of the King

We find the following dispute in *Sifrei Devarim* regarding the appointment of the king:

> "And you shall say, I will set a king over me."
>
> Rabbi Nehorai said: "This is a shameful thing for Israel, as is said: 'For they have not rejected you, but they have rejected Me from being king over them'" (1 Samuel 8:7).
>
> Rabbi Judah said: "But is it not a commandment from the Torah for them to ask for a king, as is said: 'You may indeed set a king over you' (Deuteronomy 17:15)? Why then were they punished in the days of Samuel? Because they advanced it."
>
> "Like all the nations which are round about me."
>
> Rabbi Nehorai said: "They did not seek a king except so that they might worship idols, as is said, 'that we also may be like all the nations, and that our king may govern us and go out before us and fight our battles'" (1 Samuel 8:20).[2]

---

2   *Sifrei Devarim*, 156 (ed. Finkelstein, p. 208). At the beginning of this section, we find the following homily: "'When you come into the land' – a positive mitzvah stated in a matter in reward for which you shall enter into the land." It is reasonable to assume that the formula, "a positive mitzvah … in reward for which," which appears in a number of places in relation to the biblical language, "When you go into the land" (see *Sifrei Devarim* 170, 297 [ed. Finkelstein, pp. 217, 316 respectively]), also applies to the language that opens the Commandment of the King – even though it is clear that it is not related to this matter, for what relation is there between the

It would appear that, according to the Chapter of the King in Deuteronomy (17:14–20; sometimes referred to as the "Commandment of the King"), particularly its opening verse – "and you shall say, I will set a king over me" – the appointment of a king is not an absolute obligation but rather depends upon the will of the people. Even though the next verse uses seemingly more definitive language – "you may indeed set a king over you" – according to the Book of Deuteronomy there is no obligation to appoint a king; it is only stated here that one is permitted to appoint a king. The passage was understood thus by almost all of the bible commentators and scholars, and also by R. Nehorai.[3]

However, unlike the majority of exegetes, R. Nehorai sees in the realization of the possibility offered by the Torah a "shameful thing," expressing a rejection of the kingdom of Heaven, along the line of God's words in his response to Samuel after the people (or the elders of Israel) ask, "Appoint for us a king to govern us like all the nations" (Samuel 8:5). From R. Nehorai's words further on in this passage, commenting on the

appointment of the king and entering the Land? It seems apparent from all the tannaitic sources that the appointment of the king occurred specifically after they entered the Land. Moreover, while the appointment of the king might seem to be a precondition or necessity for conquering the land, the phrase, "in reward for which you shall enter the Land" does not fit this meaning (compare *Sifrei Devarim*, 156). Nevertheless, it is possible that the editor of *Sifrei* applied this wording also to the phrase "When you come into the land" in the Chapter of the King, in order to indicate the great importance of the mitzvah of appointing a king.

3   Concerning the words, "You shall surely place [a king]," Ibn Ezra comments, "It is permitted to do so." Similarly, Rav Sa'adya Gaon writes, "You are allowed to place a king upon yourselves." Nahmanides cites the rabbinic statement inferring that one is commanded to appoint a king ("According to the opinion of our Sages, as in 'And you shall say … say … I shall place upon myself a king.' And this is a positive commandment, which obligates us to speak thus after inheriting and settling [the Land], similar to the phrase, 'you shall make a parapet for your roof' [Deuteronomy 22:8]"). He then adds that, in his opinion, the language of this section is "an allusion to what shall happen in the future, for thus it was when they asked [for] Saul," concluding: "For what reason can there be that the Torah would say in [the context of] a commandment 'like all the nations that are round about me,' and it is not fitting for Israel to learn from them nor to envy those who do iniquity. Rather, this is an allusion to a certain matter that shall be in the future; therefore this chapter is formulated in present tense." Similarly the *Natziv* (R. Naftali Zvi Yehudah Berlin; nineteenth-century Lithuania); see his *Ha'amek Davar* on Deuteronomy 17:14; and cf. S. R. Driver, *Deuteronomy* (Edinburgh, 1901), pp. 209–211; Blidstein, "The Monarchic Imperative in Rabbinic Perspective," p. 16.

verse "like all the nations which are round about me" (Deuteronomy 17:14), it would seem that he associated the appointment of a king with idolatry. R. Nehorai's language is rather surprising, for it seems to imply that the entire intention of the elders in asking for a king was in order to engage in pagan worship. While the tanna's intention may simply have been to say that the appointment of a king would indirectly lead to the abandonment of God, it is nevertheless difficult to see how the very establishment of the institution of the monarchy per se was idolatrous. Moreover, the verse used by R. Nehorai as a proof text – "that we may also be like all the nations, and that our king may govern us and go out before us and fight our battles" (1 Samuel 8:20) – makes no allusion to such a relationship; on the contrary, it follows that the intention of the elders/people in making the demand – "No! But we will have a king over us" – was focused on the sociopolitical level, on matters of war and of law.

A possible solution to this difficulty may be found in the assumption that R. Nehorai's words – "they did not seek a king, except so that they might engage in pagan worship" – imply some version of royal theology and the cult of the king that derives from it. As discussed earlier, this cult was widespread both in the Bible and in the Greco-Roman world of the tannaitic period.[4] In those religio-political cultures, each in its own way, the cult of the king and the cult of the gods were almost inseparably interwoven with one another. Thus, for example, the gods were frequently worshiped by means of a statue or image of the king.[5] According to R. Nehorai, what the people were requesting, whether consciously or by ignoring the implication, was a king "like all the nations." This would be a king to be worshiped as a kind of god, as in the great cultures of the ancient world (Egypt and Mesopotamia) and in later Antiquity (the Hellenistic kings and the Roman emperors), where the institution of the monarchy was based upon a political theology that was thoroughly "idolatrous." According to this conjecture, the "idolatry" that the king caused them to practice was none other than the cult of the king himself. In R. Nehorai's eyes, the appointment of a king and "the Kingdom of Heaven" (i.e. direct theocracy, to use Buber's terms) are two

---

4   See Blidstein, "The Monarchic Imperative," pp. 16–17. On the cult of statues of the kings in Late Antiquity, see L. R. Taylor, *The Divinity of the Roman Emperor* (Middletown, Conn., 1931). A number of bible scholars interpreted the people's request for a king in Samuel in similar fashion. See, for example, P. K. McCarter, *I–II Samuel* (Garden City, NY, 1985), p. 160; and compare M. Elat, *Samuel and the Foundation of Kingship* (Jerusalem, 1998), p. 60 n. 11.

5   See above, the studies cited in Chapter 1, n. 72.

mutually exclusive forms of government; with every king is the danger of deification. In his opinion, no intermediate option is possible – not even that suggested by the Book of Deuteronomy, according to which the king is not a god (thus greatly limiting the authority of the king).[6]

As far as we know, R. Nehorai's opinion is an isolated one within tannaitic literature. In contrast, in *Sifrei Devarim,* we find the view of Rabbi Judah – which is evidently joined (according to other sources) by that of other sages – according to which the appointment of a king is (to use the language of R. Naftali Zvi Yehudah Berlin) a categorical commandment. R. Judah's opinion is based on the language of the verse: "you shall surely place upon yourself a king." It is difficult to determine whether R. Judah relies here on the language of the verse, which seems decisive ("you shall surely place"), or whether this language merely serves as a proof text and that his opinion derives from another tradition. In either event, this language too does not change the clear impression that emerges from the passage: that the appointment of a king is only seen as something permitted.[7]

It would appear, moreover, that R. Judah does not interpret the phrase "and you shall say: I shall place " as descriptive language – "alluding to the future" (to quote Nahmanides' view) – but rather as couched in the imperative, that is, as an obligation incumbent upon the public (the people or the elders) to seek a king.[8] In other words, according to R. Judah, the commandment to appoint a king is not addressed to a

---

6   It was not for naught that R. Nehorai says elsewhere regarding the Chapter of the King in Samuel, in which the prerogatives of the king are described: "This portion was only said because of the controversy, as is said, 'And you shall say: I will place upon myself a king'": *Tosefta Sanhedrin* 4.5 (ed. Zuckermandel, p. 421); and cf. on this below. R. Nehorai's approach regarding the question of the king corresponds to his approach in the Mishnah, *Mishnah Kiddushin* 4.14: "R. Nehorai said: 'I would leave aside all skills in the world and not teach my son anything but Torah, for a person enjoys its reward in this world, and the main part thereof endures to the World to Come. But other crafts are not thus, for when a person is ill or becomes old or undergoes sufferings and is unable to engage in labor he dies of starvation. But the Torah is not thus; rather, it protects him from all evil in his youth, and it gives him an end and hope in old age.'" Blidstein comments on this, "The Monarchic Imperative," p. 31. However, contrary to his suggestion, there is no necessary connection between these things and R. Nehorai's attitude to the Bar-Kokhba rebellion; and cf. below, near n. 37.

7   See above, Chapter 1.3 (near n. 89).

8   See Nahmanides' *Commentary on the Torah,* Deuteronomy 17:14 (ed. Chavell, p. 424).

prophet with the people remaining passive; rather, the Commandment of the King is incumbent first and foremost on the people, and its matter is to seek a king, evidently by means of a priest or prophet.[9] This likewise follows from the words of R. Eleazar b. Yossi in *Tosefta Sanhedrin:*

> The elders asked properly, as it says, "Give us a king to judge us,"[10] – that is to say, they fulfilled the mitzvah properly – but the ignorant people turned and behaved improperly, as is said, "And we shall be like all the nations, and our king will judge us and go out before us and fight," etc. [11]

Thus, R. Eleazar b. Yossi also thinks that there is a commandment to appoint a king and that the obligation is incumbent upon the people or its representatives (the elders).

The commandment to appoint a king follows likewise from other, anonymous midrashim in *Sifrei Devarim*: "'You shall surely set.' If he dies, appoint another in his place ... Something else: 'You may indeed set a king' over you – this is a positive command. ['You may not put a foreigner over you' – that is a negative commandment]."[12]

The obligation, upon the death of a king, to appoint a new one in his place, derives from the basic obligation to appoint a king. Continuity, essential to every political system, is one of the striking characteristics of royal rule, in which the dynastic element generally plays a substantial role.[13] And, indeed, the midrash in *Sifrei Devarim*, in the wake of Scriptures, emphasizes: "'[That he may continue long upon his kingdom,] he and his children.' If he dies, his son comes in his place."[14] The issue of

---

9   See *Sifrei Devarim* 157 (ed. Finkelstein, p. 208: "'Which the Lord your God shall choose' – according to a prophet."

10   Compare the version of the *beraita* in *Babylonian Sanhedrin* 20b: "We have taught: R. Eleazar b. R. Yossi taught: The elders of the generation asked properly, as is said, 'Give us a king to judge us.'"

11   *Tosefta Sanhedrin* 4.5 (ed. Zuckermandel, p. 421). Cf. the language of the Genizah passage from *Mekhilta Devarim*, in S. Schechter, "Mekhilta Le-Devarim, Parashat Re'eh" (in Hebrew), in M. Brann and J. Elbogen (eds.), *Festschrift zu Israel Lewy's Siebzigstem Geburtstag* (Breslau, 1911), pp. 187–192; "Demand a king"; and cf. below, Chapter 2.2 (near the reference to n. 31).

12   *Sifrei Devarim*, 157 (ed. Finkelstein, pp. 208–209).

13   See the remarks by M. Walzer in M. Walzer et al., *The Jewish Political Tradition* (New Haven, Conn., 2000), pp. 109–116.

14   *Sifrei Devarim*, 162 (ed. Finkelstein, pp. 212–213) and the continuation of the midrash there: "I only know regarding this one alone; from whence do I know that all the leaders [*parnasim*] of Israel are succeeded by their sons after them?

dynastic succession clarifies the extent to which these tannaim adopted the institution of monarchy as it appears in the Book of Deuteronomy while rejecting direct theocracy, which fundamentally rejects the element of dynastic continuity.[15] This element of continuity, rooted in the notion of dynasty, is negated by direct theocracy even more strongly than the one-time existence of an authoritative ruler, since when a judge rules he is no different in substance from the "limited king" of Deuteronomy, and at times his powers and authority may be even broader.

While the commandment to appoint a king is not explicitly mentioned in the Mishnah, it nevertheless appears that this obligation underlies the basis of the halakhot brought on this subject (*Mishnah Sanhedrin* 2.2–5). In the final analysis, the Mishnah does not explicitly state that there is a commandment to set up a Sanhedrin, nor does it explicitly state the requirement to appoint a high priest (a subject discussed in *Mishnah Sanhedrin* 2.1).[16] The first part of *Mishnah Sanhedrin* (parallel to Deuteronomy 16:18–18:22) enumerates those laws pertaining to all branches of government: the local courts, Sanhedrin, high priest, and king.[17] Even though the editor of the Mishnah does not say so explicitly, he evidently thinks that there is an obligation to set up all these institutions, including the appointment of a king.

In this context, I should note that the editor of the Mishnah does not seem to incorporate in his work all matters relating to the king. He brings the laws pertaining to the monarchy in the course of his discussion of the authority of the courts (of 3, of 23, and of 71 [the Sanhedrin]) in Chapters 1–3 of *Mishnah Sanhedrin*. The section dealing with the king begins with the law, "The king does not judge and is not judged," its main concern the relationship and degree of subjugation of the king to the courts. This law will be discussed at length below. Even though the Mishnah's discussion of the king seems tangential, and possibly fragmented, it will become clear from the following discussion that one can discern therein the principles by which the editor of the Mishnah arranged the relevant laws.[18] As mentioned, while

Scripture says: 'He and his sons within Israel' – whoever is in Israel is succeeded by his son."

15   See Gideon's words in Judges 8:23.

16   See Blidstein, "The Monarchic Imperative," p. 21, n. 16; and compare B. Z. Bacher, *Aggadot ha-Tannaim* (Berlin, 1922), vol. II, p. 141, n. 13.

17   Further along in this tractate mention is also made of the matter of the prophet; see *Mishnah Sanhedrin* 11.5–6.

18   Thus, for example, the entire process of appointing the king, including anointment, is absent from the Mishnah; see Chapter 2.7 below.

the statement that it is obligatory to appoint to a king (as well as the controversy surrounding this issue) does not appear in the Mishnah, it appears that the commandment to establish the institution of the monarchy is implied therein.

It seems that according to the approach of Rabbi Judah (and most of the tannaim), the Law of the Kingdom in Samuel is more difficult than the language of Deuteronomy, since, according to the literal sense of the chapter in Samuel, the appointment of the king is (to quote the language of R. Nehorai) "a shameful thing for Israel."[19] According to R. Judah, the people of Israel were "punished in the days of Samuel," not because of the request for a king per se but because "they advanced it with their own hands" (*le-fi she-hikdimu 'al yadam*). The phrase "they were punished" is not altogether clear, as the Bible does not mention any specific punishment imposed upon Israel at the time of Samuel due to their demand for a king. It does not make sense that R. Judah is merely referring here to the words of chastisement that God and, in turn, Samuel addressed to them (1 Samuel 8:6–18) regarding the request of the king as such. There may have been an element of punishment in rainfall during the wheat harvest in Gilgal at the time of "renewal of the kingship," as related in 1 Samuel 12:17:

> Is it not wheat harvest today? I will call upon the Lord, that He may send thunder and rain; and you shall know and see that your wickedness is great, which you have done in the sight of the Lord, in asking for yourselves a king.[20]

R. Judah's phrase, "because they advanced it with their own hands," remains cryptic; exegetes and scholars alike have attempted to decipher it, and none of the solutions suggested seem successful.[21]

---

19 It may be that R. Judah is reacting directly to the opinion of R. Nehorai. See Blidstein's discussion, "The Monarchic Imperative," p. 19, n. 11.

20 This verse, which appears at the end of Samuel's words at Gilgal at the time of "renewing the kingship," is surprising, since what preceded it is a kind of acceptance or at least reconciliation with the appointment of the King (provided only that the people and the king follow "after the Lord"). The falling of rain initially appears to be a sign from Heaven ("this great thing that the Lord does before your eyes") of God's agreement, but in the next verse it is interpreted as a punishment. See Elat, *Samuel and the Foundation of Kingship*, pp. 138–139, and the references there, n. 36.

21 See Blidstein's discussion, "The Monarchic Imperative," pp. 32–35. Blidstein rather hesitantly raises the possibility that R. Judah's words are related to his

2.2 Three Commandments

Another expression of the view that the appointment of a king is a commandment follows from a group of tannaitic sources, which note three "national" commandments that Israel was commanded upon entering the Land or after conquering it. Rabbi Judah's words in *Sifrei Devarim* regarding the Chapter of the King are related to his words in another passage in *Sifrei Devarim:*

> "When you shall cross over the Jordan and dwell in the land." Rabbi Judah said: Israel were commanded three commandments upon entering the Land: to appoint over themselves a king; to build a Temple; and to destroy the seed of Amalek.
>
> I do not know which one comes first: to appoint a king, to build the Temple, or to destroy the seed of Amalek? Scripture says: "And he said, 'A hand upon the throne of the Lord; the Lord will have war with Amalek'" (Exodus 17:16). Once there is a king seated upon the throne of the Lord, you must cut off the seed of Amalek.

words in *Sifrei Devarim* 67 (and cf. *Tosefta Sanhedrin* 4.5 [ed. Zuckermandel, p. 421]; *Babylonian Sanhedrin* 20b; and see below) concerning the three mitzvot that the people of Israel were commanded on entering the land – the appointment of a king, the building of the Temple, and the destruction of Amalek – and the dispute between R. Akiva and R. Ishmael concerning the time when they became obligated in these (and other) mitzvot: immediately upon entering the Land (R. Akiva) or only after its conquest (R. Ishmael); concerning this matter see J. N. Epstein, *Introductions to the Tannaitic Literature* (in Hebrew) (Jerusalem, 1957), pp. 539–541. It may be that the tanna who asked "Why were they punished in the days of Samuel?" and answers, "Because they did so too early" – who is not R. Judah (see Blidstein, "The Monarchic Imperative," n. 27) – may think that their request for a king at that time was premature and that they ought to have waited until the time of David. Compare Maimonides' explanation in *Hilkhot Melakhim* 1.2: "Because they asked in a contrary manner, and did not ask in order to fulfill the mitzvah, because they were fed up with Samuel the prophet, as is said: 'For it is not you whom they have rejected, but Me that they reject.'" Another possibility emerges from a passage from *Midrash Tannaim* to Deuteronomy (ed. Hoffman, p. 104): "If so, why were they punished in the days of Samuel? Because they asked too early and requested in a contrary way and did not seek a king for the sake of Heaven." This midrash draws a contrast between "they asked too early" and "for the sake of Heaven." In his commentary on the *Tosefta Shabbat* 17.2, Lieberman explains that the phrase הקדימו על ידם means "to do so too early." It may be that here too is a similar opposition/contrast. I thank Amihai Radziner for suggesting this possibility to me.

> And from whence do we know that the throne of the Lord is the king? It says: "Then Solomon sat upon the throne of the Lord as king" (1 Chronicles 29:23).
>
> And still I do not know which takes precedence: whether to build a Temple or to destroy Amalek? Scripture says: "which the Lord your God gives you as an inheritance," and it says "Now when the king dwelt in his house, and the Lord had given him rest from all his enemies round about," and it says: "And the king said to Nathan the prophet: 'See now, I dwell in a house of cedar, but the ark of God dwells in a tent'" (2 Samuel 7:1–2).[22]

According to Rabbi Judah, the commandment to appoint a king is bound up with two other "national mitzvoth": to destroy Amalek and to build the Temple. Further on in this passage, R. Judah raises the question of their proper order. The solutions to this question proposed by the sages involve a number of difficulties, which I shall not discuss at length here, except to note that the precedence given to appointing a king over the other commandments seems natural, just as it seems logical that only upon the establishment of a central government is it possible to maintain an army that will involve the entire people and destroy Amalek, and only then will it be possible to execute a "national" project of broad scope such as the building of the Temple.[23] Moreover, the destruction of Amalek and the building of the Temple are, as mentioned, "national" mitzvot, the implementation of which is imposed upon the nation as such; only upon the enthronement of a king – who (evidently) embodies in his function and status the entire people – is it possible to fulfill these commandments.[24]

It is interesting to note the manner in which R. Judah infers that the commandment of appointing the king precedes the destruction of Amalek. The wording of Exodus 17:16 – "A hand upon the throne of the Lord; the Lord will have war with Amalek" – which literally means that God takes an oath upon His throne ("a hand upon the throne of God") that He will take vengeance against Amalek, is interpreted by R. Judah as applying to the king: "once the king sits upon the throne of the Lord."

---

22 *Sifrei Devarim* 67 (ed. Finkelstein, p. 132); and see *Tosefta Sanhedrin* 4.5 (ed. Zuckermandel, pp. 420–421); *Babylonian Sanhedrin* 20b, in the name of R. Yossi.

23 See Blidstein, "The Monarchic Imperative," pp. 32–35.

24 The precedence of the commandment to appoint a king over that to destroy Amalek follows clearly from 1 Samuel 15. Scripture places the anointing of Saul (1 Samuel 15:1–4) adjacent to God's command to smite Amalek, as if to say that the anointing of the king is in order to destroy Amalek. I thank Amihai Radziner, who brought this matter to my attention.

"The throne of the Lord" is a metonym for God Himself, and the verse from the First Book of Chronicles – "Solomon sat upon the throne of the Lord as king" (1 Chronicles 29:23) alludes to the close relationship between Solomon and God. Thus, according to his approach, the king sits upon the throne of the Lord! It does not seem plausible that R. Judah's words were merely intended to provide a basis for the (practical) halakhah that the appointment of the king precedes the destruction of Amalek. It is difficult to escape the impression that his exegetical move, with all its components, is rooted in some version of the idea of a divine king. In the final analysis, the identification of the throne of the king with the throne of God is a basic principle of royal theology. Even the proof text from Chronicles alludes to this idea for, as noted above, Solomon is the ultimate biblical embodiment of royal theology (in its sacral version).

Maimonides, who rules like R. Judah (and like R. Yossi and the Babylonian Talmud, Sanhedrin), brings different biblical proof texts in support of this halakhah and does not at all mention the exegetical path of the tanna in the Midrash:

> The appointment of the king precedes the war against Amalek, as is said: "The Lord sent me to anoint you king … now go and smite Amalek" [1 Samuel 15:1, 3]. In his view, the destruction of Amalek precedes the building of the Temple, as is said, "Now when the king dwelt in his house, and the Lord had given him rest from all his enemies round about; the king said to Nathan the prophet: I dwell in a house of cedar."[25]

Maimonides, who is extraordinarily sensitive to the mythic elements in the Bible and midrash, evidently identified the background for R. Judah's halakhah and chose to give it another biblical source.[26] Moreover, his sources indicate that R. Judah presented a reasonable alternative by interpreting the literal sense of the verses, as according to the biblical narrative the order was: king, Amalek, Temple. It is therefore reasonable to assume that the exegetical path taken by R. Judah is not merely technical.

25 *Hilkhot Melakhim* 1.2.
26 See my paper, Y. Lorberbaum, "'The Doctrine of Corporeality of God Did Not Occur Even for a Single Day to the Sages, May Their Memory Be Blessed' (The Guide of the Perplexed I, 46): Anthropomorphism in Early Rabbinic Literature – A Critical Review of Scholarly Research" (in Hebrew), *Jewish Studies*, 40 (2000): 3–54.

It is difficult to ignore the tension, and possibly even the contradiction, between the homily of R. Judah – based upon a verse that explicitly expresses a royal theology – and the opposite tendency of the Mishnah and the halakhic midrashim, which tends to support a limited earthly monarchy. This opposition is concrete, since R. Judah's homily does not nullify the meaning of the verse about Solomon sitting upon the throne of the Lord but specifically emphasizes its original, mythic-sacral meaning. It may be that in order to provide a basis for the argument that there is a commandment to appoint a king, R. Judah turns from the Chapter of the King in Deuteronomy – according to which, as stated, there is no commandment to do so – to biblical sources that express a royal theology (or the idea of a sacral monarchy), since only therein does this "commandment" receive explicit expression.

The relationship between an earthly monarch and the throne of God likewise emerges from a homily found in *Mekhilta de-Rabbi Yishmael,* attributed to R. Joshua:

> "And he said: 'A hand upon the throne of the Lord, the Lord will have war … '" R. Joshua said: When the Holy One blessed be He sits upon the throne of His kingdom, and his monarchy shall be, at that time there is a war of the Lord against Amalek.[27]

As has been argued by Menahem Kahana, the phrase "and his monarchy shall be" (ותהי ממלכתו) is truncated; it should be read as it does in the internal text in the Lauterbach edition (based upon manuscripts): "and the monarchy shall be His" (ותהי הממשלה שלו).[28] Kahana also showed that, according to the manuscript of the *Mekhilta,* the reading is "When the king sits [and not "God"] upon the throne of his kingdom." Moreover, similar to R. Judah's statement in *Sifrei Devarim* 67, this homily should not be interpreted as referring to the King of Kings and the Eschaton but rather to a human king; R. Joshua is speaking in the present.[29] The phrase "the throne of the Lord [or Jah]" is therefore interpreted here as well

27   *Mekhilta de-Rabbi Yishmael, Amalek* 2 (ed. Horowitz and Rabin, p. 186).

28   *Mekhilta de-Rabbi Ishmael* (ed. Lauterbach), p. 160.

29   See M. I. Kahana, *The Two Mekhiltot on the Amalek Portion: The Originality of the Version of the Mekhila D'rabbi Ishma'el with Respect to the Makhilta of Rabbi Shim'on Ben Yohay* (in Hebrew) (Jerusalem, 1999), pp. 56–57; and compare J. R. Elbaum, "'Eleazar Hamodai and R. Joshua on the Amalek Pericope" (in Hebrew), in I. Ben-Ami I. and J. Dan (eds.), *Studies in Aggadah and Jewish Folklore,* 7 (Jerusalem, 1983), pp. 99–116, at p. 110.

as referring to a human kingdom; again, consistent with the pattern of thought characteristic of royal theology, the king is presented here as a kind of long hand of God.[30]

The commandment to appoint a king also follows from a midrashic fragment from the [Cairo] Genizah published by Solomon Schechter, which he identified as part of the *Mekhilta* to Deuteronomy. This passage revolves around the phrase, "to make His habitation there" (Deuteronomy 12:5):

> "To make His habitation there." The Scripture speaks after the inheritance and settling of the land. Once you shall conquer and inhabit and dwell therein, build a Temple, office sacrifices, ask a king, and destroy the memory of Amalek ... [31]
>
> The Temple precedes the king, and it is logical. It speak[s of fear of He]aven and fear of earth; it speaks of the kingdom of Heaven and the kingdom of earth. We find that ... fear of Heaven [is prior to] fear of earth. Thus, the kingdom of Heaven precedes the kingdom of earth.
>
> But I do not know which one precedes, whether the king or the destroying the memory of Amalek?
>
> Scripture says: "And say: 'A hand upon the throne of the Lord ...'" When the king shall sit upon the throne of God and the sovereignty of God shall be in his hand, at that time "the Lord will have war with Amalek from generation to generation."
>
> For we have found that when they sought to anoint ... a king ... to ... as is said, "For they have not rejected you, but they have rejected Me ..." (1 Samuel 8:7).
>
> [R. Jo]nathan said: The king precedes the Temple, as is said, "When you come to the land which the Lord your God gives you, and you possess it and dwell in it, and then say: I will set a king over me."[32]

---

30 However, it is still possible that in R. Joshua's statement in the *Mekhilta* the word מלך ("king") refers to God and not to an earthly king. According to this interpretation, the saying deals with the complete kingship of God (in the eschatological future), in keeping with the approach of the amoraic midrash in *Pesikta de-Rav Kahana*, 3.16 (ed. Mandelbaum, p. 53): "So long as the seed of Amalek exists in the world, God's name is not complete, nor is His throne complete." Cf. A. Schremer, "Eschatology, Violence and Suicide: An Early Rabbinic Theme and its Influence in the Middle Ages," in A. Amanat and J. J. Collins (eds.), *Apocalypse and Violence* (New Haven, Conn., 2004), pp. 19–43, at n. 22.

31 See Rashi to *Babylonian Sanhedrin* 20b, s.v. *shalosh mitzvot*.

32 Thus suggests Schechter, "Mekhilta Le-Devarim."

Still, I do not know which takes precedence: the Temple or the destruction of the memory of Amalek? Scripture says: "Therefore, when the Lord your God has given you rest from all your enemies round about, in the land which the Lord your God gives you for an inheritance to possess, you shall blot out the remembrance of Amalek from under heaven; you shall not forget." That is, the king precedes the Temple, and the Temple precedes the destruction of Amalek.

If so, why does the Scripture say: "For they have not rejected you, but they have rejected Me . . ."? This teaches that they did not seek a king for the sake [of Heaven], but rather sought a king for their own sakes ... as is said ... "that we also may be like all the nations," etc.[33]

This passage also suggests that there is a commandment to appoint a king and that this commandment is related to two other national commandments: the building of the Temple and the eradication of Amalek. It differs on several points, however, from the midrashic passage in *Sifrei Devarim*. First, it states that these mitzvot do not apply immediately upon their entering into the land (as is the opinion of R. Judah in *Sifrei Devarim*) but only after its conquest and inheritance; second, as opposed to the opinion of R. Judah and other tannaim – who think that the correct order is: king, Amalek, Temple – according to the former opinion in this passage, the appointment of the king follows the building of the Temple, and only thereafter the eradication of Amalek.[34]

33   This reconstruction is suggested by Schechter, "Mekhilta Le-Devarim," pp. 191–192. On this passage, see Kahana's introductory remarks, *The Two Mekhiltot*, pp. 187–188. The manuscript of these pages of *Mekhilta Devarim* were evidently lost; see M. Kahana, *Manuscripts of the Halakhic Midrashim: An Annotated Catalogue* (in Hebrew) (Jerusalem, 1995), pp. 110–111. The passage is discussed by Blidstein, "The Monarchic Imperative," pp. 25–27; and by Kahana, *The Two Mekhiltot*, p. 83 and n. 116 there. The homily that preceded the above passage is: "'Seek that he may dwell there' [Deuteronomy 12:5]. Scripture speaks after inheritance and settling. You might ask: Does Scripture speak of after inheritance and settling, or does it speak immediately upon their entering the Land? Scripture says, 'and you shall inherit it and settle there.'"

34   See the passage deleted above (from the first paragraph), indicated by square brackets: "Or does it only speak immediately upon their entering the land? Scripture says: 'You shall cross over the Jordan and settle in the land,' etc. 'And the place which the Lord your God shall choose' [Deuteronomy 12:10–11]." On this dispute, see Epstein, *Introductions to Tannaitic Literature*, pp. 539–541; Blidstein, "The Monarchic Imperative," p. 24.

It is not clear what lies at the basis of the controversy concerning the order in which these national commandments should be fulfilled: that is, do the exegeses of the verses dictate the various opinions or are there inherent differing views as to the rationales for these commandments and the nature of the relations among them, which in turn dictate the order of their performance.[35] Even if the second possibility is correct, it is difficult to extract from this saying (and its parallels) the nature of these competing reasons and relations, as the rival explanations are all equal. Gerald Blidstein suggests reading this controversy – both regarding the commandment to appoint a king (i.e. the dispute among R. Nehorai, R. Judah, and the sages) and regarding the order of the commandments – against the background of the Bar Kokhba Rebellion. According to his suggestion, the sages' words are to be read and interpreted as an encouragement to rebel against the Romans or as justification of the rebellion in retrospect. However, as he himself repeatedly notes, this suggestion does not shed light upon the controversy, as the different opinions are all open to different and even contradictory explanations.[36]

The midrashim in this passage are interesting in this context because, no less than those of R. Judah in *Sifrei* and that of R. Joshua in *Mekhilta,* they are suffused with the imprint of sacral monarchy. An anonymous preacher infers the precedence given to the building of the Temple over the appointment of a king on the basis of the parallel between fear of Heaven/kingdom of heaven, and fear of the earth/kingdom of the earth. It is not clear from where he derives this parallel; perhaps, as Schechter has suggested, he learns it from Proverbs 24:21: "My son, fear the Lord and the king." In any event, it would appear that the parallel drawn in this midrash between the kingdom of Heaven and the kingdom of earth – like most parallels between heaven and earth, which are extremely common in rabbinic literature – also pertain to the connection between them.[37] The midrash may be implying that there is a connection between the king and the kingdom of Heaven – and possibly also that the Temple must precede the king, because one of the conditions of the king's rule

35 See Rashi to *Babylonian Sanhedrin* 20b, s.v. *shalosh mitzvot.*
36 See Blidstein, "The Monarchic Imperative," pp. 29–33.
37 On the parallels between the upper and lower realms in rabbinic literature, see V. Aptowitzer, "The Heavenly Temple in the Aggadah" (in Hebrew), *Tarbiz,* 2 (1931): 137–153, 257–287; and, in other contexts, see Y. Lorberbaum, *Image of God,* Chapter 6.

is the dwelling of the divine presence upon him via the Temple.[38] As for the king's appointment preceding the destruction of Amalek, here too the author utilizes a motive that appears in R. Judah's homily in *Sifrei* (and in that of R. Joshua in *Mekhilta*) – namely, that the king sits upon the throne of God.

The last part of this passage ("If so, why does Scripture say") is not a continuation of what precedes it, and hence not part of the words of R. Jonathan, but rather returns to the opening homily of the passage. Here, the phrase "for they have not rejected you, but they have rejected Me" is interpreted in a rather surprising manner. Whereas, according to Scripture, the opposition is between the kingdom of Heaven and an earthly king, here the opposition is between a human king who rules "for the sake of Heaven" (assuming we accept Schechter's plausible reconstruction of the text) and a human king who reigns "for their own sake." It may be that, by referring to a king who rules "for the sake of Heaven," the midrash is alluding to one who does so for the sake of the mitzvah, and not for worldly political goals.[39] However, it is also possible that, as in several other places in rabbinic literature, the meaning of the idiom is literal.[40] According to this reading, the move in this sermon is explicitly associated with an approach of royal theology.[41]

---

38   The relation between the king and the Temple also follows from the following passage from *Sifrei Devarim* 6 (ed. Finkelstein, p. 14: "'And the Lebanon' [Deuteronomy 3:25]. He said to them: When you enter into the land, you must set up for yourselves a king and build yourselves a Temple. From whence do we know that 'Lebanon' refers to a king? As is said, 'came to Lebanon and took the top of the cedar' [Ezekiel 17:3] and it says, 'a thistle on Lebanon' [2 Kings 14:9]. And Lebanon is none other but the Temple, as it says 'You are My witness, head of the Lebanon' [Jeremiah 20:26] and it says, 'He will cut down the thickets of the forest with an axe, and Lebanon with its majestic trees shall fall' [Isaiah 10:34]." It would therefore appear that the fact that "Lebanon" is a term used both for the king and for the Temple suggests that this author identified a real connection between them; see also *Sifrei Bamidbar* 134 (ed. Horowitz, p. 181) and the bibliography brought by the editor in *Sifrei Devarim*.

39   See *Midrash Tannaim* on *Devarim* (ed. Hoffman, p. 104): "If so, why were they punished in the days of Samuel? Because they did so prematurely, and asked in a complaining manner and did not ask for a king for the sake of Heaven."

40   See, for example, *Avot de-Rabbi Nathan*, Version B (ed. Schechter, p. 66); and cf. Lorberbaum, *Image of God*, pp. 173–177.

41   The practical significance of the first reading may be that the king is intended to fulfill a primarily symbolic function or office and that he is lacking in political authority, while according to the second reading he has extensive political authority.

If the relationship between the king and the Temple in the Genizah fragment discussed above is not fully clear, the closeness between them, characteristic of royal theology, follows explicitly from the following passage in *Sifrei Devarim*:

> "And the Lebanon" (Deuteronomy 1:7). He said to them: When you enter the Land, you need to place upon yourself a king and to build yourself a Temple.
>
> From whence do we know that Lebanon refers to none other than the king? As is said: "He came to Lebanon and took the top of the cedar" (Ezekiel 17:3), and it says, "a thistle on Lebanon" (2 Kings 14:9).
>
> And Lebanon is naught but the Temple, as is said: "You are as Gilead to me, as the summit of Lebanon" (Jeremiah 22:6), and it says, "He will cut down the thickets of the forest with an axe, and Lebanon with its majestic trees will fall" (Isaiah 10:34).[42]

In this homily, "Lebanon" serves as a joint code word for both the Temple and the king: the author identifies "Lebanon" in Deuteronomy 1 with the image of "Lebanon" in the proverbs of Ezekiel (17:3) and of Amaziah king of Judah (2 Kings 14:9), in which the object of the parable is the kings of Judah and Israel. But "Lebanon" is also an image for the Temple (thus in Isaiah 10:34 and in many other places).[43] It would seem that our preacher is thereby establishing a relationship between the king and the Temple.[44]

---

42   *Sifrei Devarim* 6 (ed. Finkelstein, p. 14). For alternative readings of this passage, see M. I. Kahana, *Sifre Zuta on Deuteronomy: Citations from a New Tannaitic Midrash* (in Hebrew) (Jerusalem, 2002), p. 137; and cf. Epstein, *Introductions to Tannaitic Literature*, p. 625. Kahana, *The Two Mekhiltot*, p. 135, notes the parallel in *Sifrei Zuta Devarim* 1.7,11.7–12: "'And the Lebanon' (Deuteronomy 1:7). He said to them: When you enter the land, you need to appoint over yourselves a king and establish for yourselves a dwelling place for the Divine Presence. And from whence do be know that 'Lebanon' refers to kingship? It says. 'The thistle on Lebanon' etc. and 'Come to Lebanon,' etc. And from whence do we know that Lebanon is none other than the Temple? He said: 'Gilead, you are mine, head of the Lebanon, opening of Lebanon' etc. and 'There shall be knocked down the thistles of the forest.'" On the idiom בית השכינה ("a dwelling place for the Divine Presence"), which is unique to *Sifrei Zuta Devarim,* see Kahana, *Sifre Zuta on Deuteronomy*, Chapter 2, Section 2.3 (56), and pp. 142–143 on the parallels from *Sifrei Devarim* and the *Mekhiltot* to Deuteronomy.

43   See Kahana, *Sifre Zuta on Deuteronomy*, pp. 143–144.

44   Cf. *Sifrei Bamidbar* 134 (ed. Horowitz, p. 181), and the editor's bibliography in *Sifrei Devarim*.

A similar relationship between the king and the Temple, or possibly even the same one, also follows from a passage in *Midrash Shmuel*:

> "And the Lord said to Samuel: Hearken ..." etc. (1 Samuel 8:7). Rabbi Shimon b. Yohai taught: "they have rejected Me" – Me too they have rejected, because Me too they have rejected. He said to him: In three things they shall reject: [in the kingdom of Heaven, and the kingdom of the Davidic house], and in the building of the Temple.
>
> When did they reject all three of them? In the days of Rehoboam. It is written there, "And when all Israel saw ... [the people answered], What portion have we in David?" (1 Kings 12:16) – this refers to the kingdom of Heaven. "Nor an inheritance in the son of Jesse" (1 Kings 12:16) – this refers to the Davidic house. "[To your tents,] O Israel! Look now to your own house, David" (1 Kings 12:16) – this refers to the building of the Temple.
>
> Rabbi Shimon b. Menasiah said: Israel will never see any sign of blessing until they return and seek all three, as is written, "Afterward the children of Israel shall return and seek the Lord their God" (Hosea 3:5). This is the kingdom of Heaven.
>
> "And David their king" (Hosea 3:5) – this is the kingdom of the Davidic house. "And they shall come in fear to the Lord and to His goodness in the latter days" (Hosea 3:5) – this is the building of the Temple.[45]

According to the words in this passage attributed to Rabbi Shimon b. Yohai, God's reply to Samuel regarding the people's request ("Appoint for us a king to govern us") alludes to three things that Israel will reject in the future, after several generations (i.e. in the days of Rehoboam). How the midrash infers these "three rejections" is not entirely clear, but it is clear that it expounds the phrase, "they have not rejected you, but they have rejected Me" as a conjuncture: they have rejected you, as well as Myself.[46] As in the Genizah passage discussed earlier, here too God's words – "for they have rejected Me" – are interpreted not only as a rejection of the kingdom of Heaven but also as a rejection of the earthly kingdom, that of the Davidic monarchy. Moreover, it appears that this midrashic author identifies between the two kingdoms, as the rejection

---

45   *Midrash Shmuel* 13.4 (ed. Buber, p. 84). For a discussion of this passage from other points of view, see Blidstein, "The Monarchic Imperative," pp. 27–29.

46   See Buber's note in *Midrash Shmuel* (p. 84).

of the Davidic kingdom as such is also seen as a rejection of the Heavenly rule; he evidently believes that the Davidic dynasty is the representation and embodiment of the kingdom of God.[47] This conclusion follows from the course of the homily, which identifies both of them with the name "David" and with the phrase "the son of Jesse": "'We have no portion in David' (1 Kings 12:16) – this refers to the kingdom of Heaven. 'Nor an inheritance in the son of Jesse' (1 Kings 12:16) – this refers to the Davidic house" (1 Kings 12:16). Moreover, the Temple itself is inferred from a homily on the same name: "'[to your tents] O Israel; see to you own house, O David' (1 Kings 12:16) – this refers to the building of the Temple." It would seem that, like the other midrashic passages discussed earlier, the structure of thought underlying this fragment is rooted in royal theology, which connects the kingdom of God with the earthly kingdom, and both of them with the Temple and the cult conducted there.[48]

Even though all the sources discussed thus far use concepts, images, and midrashic methods rooted in what might be identified as royal theology, when one examines the authority given to the king, and particularly the limitations that apply to him, it becomes clear that in the realm of the halakhah – in the Mishnah, *Tosefta,* and halakhic midrashim – the sages reject royal theology and adopt the limited monarchy of the Book of Deuteronomy. This is the case regarding both the political power of the king and his relationship to the judicial system, matters to be discussed in the next chapter. It would appear that echoes of the royal theology are preserved in those places that establish the commandment to appoint a king; the reliance on these sources may derive from the fact that there is no specific commandment to appoint a king in the

47   The midrashic author interprets the word מאס in Samuel as "rejection"; however, in the biblical context it seems that its meaning is "contempt," as in Numbers 11:20: "because you have rejected the Lord" – that is, you have exhibited contempt for God's ability to provide you with meat. And indeed, further on an answer is given: "Is God's hand limited?" (Numbers 11:23). See Elat, *Samuel and the Foundation of Kingship,* p. 67. Elat comments that there is no correspondence between 1 Samuel 8:7 ("for they have not rejected you, but it is Me they have rejected") and the claim in the subsequent verse expressing the people's rejection of God ("like all the deeds that have been done … and they have abandoned me and served other gods"). He therefore adopts the theory that this verse is not by the author of Samuel, but rather by the Deuteronomistic redactor.

48   The relationship between the Temple and the Davidic monarchy also follows from *Mekhilta de-Rabbi Yishmael, Amalek* (ed. Horowitz-Rabin, p. 201): "Three things were given on condition: the Land of Israel, the Temple and the Davidic monarchy."

Chapter of the King in Deuteronomy, whereas the "historical" sources, based on a theological or sacral understanding of the monarchy, relate positively to the institution of the monarchy. It is likewise possible that these sources indicate that the sages had not entirely freed themselves from this approach in relation to the monarchy and even suggest a secret longing for a "divine," or at least a sacral king. Nevertheless, insofar as these matters relate to the authority of the king and his governmental powers, tannaitic halakhah in the Mishnah and in the halakhic midrashim adhered to the model of a king with limited authority as depicted in Deuteronomy – even if it made certain changes to this model.

2.3 The Law of the Kingdom in the Book of Samuel

In the chapter of the Book of Samuel relating to the establishment of the monarchy, Samuel proposes the "Law of the Kingdom" (*mishpat ha-melekh*), a document known by scholars as the "Constitution of the Monarchy." This "law" or "constitution" states the rights of the king and the social and economic platform characteristic of royal rule.[49] Samuel describes the Law of the King (evidently as dictated by God) as follows:[50]

> He said: These will be the ways of the king who shall reign over you: He will take your sons and appoint them to his chariots and to be his horsemen, and to run before his chariots. And he will appoint for himself commanders of thousands and commanders of fifties, and some to plow his ground and to reap his harvest, and to make his implements of war and the equipment of his chariots. He will take your daughters to be perfumers and cooks and bakers. He will take the best of your fields and vineyards and olive orchards and give them to his servants. He will take the tenth of your grain and of your vineyards and give it to his officers and to his servants. He will take your menservants and maidservants, and your young men and your asses, and put them to his work. He will take the tenth of your flocks, and you will be his slaves.
>
> (1 Samuel 8:11–17)

---

49   See S. Talmon, "The Law of the King" (in Hebrew), in *Sefer Biram* (Jerusalem, 1956), pp. 45–56; also published as *The Beginnings of the Israelite Monarchy and Its Impact upon Leadership in Israel* (Jerusalem, 1975), pp. 16–27, at p. 16; Elat, *Samuel and the Foundation of Kingship*, p. 72.

50   See the language used in the Bible: "And Samuel said all the words of the Lord to the people, who had asked of him a king" (1 Samuel 8:10).

I will analyze this law as articulated by Samuel further on, in the framework of our discussion of the Talmudic sources that relate to it. The Law of the Kingdom is discussed, among other places, in the following passage in *Tosefta Sanhedrin:*

> R. Yossi said: Everything stated in the Chapter of the King, the king is permitted therein. R. Judah said: This chapter was only said in order to frighten them, as is said: "You shall surely set a king over you."
>
> Thus said R. Judah: Israel were commanded three commandments when they entered the land: they were commanded to appoint a king …
>
> R. Nehorai said: This chapter was only said because of their protesting, as is said, "And you shall say, 'I will set a king over me.'"[51]
>
> R. Eleazar b. R. Yossi said: The elders asked properly, as is said: "Give us a king to judge us." But the common people turned about and spoiled matters, as is said: "That we also may be like all the nations, and that our king may govern us and go out before us and fight our battles," etc.[52]

The dispute between R. Yossi and R. Judah – who were later joined by the amoraim Rav and Shmuel (see *Babylonian Sanhedrin* 20b) – is rooted among other things in the vagueness that surrounds the Law of the Kingdom in Samuel – a vagueness that relates both to the frame story in which the law is given and to its content. As for the place of the law in the course of the narrative, it is not clear what function this law plays in the exchange between Samuel and the people: was it rhetoric intended to frighten and

---

51 E. E. Urbach for some reason reads here as follows: "R. Nehorai says: This passage, 'You shall surely place upon yourselves a king,' was not stated as a commandment, but against their complaints. For it was revealed before Him that they would complain about this in the future and say: let us also be like all the nations; [so it was] rather because of the complaint, that it says, 'And you shall say.'" See E. E. Urbach, "The Biblical Monarchy as Viewed by the Sages" (in Hebrew), in A. Rofe and Y. Zakovitch (eds.), *Isaac Leo Seeligmann Volume: Essays on the Bible and the Ancient World* (Jerusalem, 1983), pp. 439–451; at p. 440 (his *The World of the Sages: Collected Studies* [in Hebrew] [Jerusalem, 2002], pp. 363–375). I have not found any support for this reading, and it seems to me that Urbach conflated here – as in the *Tosefta* version – Rashi's commentary on the parallel in *Babylonian Sanhedrin* 20b, s.v. *lo ne'emrah parashah zo.*

52 *Tosefta Sanhedrin* 4.5 (ed. Zuckermandel, p. 421); and see *Bavli Sanhedrin* 20b.

dissuade the people or was it a realistic description of the nature of royal rule?[53] As for the content: even though it is suitable to how kings rule (in the ancient Near East generally and of the kings of Israel in particular), the law describes the rule of a greedy tyrant who knows no limits, whose path seemingly contradicts the commandment of the king in the Book of Deuteronomy. For all these reasons, many commentators and scholars think it unlikely that Samuel intended here to establish a royal rule.

To elaborate on this point: in the Book of Samuel God describes the people's request to appoint a king as a rejection of Him ("for they have not rejected you, but they have rejected Me from being king over them"). Nevertheless, He accepts their request ("Hearken to the voice of the people in all that they say to you ... Now then, hearken to their voice"; 1 Samuel 8:7, 9). God's initial response indicates that He is reconciled to their request, and He encourages Samuel: "Only you shall surely warn them (הָעֵד תָּעִיד), and show them the ways of the king" (1 Samuel 8:7, 9). It would appear that, from God's viewpoint, the law of the kingdom, rather than being intended to dissuade the people and to cause them to renege on their request, is intended to prepare them for the introduction of royal rule; the "testimony" or "warning" regarding the law of the kingdom intends to make the people aware of the nature of the rule to be established and to prepare the ground for it. It should be mentioned here that the significance of the terms עוּד and תָּעִיד in the Bible is, among other things: giving of testimony (Psalms 50:7); establishment of law and regulation (2 Kings 17:15; Nehemiah 9:34); and warning directed to those who would accept upon themselves the fulfillment of the law (Jeremiah 11:7; Nehemiah 9:26). It would thus appear that the meaning of the words הָעֵד תָּעִיד in the Chapter of the King has one of the two latter meanings.[54]

---

53   As defined by Talmon, "The Law of the King," p. 18.

54   See Talmon, "The Law of the King," p. 19. Talmon opposes the view, according to which the law of the king in Samuel is a later, critical description by the opponents of the monarchy, whose political approach was one of direct theocracy. In his view, the description in the Book of Samuel originated during the formative period of Israelite kingship (i.e. in the days of David and Samuel). Accordingly, Samuel's speech does not negate or reject the monarchy per se; rather, it reflects the actual or concrete life of the people in their day. I tend to accept the analysis that he proposes for this passage, without accepting his historical conclusions. Talmon does not properly interpret the words of Rav in *Babylonian Sanhedrin*. According to his interpretation, the amora Samuel (who stated that "everything that is stated ... the king is permitted to do," *Babylonian Sanhedrin* 20b), thinks that this establishes the law of the king, whereas Rav (who stated, "This section was only

But God's viewpoint regarding the law of the kingdom is not necessarily the same as that of Samuel. In light of God's response, it should be understood as a kind of suggested or draft constitution, whereas from Samuel's viewpoint the matters are (also) intended to warn the people and to encourage them to withdraw their request for a king. While God is reconciled to the request, Samuel has still not given up; he portrays a tyrannical king, who dominates his people and appropriates all the wealth of the land for himself. It is as if to say, you want a king who will fight your battles, expand your borders, increase your resources, and perform righteousness and justice – but in the end you will receive a tyranny marked by poverty and want. This reading is reinforced by the end of his speech: "And in that day you will cry out because of your king, whom you have chosen for yourselves; but the Lord will not answer you on that day" (1 Samuel 8:18)[55] – and by the people's response: "But the people refused to listen to the voice of Samuel, and they said, 'No! But we will have a king over us'" (1 Samuel 8:19).[56] The people's refusal indicates that they

said in order to frighten them, as is said: 'You shall surely place upon yourselves a king' – that his fear shall be upon you," *Babylonian Sanhedrin* 20b), opposes the monarchy. However, the literal sense of Rav's words is that one is commanded to appoint a king, and that this is Samuel's stance; however, the law of the king is not a constitution charter but rather a rhetorical-psychological move, intended to instill fear of the king. In all events, there is no opposition here to the institution of monarchy as such. Talmon asks what caused this law of the king, which was understood by earlier commentators in a positive manner (thus even R. Judah, who spoke like Rav but stated that there is an obligation to appoint a king, this being one of the three commandments that they were commanded upon entering the land), was completely rejected by later interpreters? He emphasizes that Samuel's words do not cause the elders to argue with him, nor with their response, "No, for a king shall rule over us." Samuel did not tell the elders anything that they did not already know. They wish to solve a practical problem: they want a king to set up an army in order protect the people against the Philistines. Samuel's words are based upon three assumptions, rooted in the social, political, and economic circumstances of Israelite society before the period of David and Solomon, in whose day decisive changes occurred in the internal structure of society.

55 1 Samuel 8:18. It is possible that the word מלככם ("your king") is deliberately ambiguous. The people cry out about their trouble before the king whom they have chosen (as if he is the proper address), while God – their true king – does not answer them. It would appear that the idiom ביום ההוא ("on that day") is intended to emphasize that, as opposed to responding now without offering any alternative, God will ignore their plea in the future, when they will groan under the yoke of the king.

56 1 Samuel 8:19. God's response to their request to appoint a king – as against Samuel's efforts to prevent the dramatic change in the structure of government

properly understood Samuel's words as an attempt to dissuade them from their request.

There is not necessarily any contradiction between the claim that "the law of the kingdom" is a kind of constitution and Samuel's intention to discourage the people by its means. Samuel may have attempted to discourage them from their request specifically by means of a realistic and even "obligatory" description of royal rule – as if to say, if you want a king, you should know that this is what his rule will be like; the king and the law of the kingdom are one and the same. In other words, there is no middle ground between the king whose authority is described in the law of the kingdom and direct theocracy. And, indeed, as we hinted earlier, bible scholars have noted the similarity between the prerogatives listed in the law of the kingdom and the actual rule of kings – in the other nations of the ancient Near East and in Judah and Israel. Kings in both were accustomed to forcing people into their service ("he will take your sons and appoint them to his chariots and to be his horsemen ... as commanders over thousands ... He will take your daughters as perfumers and cooks," 1 Samuel 8:11–13), taking the property of their subjects in order to sustain their courts ("He will take the best of your fields and vineyards ... and give them to his servants; He will take the tenth of your grain and of your vineyards and give it to his officers and to his servants," 1 Samuel 8:14–15), and imposing a tax upon the fruit of their subjects' labor ("He will take the tenth of your flocks," 1 Samuel 8:17).[57] One cannot ignore the negative tenor in Samuel's words regarding the law of the kingdom, but his critical description describes manners of rule characteristic of every king, not necessarily a tyrannical and greedy one.[58] In the final analysis, what is a king without a mechanism of court and army, to which he drafts the best of the young men of the kingdom,

---

– follows from the end of the passage as well (1 Samuel 8:22): "And God said to Samuel: 'Listen to their voice and make a king to reign over them.'" The reason for Samuel's objections follows from the continuation of the verse, which also ends the section: "And Samuel said to the people of Israel: Let each man return to his city."

57   See Elat, *Samuel and the Foundation of Kingship*, pp. 73–80; Talmon, "The Law of the King," pp. 23–26. Elat and Talmon point out the manner of rule of the foreign kings and of the kings of Israel in relation to the law of the king.

58   This tension brought certain scholars to argue that "The law of the king reflects the opinion of those opponents of the kingship who already emerged in the days of Saul, or even prior to its establishment"; see Elat, *Samuel and the Foundation of Kingship*, p. 79, and the references there in n. 118; and see also Talmon, "The Law of the King," p. 26.

and in order to maintain which he takes property, tithes and taxes from the people? Shemaryahu Talmon was correct in observing that "Samuel's words testify to a king who will draft the people ... This will not be interpreted by the people as an edict, but as the fulfillment of their hearts' desire." Samuel's opposition to the institution of the monarchy is therefore based not on the fear that the institution will deteriorate to tyranny but on principled reasons that lead him to prefer another system of rule. This analysis strengthens the possibility that, according to the Law of the Kingdom in Samuel, when a king is established he is permitted to do everything stated therein.[59]

Let us return now to the passage in *Tosefta Sanhedrin*. The various possible ways of reading the law of the king declaimed by Samuel – as a warning, as a threat, or as an obligatory constitution – is found in various opinions in that same passage. Rabbi Yossi thinks that "Everything said in the Law of the Kingdom, the king is permitted to do." In his opinion, this chapter presents, in concise form, the prerogatives of the king. This is doubtless a plausible reading of the chapter as it is consistent with the viewpoint of God, who orders the prophets to warn the people; in the final analysis it also fits Samuel's viewpoint. R. Yossi's words also reflect not only the prerogatives of the kings (both foreign and Israelite) according to the Bible but also the conduct of the kings during the Hellenistic and Roman era.[60] His view is likewise consistent with the view that the appointment of the king is a mitzvah, but it is not necessarily based thereupon. On the other hand, it is also possible that, according to the view of R. Yossi, the appointment of a king is (only)

---

59 See 1 Samuel 10:25: "And Samuel said to the people the law of the king, and wrote it in a book, and placed it before the Lord." Elat, *Samuel and the Foundation of Kingship*, p. 106, n. 39, thinks that the "Law of the King" referred to here is not the "Law of the King" stated in 1 Samuel 8:11–17, as "There the rule of the king is arbitrary and greedy, for which reason he warned against it and sought to convince the people not to ask for themselves a king of flesh and blood"; see also the references to the studies of Weiser, McCarter, Segal and Cruseman. However, in light of the above analysis, this argument is not necessary; see Talmon, "The Law of the King," p. 22 and n. 27 there. On the entire matter, compare Garsiel, "The Dispute Between Samuel and the People," and the literature there.

60 The famous Greek saying: *para basileos nomos agraphos* ("the king has no written law") was well known to the sages. See *Leviticus Rabbah*, 35.3 (ed. Margaliot, p. 820); and see S. Lieberman, *Greek in Jewish Palestine,* 2nd edn, New York, 1965), p. 38, n. 51; and see E. E. Halevi, "The Authority of Kingship" (in Hebrew), *Tarbiz*, 38 (1969): 225–230, at p. 226. I will discuss this paper below, in Chapter 3.3 (near the reference to n. 76).

permissible and not obligatory; however, once he has been appointed, his powers and authorities are those mentioned by Samuel in the law of the kingdom.[61] In *Babylonian Sanhedrin*, R. Yossi's view is attributed to the amora Samuel.[62] To be discussed below is the question of the relationship between R. Yossi's approach and the limitations placed on the king – regarding the quantity of property and of gold and silver that the king is allowed to accumulate, the number of women he is allowed to marry, and the size of the army he is allowed to organize – all of which are mentioned in the Midrash and in the halakhic midrashim (following the Book of Deuteronomy).

Unlike R. Yossi, R. Judah thinks that this chapter was only written in order to frighten the people. The amora Rav, in the *sugya* of the Babylonian Talmud in Sanhedrin, holds a similar position. According to this approach, those things stipulated in the Law of the Kingdom are not in fact permitted to the king. The purpose of Samuel's speech was not to interpret the Chapter of the King but to frighten the people or to ensure, in the words of Rashi, "that the fear of their king might be upon them." But, unlike the initial impression, the phrase "that his fear might be upon them" does not mean to dissuade them from seeking a king. On the contrary, Samuel's speech is intended to prepare the ground for a supreme political authority, which did not exist until that time. The very essence of such an authority, particularly when speaking of a king, is the power given him and the fear that he imposes. According to the views of both R. Judah and the amora Rav, the fear of the king serves a positive function, as a necessary condition for a political authority that purposes to impose law and order and to protect against both internal

---

61   Halevi thinks that, according to R. Yossi, "A monarchic regime is a cruel and improper form of government, for any person is capable of changing, to become tyrannical and to enslave others ... And whoever chose a royal form of government is as if he agreed in advance to every action on the part of the king, and he can only complain of his own foolishness and not against the king." Halevi identifies R. Yossi's opinion with that of R. Nehorai ("that having a king is a shame to Israel"): see Halevi, "The Authority of Kingship," pp. 225, 229, n. 24. However, in light of the above analysis, these conclusions are in no way necessary.

62   *Babylonian Sanhedrin* 20b. In this context it is interesting to note that the amora Samuel was the author of the rule, "the law of the land is the land," that acknowledges the extensive authority of a foreign king (in his day the kings of Persia), particularly in matters of property and taxation. See G. J. Blidstein, "The Israeli Legal System as Viewed by Contemporary Halakhic Authorities" (in Hebrew), *Dinei Israel* (New York and Tel Aviv, 1986–1988), vols. XIII–XIV, pp. 21–42. I thank Amihai Radziner for calling my attention to this issue.

and external enemies.[63] As I shall show below, this view was shared by other sages as well.

In contrast, R. Nehorai thinks that "this chapter was only said because of the controversy" (*Tosefta Sanhedrin,* Chapter 4). By "this chapter" R. Nehorai is referring not to the Chapter of the King in Deuteronomy (as has been suggested by a number of commentators and scholars) but to the law of the kingdom in Samuel, which the subject of the entire chapter in *Tosefta Sanhedrin.*[64] The word *tar'omet* (translated here as "controversy") refers to a complaint or grievance directed against the other. In the language of the sages, *tar'omet* may be justified or, at times – as in the present case – may not be unjustified.[65] According to R. Nehorai, the people ask for a king improperly – a line of interpretation following from his approach, that the request for a king was "a shameful thing for Israel," as "they only sought a king in order to worship idols"

---

63 Compare Talmon, "The Law of the King," p. 19, and the discussion in n. 55 above; and also Halevi, "The Authority of Kingship," p. 227, who interprets the purpose of frightening them as "to deter them from their request [of a king] … And perhaps he [R. Judah, who said 'because they asked prematurely'] thinks that the kingship refers only to the Davidic dynasty, and the time has not yet come for this house." It should be noted that the Torah does not explicitly require the people to listen to the voice of the king, while such a command does appear in relation to the Great Court and in relation to the prophet: see Deuteronomy 17:10–12; 18:19. The sages therefore emphasize that which the Torah refrained from emphasizing, perhaps because in relation to the king there is no need for this, or perhaps because of their reservations about the institution of the monarchy. Regarding the fear of the king, see below, Chapter 4.1.

64 There are those who think (Rashi in *Babylonian Sanhedrin* 20b; Urbach, "The Biblical Monarchy," p. 440; Halevi, "The Authority of Kingship," p. 225) that the words of R. Nehorai in *Tosefta Sanhedrin* relate to the Chapter of the King in Deuteronomy; however, both on the basis of its language and that of the subject, his words clearly relate to the subject of the king as it appears in Samuel. See below.

65 For an example of justified "complaint," see *Mishnah Bava Metzi'a* 6a: "One who hires artisans, and they deceived one another, they have naught against one another except grievance." For an example of unjustified complaint, see *Mekhilta de-Rabbi Yishmael, Vayisa* (ed. Horowitz-Rabin, p. 155): "'And the people complained against Moses.' R. Joshua says: Israel ought to have gone first to the greatest one among them to say, 'What shall we drink?' But they stood and said words of complaint against Moses. R. Eleazar ha-Modai said: The people of Israel were accustomed to say words of complaint against Moses; and not against Moses alone did they say them, but also against the [divine] Power. Therefore it is said: 'saying, what shall we drink?'" See the entry "*Tar'omet*" in E. Ben-Yehudah's *The Dictionary of the Hebrew Language, Old and New,* 17 volumes, 1910–1958, vol. XVI, p. 7919.

(*Sifrei Devarim*, 156). The language in Deuteronomy – "and you shall say, ['I shall place upon myself a king']" – is interpreted here by R. Nehorai not necessarily as referring to a possible request on the part of the people nor as an imperative (as in the opinion of R. Judah), but as descriptive language, anticipating a future in which the people will address complaints to Samuel, improperly demanding a king.[66] According to R. Nehorai, Samuel purposes not to establish the monarchy nor to create the psychological-social framework for the creation of royal rule, but simply to dissuade the people from seeking a king. The law of the kingdom, anchored in the actual practice of kings in the ancient Near East, could be an effective means of doing this.

R. Eleazar b. Yossi, like R. Judah, thinks that the Torah commands the appointment of a king and that hence "the elders asked properly" (i.e. "and you shall say, 'I will place upon myself a king'").[67] In order to bridge the gap between the law of the kingship in Samuel and the Chapter of the King in Deuteronomy, he draws a distinction between the elders (who asked properly) and the people of the land, who "returned and behaved improperly," placing in their mouths the complaint, "that we also may be like all the nations, and that our king may govern us and go out before us." R. Eleazar b. Yossi may have attributed to the elders a legitimate request for a king, within the limited framework of Deuteronomy, according to which the king is subject to the Torah and his powers are limited; the people, on the other hand, wanted a king in the framework customary in the ancient Near East, that of a sacral monarchy (or even a divine king). According to R. Eleazar b. Yossi's interpretation, like that of R. Nehorai, Samuel's speech is thus an attempt to dissuade the people from seeking a king. But, unlike R. Nehorai, R. Eleazar's interpretation is not based on the principled position that seeking a king is a shameful thing for Israel but rather on the language of the request made by the people and its motivations ("and we shall be … like all the nations").

The relationship between the approaches to the monarchy found among the tannaim and those approaches identified above in the Bible must be evaluated in light of the entire complex of tannaitic statements regarding the king. However, already at this stage of the discussion it is noteworthy that, among the various approaches to the Law of the Kingdom in Samuel, it is difficult to arrive at any clear conclusions regarding the approach to monarchy adopted by the sages. This claim is also true regarding those sages who think that "Everything stated in the Chapter

66   See Chapter 2.1 above.
67   See Chapter 2.1 above.

of the King – he is permitted to do." In the final analysis, this chapter does not relate to the ritual functions of the king nor to his functions in the judicial area ("doing justice and righteousness"). This chapter is only concerned with the prerogatives of the king regarding matters of property, administration, tax collection, taxes, and the like. This is thus a rather limited statute, which does not tell us much about the functions of the king in other areas. Indeed, this chapter leaves the impression that, at least according to some tannaim, the Israelite king is not restricted at all – and in that respect he is similar to the other kings of the ancient Near East (or to the Hellenistic kings and Roman emperors). However, if we turn to other tannaitic sources it becomes clear that in other areas – and in practice even in those areas to which the law of the kingdom in Samuel pertains – his power and authority are extremely limited.

2.4 Limitations on the King

We noted above the seeming opposition between the law of the king in Samuel and the restrictions placed on the king in the Chapter of the King in Deuteronomy. To recall, Deuteronomy 17:16–17 states:

> Only he must not multiply horses for himself, nor cause the people to return to Egypt in order to multiply horses, since the Lord has said to you: You shall never return that way again. And he shall not multiply wives for himself, lest his heart turn away; nor shall he greatly multiply for himself silver and gold.

The words of Samuel, in contrast, indicate that there are no restrictions upon the king regarding what he is allowed to take from the people in order to increase his army or to augment his property. While Samuel does not mention the matter of wives, one nevertheless feels the tension (if not the opposition) between the "constitution" that he interprets and the instructions in the Book of Deuteronomy – at least regarding horses (i.e. the size of his army) and gold and silver. In *Sifrei Devarim*, the restrictions on these matters in Deuteronomy are interpreted as follows:

> "Only he must not multiply horses for himself." Might it be that he may not increase them even for his chariots and his horsemen? Scripture says "to him." For himself he does not increase, but he is allowed to increase for his chariots and his horsemen. If so, why does it say "must not multiply horses"? Horses that are idle.

> From whence do we know that even for one horse that is idle he might return the people to Egypt? Scripture says, "Only he must not multiply horses, nor cause ... to return ..."[68]
>
> "Nor shall he greatly multiply for himself silver and gold." Might it be that he shall not increase them, even to give to his army storehouses? Scripture says, "He shall he greatly multiply for himself" – for himself he does not increase, but he may increase in order to give to his army.[69]

The midrashic author in *Sifrei* limits the prohibition upon the king to "increase horses" to those horses intended for his own personal use or to glorify his name – and not those needed for military or administrative purposes. It is thus that one ought to understand the expression "for his chariots and his horsemen." It would appear that, unlike the meaning of the scriptural verses – in which no distinction is made between the national-public realm and the private realm, and which therefore refers to both – the tanna allows the king to increase the number of his horses without restriction in order to strengthen his army, for "he does not multiply for himself" but only for his chariots and horsemen.[70] Moreover, it is possible that the formula "he multiplies for his chariots and his horsemen" alludes to the idea that the king is allowed to increase horses even for quasi-personal purposes, which are not explicitly military. A similar move appears in the *Mishnah Sanhedrin* 2.4: "'He shall not multiply horses' except for the needs of his chariots."[71] In *Sifrei Zuta* to Deuteronomy, which was recently published by Menahem Kahana, the wording is somewhat different: "'He shall not multiply horses' – [but he

---

68 *Sifrei Devarim,* 158 (ed. Finkelstein, p. 209). Further on, we read: "and are not matters *a fortiori?* If, regarding Egypt, about whom a covenant was made, [only] transgression returns them there, the other lands, about which there is no covenant, is it not all the more so?!"

69 *Sifrei Devarim* 159 (ed. Finkelstein, p. 210). And cf. *Mishnah Sanhedrin* 2.3; *Babylonian Sanhedrin* 21b; *Midrash Tannaim* (ed. Hoffman, p. 105); and *Sifrei Zuta, Devarim* (ed. Kahana, p. 258). Further on in the passage from *Sifrei* an additional homily is brought, whose conclusion is similar: "Something Else: [May he multiply] so as to place in the storehouse? Scripture says, 'He shall not multiply' – for himself he may not increase, but he may increase for the storehouse. And thus did David, as is said 'With great pains I have provided for the house of the Lord ... ' (1 Chronicles 22:14). But Solomon changed, as in the matter said. 'And the king made silver as common in Jerusalem as stones' (1 Kings 10:27)."

70 See Kahana, *Sifrei Zuta, Devarim,* p. 256.

71 Cf. *Babylonian Sanhedrin* 21b; and *Midrash Tannaim* (ed. Hoffman, p. 104), where the example from David and Solomon is added.

increases for the kingdom" – and, as Kahana comments, the permission here may be limited to the needs of the kingdom alone.[72]

As in the matter of horses, so too regarding the prohibition against increasing silver and gold: whereas the Torah limits the accumulation of wealth, both for personal needs and for national-social goals, the tanna restricts this prohibition to the accumulation of wealth for personal purposes, again using the same exegetical technique – "'he must not multiply for himself' – for himself he does multiply, but he may multiply so as to give to his army storehouses." The two matters are interrelated, for, according to our midrashic author, the permission to accumulate wealth is connected to military purposes intended for the storehouses – that is, for salaries of military personnel.[73] On this matter, *Mishnah Sanhedrin* (2.4) is similar to the homily in *Sifrei:* "'Nor shall he greatly multiply silver and gold' – except so as to give to the storehouse [*aspanya/afsanya*]." In *Sifrei Zuta* to Deuteronomy, the homily is somewhat different: "'Nor shall he greatly multiply silver and gold' – he may multiply it for the kingdom. Might it be that he may not increase it to give to the storehouses? It says 'very much' – he may increase it to distribute to the stores."[74] This homily does not limit the prohibition against increasing gold and silver to what is needed to support the army but, as in the matter of the horses, establishes a general permission, once again by a fine turn of phrase

---

72 Kahana, *Sifrei Zuta, Devarim,* p. 257. In this work an additional homily is brought concerning this matter: "Is he allowed to multiply for his *compon?* it says, 'Only' – me does not multiply for his *compon.*" *Compon* refers to a hypodrome intended for horse races (see Kahana, *Sifrei Zuta, Devarim,* and his references there to the exegetes and researchers). As Kahana explains, the author of the homily in *Sifrei Zuta* emphasizes that the increase in the number of horses for purposes of the kingdom does not include race horses, but this restriction is not included in the *Sifrei,* which emphasizes the prohibition against multiplying the number of idle horses, specifically. So too in *Tosefta Sanhedrin* 4.5 (ed. Zuckermandel, p. 421): "'He shall not increase his horses' – not even one horse that is idle, as is said 'that he might increase his horses.' R. Judah said: It says, 'Solomon had forty thousand stalls of horses,' and he did properly, as is said 'Judah and Israel were as many as the sand by the sea' (1 Kings 4:19). When it says, 'Twelve thousand cavalry riders' you might think that the rest are idle. But an ordinary person is allowed to have all these." And cf. *Mekhilta Decarim*; Epstein, *Introductions to Tannaitic Literature,* p. 722. Regarding the verse on Solomon in 1 Kings 4, see Kahana's comment, *Sifrei Zuta, Devarim,* 258 and n. 11.

73 See H. Albeck (ed.), *Shishah Sidrei Mishnah* (Jerusalem, 1953), *Sanhedrin* 2.3 (175); Kahana, *Sifrei Zuta, Devarim,* p. 260 and the bibliography there. In *Palestinian Sanhedrin* 2.6 (20c), Rabbi Joshua ben Levi limits it to "storehouse for this year alone."

74 *Sifrei Zuta, Devarim* (ed. Kahana, p. 258).

inferred from the word *lo*, "to him": he may not increase for himself but "he increases for the kingdom." Only thereafter, evidently influenced by the homily in *Sifrei* (*Devarim*), does he infer from the word *me'od*, "very much" – that "he increases to distribute to the storehouses."[75]

As in the matter of the horses and the gold and silver, tannaitic halakhah expands the options available to the king regarding the matter of marrying many women. Unlike the language of Scripture ("and he shall not multiply the number of his wives, lest they turn his heart astray"), which implies that it is forbidden for the king to marry many wives, possibly even more than one, the Mishnah and the Midrash go far in increasing the options of the king in this area:[76]

> "And he shall not multiply wives" – only eighteen.
>
> R. Judah said: he is allowed to multiply, provided that they not lead his heart astray.
>
> R. Shimon said: Even one, if she leads his heart astray he should not marry her. If so, why does it say, "And he shall not multiply wives." Even like Abigail.[77]

There would seem to be three different opinions in this mishnah regarding the relation between the two halves of the biblical verse. The first opinion, the *tanna kamma*, assumes a direct relationship between the number of wives that a man marries and "lest his heart turn away" – resembling the view that "He who increases wives increases lewdness."[78] But, unlike the literal meaning of the verse, the *tanna kamma* is unusually generous in

---

75   On the difficulty in this homily, which seems superfluous, see Kahana's discussion, *Sifrei Zuta, Devarim* (ed. Kahana, pp. 261–262).

76   See below for the comparison to the *Temple Scroll*.

77   *Mishnah Sanhedrin* 2.4; *Sifrei Devarim* 159 (ed. Finkelstein, p. 210); J. N. Epstein, *Introduction to the Mishnaic Text*, 3rd edn (in Hebrew) (Jerusalem, 2000), p. 72 notes that *Mishnah Sanhedrin* 2.4–5 is based upon the halakhic midrash in *Sifrei Devarim* 157–161 (cf. ed. Finkelstein, p. 732); and cf. *Tosefta Sanhedrin* 4.5 (ed. Zuckermandel, pp. 420–421), which only brings the opinion of R. Judah: "'He shall not multiply his wives' – like Jezebel, but if they are like Abigail it is permitted – these are the words of R. Judah." And cf. *Midrash Hagadol, Devarim*, 401; and *Sifrei Zuta, Devarim* 17:17 (ed. Kahana, p. 258); and see below.

78   See *Mishnah Avot* 2.7: "He [Hillel] used to say: ... He who multiplies wives multiplies witchcraft; he who multiplies maidservants multiplies lewdness." The biblical prohibition is evidently related to the widespread connection between the marriages of the king and political alliances with neighboring kingdoms, which are liable to bring harmful cultural and religious influences in their wake: see H. Albeck (ed.), *Introduction to the Mishnah* (in Hebrew) (Jerusalem, 1979), p. 359.

the number of wives he allows the king. The number eighteen is evidently derived from the number of women David married and from the desire to justify him.[79] In contrast, R. Judah introduces two innovations: first, he sees the wording of the phrase, "lest they turn his heart away" as the main point of the biblical commandment, whereas the instruction, "he shall not multiply his wives" is seen as subsidiary to it; second, this phrase ("and they shall not lead his heart astray") pertains to the nature of the women whom the king wishes to marry (and not necessarily to the number of women, whatever their nature, as leading his heart astray).[80] According to this approach, the prohibition against increasing the number of wives only applies to women who "lead the heart astray," such as Jezebel, whereas it is permitted for him to marry "kosher" women, such as Abigail, without restriction.[81] R. Shimon thinks that R. Judah thereby empties the rule, "and he shall not multiply wives" of all contents, for if it is concerned with women who lead his heart astray, what does the number matter? He should not even marry one such! In other words, it is impossible to base the prohibition against "multiplying" wives only on the principle of leading the heart astray. Nevertheless, R. Shimon continues to adopt the distinction drawn by R. Judah between different kinds of women, only he

79   See Kahana, *Sifrei Zuta, Devarim*, p. 260 and n. 9. And indeed, in *Babylonian Sanhedrin* 21a and *Palestinian Sanhedrin* 2.6 (20c), Rav Kahana infers the permission for the king to marry eighteen wives from the words of Nathan the prophet to David in 2 Samuel 12:8: "and I gave you your master's house, and your master's wives into your bosom … and if this were too little, I would add to you as much more [lit.: as these and these]." Some inferred from this verse the permission to marry twenty-four wives, while others inferred forty-eight.

80   This disagreement between the *tanna kamma* and R. Judah may reflect two possible understandings of "leading astray the heart" in the Bible. One possibility is to see it as rooted in the sexuality of the women; however, one may also read the Chapter of the King in Deuteronomy against the background of the tendencies of Solomon's heart (or perhaps of his policy) to marry, within the framework of various foreign alliances, foreign wives who led his heart astray (see 1 Kings 11:1–10). He also accumulated silver and gold and horses (see 1 Kings 10:10–29); hence, the prohibition against multiplying wives because of their leading astray his heart is rooted in the prohibition of idolatry.

81   R. Judah's view is brought in the Mishnah and in *Sifrei Devarim* as a response to that of the *tanna kamma*, who "restricts" the number of wives to eighteen. However, the number eighteen may not have been in the background of R. Judah's original words, and he may have based his own view on exegesis of the words of Scripture, concluding that there was no limit on the number of women the king is allowed to marry – provided only that they not lead his heart astray. This indeed follows from his words in *Tosefta Sanhedrin* 4.5 (ed. Zuckermandel, p. 421).

integrates it within the viewpoint of the *tanna kamma*. Similarly, R. Shimon restricts the number of women the king is allowed to marry to eighteen – the king may not marry more, even if they are like Abigail – but, like R. Judah, he prohibits the king from marrying even one woman like Jezebel, who led her husband's heart astray.[82]

It is interesting to compare these laws with a passage from the *Temple Scroll* (from the Judean Desert Documents) that interprets and develops the Torah's laws regarding the king. The following passage deals with the wives of the king:

> And he may not marry a wife from the daughters of the nations, but from the house of his father he shall take a wife, from the family [or clan] of his father. And he shall not take another wife in addition to her, for she alone will be with him all the days of his life, and if she dies he shall marry another from the house of his father and from his family [or clan].[83]

According to the *Temple Scroll*, evidently a sectarian work, the king is permitted to marry only one woman, and only if his wife dies may he marry another in her stead.[84] This passage emphasizes not only that he may not marry a foreign woman but also that the woman whom he is

---

82   See the formulation in *Midrash Hagadol, Devarim* (ed. Fisch, p. 401); and Kahana's notes in *Sifrei Zuta, Devarim*, p. 259 and n. 6. The dispute between R. Judah and R. Shimon is brought in *Sifrei Zuta, Devarim* to Deuteronomy 17:17 (ed. Kahana, p. 258); however, their views are attributed there to R. Hananiah and to R. Eleazar b. Matya (respectively). See Kahana's notes, *Sifrei Zuta, Devarim*, p. 259.

83   *Temple Scroll* 56 xv–xviii (ed. Qimron, p. 81). The section of the *Temple Scroll* dealing with the king is quite extensive; see *Temple Scroll* 56 xii–59 xxi (ed. Qimron, pp. 81–84). On this passage, see S. T. Fraade, "The Torah of the King (Deuteronomy 17:14–20) in the Temple Scroll and Early Rabbinic Law," in J. R. Davila (ed.), *The Dead Sea Scrolls as Background to Postbiblical Judaism and Early Christianity: Papers from an International Conference at St. Andrews in 2001* (Leiden 2003), pp. 25–60; Y. Barzilay, "The Law of the King in the Temple Scroll: Its Original Characteristics and Later Redaction" (in Hebrew), *Tarbiz*, 72 (2003): 59–84.

84   Scholars disagree as to whether the *Temple Scroll* is a sectarian or pre-sectarian work, which originated in priestly (Sadducee) circles and which was adopted, and possibly edited, by the Dead Sea sect. The predominant opinion is that of Y. Yadin, according to whom the Scroll is a sectarian work. See his *The Temple Scroll* (in Hebrew) (Jerusalem, 1977); compare L. H. Schiffman, *Law, Custom and Messianism in the Dead Sea Sect* (in Hebrew) (Jerusalem, 1993), pp. 31–33; for a survey of research in this area see Barzilay, "The Law of the King," pp. 60–63.

permitted to marry (whether as his first wife or as his second) may only be from his father's family or clan – and all this, evidently, in order to preserve his proper pedigree.[85]

The sectarian law regarding the prohibition against the king having many wives is also found in the scroll of the *Damascus Covenant:*

> The foundation of the Creation is "male and female he created them," and those who went into the ark, "Two by two they went into the ark." And concerning the *Nasi* (Prince) it is written, "He shall not multiply wives." But David did not read the Torah scroll, which was sealed and which was in the ark, for it not been opened to Israel from the day that Eleazar and Joshua died.[86]

This passage claims, evidently in a polemic manner, that multiplying wives contradicts the "foundation of the Creation," as expressed in the verses, "male and female he created them," and "two by two they went into the ark."[87] It particularly emphasizes the prohibition against the *nasi* – that is, the king – taking many wives.[88] Like the *Temple Scroll,* it interprets this in an emphatic way: one wife. The prohibition against the king taking many wives in the sectarian halakhah – interpreted, as we said, as a prohibition against marrying more than one wife – is in practice no more than a particular case of the prohibition that applies to every person in Israel against marrying more than one woman. Nevertheless, the sources particularly emphasize the prohibition against the king doing so, adding to it the limitations of family background.

An echo of the subject of the pedigree of the king's wives also appears in law in the *Tosefta:* "One does not appoint a king unless he was suitable to marry with the priestly families."[89] It would seem that this law does not restrict the king to women from priestly families but states that the pedigree of the king must be such that he would be permitted to marry women from those families. This is comparable to the passage in *Mishnah*

---

85 On this passage, see Barzilay, "The Law of the King," p. 68.

86 CD 4 xx–xx; 5 i–iv. On *The Damascus Covenant* see A. Schremer, *Male and Female He Created Them: Jewish Marriage in the Late Second Temple, Mishnah and Talmud Periods* (in Hebrew) (Jerusalem, 2003), p. 48, n. 58 and the literature cited there.

87 See Schremer, *Male and Female He Created Them,* p. 48, n. 58.

88 On the identification of the *nasi* with the king in the Bible, see, for example, Ezekiel 34:24; and see below, Chapter 6 (near n. 27).

89 *Tosefta Sanhedrin* 4.10 (ed. Zuckermandel, p. 422).

Sanhedrin: "And not all are fit to judge capital cases, but only priests and Levites, and Israelites who may marry with the priesthood."[90]

The tannaitic law departs from the literal meaning of Scripture and restricts the limitations placed upon the king regarding the matter of wives (or nullifies them in practice), whereas the sectarian halakhah clearly tends towards the opposite extreme. If we do not read the verse "he shall not multiply wives" in an emphatic way, then even the categorical prohibition against taking many wives, read as permitting the king to have only one wife, deviates from the literal meaning of Scripture.[91]

It would seem that in all of these homilies – horses, silver and gold, and wives – the sages attempted to resolve the contradiction between the law of the king in the Book of Samuel and the commandment of the king in Deuteronomy. These tannaim – who evidently hold that the appointment of the king is a mitzvah (or at least is not a scandal or shame to Israel) – modify the restrictions that the Book of Deuteronomy places upon the king and bring them into line with the Law of the King in Samuel. It would seem that the editor of the *Tosefta* thought thus, as he based his approaches to the issues of women, horses and gold upon the views regarding the status of the law of the king in Samuel:

> He shall not multiply wives like Jezebel, but like Abigail is permitted – these are the words of R. Judah. He should not increase horses – idle horses, even one, as is said … R. Judah said. Yet it says, "And Solomon had 40,000 stables of horses," and he did properly … perhaps that the rest were idle. … R. Yossi said: Everything stated in the Chapter of the King – is permitted to him. R. Judah said: This chapter was only said in order to frighten people, as is said: "You shall surely place upon yourselves a king" … [92]

At the same time, it is important to note that the exegetical moves of these sages regarding the modification of the restrictions imposed on

90 *Mishnah Sanhedrin* 4.2; cf. *Tosefta Sanhedrin* 4.7 (ed. Zuckermandel, p. 421), 7.1 (ed. Zuckermandel, p. 425). On marital connections to the priestly families in Jewish society during the period of the Mishnah and the Talmud, see the discussion of Schremer, *Male and Female He Created Them*, pp. 180–182, and see there for further sources.

91 Barzilay argues that this halakhah in the *Temple Scroll* was only part of its later editing and is not part of the early doctrine of the king. See Barzilay, "The Law of the King," p. 68.

92 *Tosefta Sanhedrin* 4.5 (ed. Zuckermandel, p. 421), with decoding of the abbreviations.

the king by Deuteronomy, as well as their attitude to the Chapter of the King in Samuel, do not derive (exclusively) from the exegetical difficulties involved in bridging the tension between the Chapter of the King in Samuel and the Chapter of the King in Deuteronomy. They are based upon political viewpoints, according to which one may extend the powers and prerogatives of the king beyond those in Deuteronomy. As we shall see below, this approach is connected to the sages' political realism and to their belief that the king must impose fear upon the people so that he may impose law and order. In order to fulfill his tasks, he needs more than the limited prerogatives granted by the Torah and must be given (within the framework of the halakhah) the means of realizing them.

The approach that says that "Everything stated in the Chapter of the King – is permitted to him" does not necessarily bring the viewpoint of those sages who adhere to it any closer to one or another version of royal theology. The expansion of the king's authority, beyond what is granted by the Book of Deuteronomy, may still be described within the framework of what we have called a limited kingship. In the final analysis, the law of the king in Samuel speaks primarily of the king's prerogatives in the area of property (collecting taxes), administration and army (i.e. foreign policy and defense); there is no reference in the entire chapter to the king's status regarding the cult, nor to his functions in terms of doing justice and righteousness – matters that are substantive to every version of royal theology or sacral kingship.

2.5 The King and War

One area, typically under the explicit authority of the king, is that of war. The decision to go to war – or, to use anachronistic terminology, foreign policy and defense – was, as we recall, the main reason given by the elders when they addressed Samuel to ask for a king ("and go out before us and fight our battles," 1 Samuel 8:20). Hence, one might reasonably expect that, specifically within this area, the king would, according to the sages, enjoy far-reaching authority; however, even regarding the decision to go to war, the Mishnah restricts his prerogatives: "And he [the king] sends them out to an optional war on the basis of the high court of seventy-one."[93] This law also appears in the previous chapter, in which the prerogatives of the various kinds of courts are discussed, including the Sanhedrin: "One does not go out to an optional war except according to the Court of seventy-one."[94]

93 *Mishnah Sanhedrin* 2.4.
94 *Mishnah Sanhedrin* 1.5.

An optional war (*milhemet reshut*) is distinguished here from a commanded war (*milhemet mitzvah*), sometimes referred to as an "obligatory war" (*milhemet hovah*).[95] According to tannaitic halakhah, the latter case includes three kinds of war: the conquest of the land by Joshua (against the seven indigenous nations), the war of Amalek, and a defensive war. An optional war is defined as a war that aims to expand in order to glorify the ruler or for economic goals.[96] The first two types of obligatory or commanded war held no practical significance already in the days of the tannaim. The war against the seven indigenous nations was of purely historical significance, as the Mishnah states (albeit in the context of converting an Amorite) that "Sannacherib already came and mixed all the nations."[97] For similar reasons also, the second type of obligatory war – the war against Amalek – no longer existed at the time of the sages.[98]

Thus, the only kind of commanded war relevant to the laws of the king is the defensive war. According to the Mishnah in Sanhedrin, the king is only allowed to initiate this type of war by himself without requiring permission from the Sanhedrin, whereas any other kind of war is conditional upon the consent of the Sanhedrin which, presumably, will curtail the steps of the king, preventing unnecessary military adventures.[99]

95   See the opinion of R. Judah in *Mishnah Sotah* 8.7; and see below.
96   *Palestinian Sotah* 9.10 (23 a); *Babylonian Berakhot* 3b; *Babylonian Sotah* 44b; *Babylonian Sanhedrin* 16a. And cf. R. Kimelman, "Laws of War and Its Limitations" (in Hebrew), in I. Gafni and A. Ravitzky (eds.), *Sanctity of Life and Martyrdom: Studies in Memory of Amir Yekutiel* (Jerusalem, 1992), pp. 233–254.
97   *Mishnah Yadayim* 4.4. Kimelman ("Laws of War," p. 233) speculates that this statement is part of the tendency to soften the severe biblical policy towards the seven nations. He also notes that the Bible itself relates that this policy was not executed in practice, even when the early Israelite kingdom was at the height of its power. It was not for naught that Maimonides emphasizes, regarding the seven nations, that "their memory has already been forgotten": *Hilkhot Melakhim* 5.4.
98   See Kimelman, "Laws of War," p. 234. On the tendency of the tannaim regarding the interpretation of the chapter of Amalek, see Kahana, *The Two Mekhiltot*, especially pp. 364 ff.
99   See Kimelman, "Laws of War," pp. 236–237. Menahem Lorberbaum has suggested that the intention of the Mishnah is that the king may not take the people out to an optional war without the permission of the Sanhedrin; he is, however, to do so with his own private army. In other words, only the conscription of the public to an optional war is supervised by the Sanhedrin – but not a war conducted by the king's private army of mercenaries. See M. Lorberbaum, *Politics and the Limits of Law: Secularizing the Political in Medieval Jewish Thought* (Palo Alto, Calif., 2001),

The question of the character of a defensive war, not requiring the approval of the Sanhedrin, is not clear from the sources. The central question is: does it refer only to a defensive war, after there has already been an enemy attack – or does the category of defensive war also include a preemptive attack? If defensive war only includes the former possibility, the king is almost entirely lacking in freedom of action. Even in the second case the king's room to maneuver is quite limited – for example, in presenting a war intended for purposes of expansion or for economic reasons as a preemptive action.

It is possible that the dispute regarding the question of whether the category of "commanded war" includes preemptive attack – or whether a defensive war is only one that follows the beginning of an attack on the part of the enemy – is implied by the following mishnah in *Tosefta Sotah:*

> To what do these things refer? To an optional war; but in the case of a commanded war, everyone goes out: even the bridegroom from his chamber and the bride from her canopy (see Joel 2:16).
>
> R. Judah said: To what does this refer? To a commanded war; but in the case of an obligatory war, everyone goes out: even the bridegroom from his chamber and the bride from her canopy.[100]

According to the sages, the possibility of returning from the battlefront – that is, to be exempt from participating in the warfare (see Deuteronomy 20:1–10) – only applies to an optional war – to a war for the purpose of territorial expansion or economic goals. The exemptions mentioned in the Book of Deuteronomy – interpreted in *Mishnah Sotah,* in the passages that precede the one quoted above (*Mishnah Sotah* 8.1–6) – do not apply in a commanded war, in which everybody must participate. R. Judah's

p. 173, n. 4. According to this theory, the limitations on the king's conduct of a voluntary or optional war are far more limited – particularly if we take into account that tannaitic halakhah (in contrast to that of Deuteronomy) does not limit the size of the king's army (see Chapter 2.4 above). However, it is difficult to accept this conjecture, as there is no mention either in the Mishnah or the other tannaitic (and Talmudic) sources of any distinction being drawn between the army of the people and that of the king. These sources impart the impression that any optional war depends on the approval of the Sanhedrin.

100 *Mishnah Sotah* 8.7. The various divergent opinions are also found in *Sifrei Devarim* 198 (ed. Finkelstein, p. 234) and 190 (ed. Finkelstein, p. 232; the view of R. Judah).

opinion, which seemingly disagrees, is not altogether clear. Epstein thinks that the difference between R. Judah and the sages is not over a concrete halakhic issue but rather a dispute concerning terminology: namely, what the sages refer to as an "optional war" is referred to by R. Judah as a "commanded war"; whereas what the sages referred to as "commanded war" is referred to by R. Judah as an "obligatory war."[101] This claim is based, among other things, upon the language used in the *Tosefta*: "R. Judah called an optional war a commanded war, but in an obligatory war everybody goes out: even the bridegroom from his chamber and the bride from her canopy."[102] A similar interpretation of R. Judah's opinion is found in the *sugyot* of both the Palestinian and the Babylonian Talmud in the name of Rabbi Yohanan: "R. Yohanan said: The meaning [i.e. of the word] is between them. R. Judah called an optional war a commanded war, but in an obligatory war everybody goes out: even the bridegroom from his chamber and the bride from her canopy."[103] Epstein bases his argument, among other things, on the fact that R. Judah's words in the Mishnah are not presented as a dispute among the sages, but as a formulation that repeats the words of the other ("To what does this refer?"), but using different terminology ("each one gave it in the language he had heard from his master").[104] One is therefore forced to conclude that, in terms of content, the opinion of both is the same.[105] There are, however, those who thought that the difference between the sages and R. Judah was not merely one of terminology. Such is the view of Ravva in the discussion in the Babylonian:

---

101 See Epstein, *Introduction to the Mishnaic Text*, p. 2; cf. S. Lieberman, *Tosefta ki-feshutah: Zera'im–Nashim* (New York, 1955–1973): *Nashim, Sotah*, p. 696.

102 *Tosefta Sotah* 7.24 (ed. Lieberman); cf. Lieberman, *Tosefta ki-feshutah*.

103 Thus in *Palestinian Sotah* 8.6 (23a); and cf. Lieberman, *Tosefta ki-feshutah*, p. 6 n. 42. And cf. *Babylonian Sotah* 44b: "R. Johanan said: That which the Rabbis consider optional is a commandment according to R. Judah; that which the Rabbis call mitzvah is an obligation according to R. Judah."

104 Lieberman, *Tosefta ki-feshutah: Nashim*, p. 696.

105 R. Judah's different terminology remains puzzling: why does he refer to a war of territorial expansion or one waged for economic purposes as a *milhemet mitzvah* ("commanded war")? Does he think that such a war becomes a commandment because the king has commanded it, or perhaps because it has been commanded by the Sanhedrin (which, as mentioned, needs to grant its permission before going to war of this sort)? On the use of the terms *reshut, mitzvah,* and *hovah* (optional, commanded, and obligatory) in rabbinic language, see G. Alon, *Studies in Jewish History* (Tel Aviv, 1970), vol. II, pp. 111–119.

> Ravva said: Joshua's wars of conquest – all agree that they were
> obligatory. The wars of the Davidic house to expand – all agree
> that they were optional. Regarding what do they differ? Not to
> include idolaters, so that they not come upon us. One called it a
> commanded [war], and the other called it an optional [war]. What
> is the implication? [The law of whether in this case] one who was
> engaged in a mitzvah is exempt from another mitzvah.[106]

According to Ravva, the sages and R. Judah agree regarding the "wars of
the house of David to expand" (that is, for economic purposes) – that they
are an optional war, and regarding the war of Joshua to conquer the land
– that it was an obligatory war, i.e. a mitzvah.[107] The sages and R. Judah
likewise agree regarding a defensive war in which the enemy has already
attacked – that it too is an obligatory war, i.e. a mitzvah. Their dispute only
revolves around a preemptive attack or, to use the language of R. Menahem
Hameiri: "They only disagreed in a case where they are fighting with the
enemy because they are afraid they will come upon them, or it is known
that they are preparing to do so."[108] According to Hameiri, a preventive
war (i.e. preemptive strike) is a "commanded war" according to the sages,
whereas R. Judah thinks that is an optional war; whereas, according to
Rashi, R. Judah thought that a preemptive war is an obligatory war, while
the sages considered it optional.[109] The halakhic consequences cited by
Ravva in terms of the distinction between these two opinions deals with
whether one engaged in (another) mitzvah is exempt from the obligation
to participate in the war, if it is defined as an optional war; it would also

---

106 *Babylonian Sotah* 44b. This may also have been the opinion of Rav Hisda in *Palestinian Sotah*: "R. Hisda said: There is a dispute between them. The Rabbis say that a 'war of mitzvah' refers to the wars of David, an 'obligatory war' refers to the wars of Joshua; R. Judah would use the term 'optional war' to refer to those to which we go out; an 'obligatory war' refers to those to which they [i.e. our predecessors] went out." See Lieberman, *Tosefta ki-feshutah*. However, this text is not altogether clear; see the edition of the *Palestinian Talmud* based upon *MS Schliger 3* (Or. 4720) found in the University of Leiden, with completions and corrections and with an introduction by J. Sussman (Jerusalem, 2001): *Sotah* 8.7 (23a), p. 942.

107 See, for example, *Leviticus Rabbah* 1.4 (ed. Margaliot, pp. 14–15): "And she said: 'I have taken help from a mighty one.' R. Abah b. Kahana said: David made 13 wars. The Rabbis said: 18. And they did not differ. The one who said 13 – [all of them] were for the needs of Israel. The one who said 18 – 5 were for his own needs, and 13 for the needs of Israel."

108 *Beit ha-Behirah* to *Babylonian Sotah* 42b; also quoted by Lieberman, *Tosefta ki-feshutah*.

109 See Rashi to *Babylonian Sotah* 42b, s.v. *ki peligei*; see Kimelman, "Laws of War," p. 234.

seem that he is permitted to avoid fighting in it if one of the exemptions enumerated in *Mishnah Sotah*, Chapter 8, apply to him.

However, it is not yet clear whether, according to Ravva's opinion, there is a difference between the opinions of the tannaim regarding the king's obligation to seek the permission of the Sanhedrin in order to engage in preemptive military initiative. Offhand, if the sages indeed think that a preemptive war is an obligatory war (according to the opinion of Hameiri), one can only conclude that the king does not need to receive the permission of the Sanhedrin in order to initiate it; whereas R. Judah, who defines such a war as an optional war (again, according to Hameiri), will explain that the king needs the permission of the Sanhedrin in order to set out on a preemptive war.[110]

If we accept the interpretations of R. Yohanan and of Epstein, according to which the difference between the sages and R. Judah is purely terminological, then, according to the tannaim, the king's authority in military matters is extremely narrow: it is limited to the case of a defensive war in the narrow sense of the term alone, while all other military initiatives are conditional upon the consent of the Sanhedrin. Even if we accept the interpretation of Ravva (which is less plausible), the king's authority – again, according to a certain opinion (that of R. Judah or of the sages) – expands only very slightly, in that he is also permitted to set out on a preventive war without the Sanhedrin's agreement. This possibility, while opening a certain door to political manipulations, also greatly limits the king's prerogatives in these matters. The subjugation of the king to the Sanhedrin in matters of foreign and defense policy is one explicit expression of the limited nature of his prerogatives in Talmudic law.[111] Regarding this matter, more so than in others (several of which also

---

110 According to Rashi, the opinions are of course switched.

111 A colorful expression of this idea appears in *Babylonian Sanhedrin* 16a–b: "'One does not go out to war except … ' From whence do we learn these things? R. Abahu said: From the verse, 'And before Eleazar the priest he shall stand.' 'He' – this refers to the king. 'And all Israel with him' – this is the priest anointed over war. 'And all the congregation' – this is the Sanhedrin. And might it be that the Torah instructed the Sanhedrin to ask of the *Urim* and *Tumim*? Rather, this is what was said by R. Ahha b. Bizna in the name of R. Shimon Hasida: A harp was suspended above David's bed. When midnight came, a north wind blew and played upon it. Immediately David would rise and engage in Torah until the morning star. Once the morning star rose, the Sages of Israel came in. They said to him: Our master the king, your people Israel need livelihood. He said to them: Go, and let them make their livelihood from one another. They said to him: The hollow does not satisfy the lion, nor is a hole filled from that which has been dug

expand his authority), Talmudic law went quite far in limiting the power of the king far beyond the concept of limited monarchy as found in the Bible.[112]

out of it. He said to them: Let them extend their hands in the troops. Immediately they took counsel with Ahitophel, and went to the Sanhedrin, and asked the *Urim* and *Tummim*. Rav Yosef said: What is the meaning of the verse, 'Ahithophel was succeeded by Jehoida the son of Benaiah and Abiathar; Joab was commander of the king's army' (1 Chronicles 27:34). 'Ahitophel' – he gives counsel; and it also says, 'and the counsel of Ahitophel which he advised,' etc. 'And Benaiah and Abiathar' – this refers to the Sanhedrin. 'Aviathar.' These are the *Urim* and *Tummim*. And it also says, 'Benaiah the son of Jehoiada over the *Keretim* and the *Pletim*.' And why are they called *Keretim* and *Pletim*? '*Keretim*' – that they cut matters. '*Pletim*' – that they are outstanding in their deeds. And after that 'the head of the king's army.'"

112 In this context, it is interesting to compare the authority of the king in Talmudic halakhah to the prerogatives of the king regarding matters of war in the *Temple Scroll*. The *Scroll* devotes an extensive discussion to the issue of the wars waged by the king; it describes the manner in which the army is organized as well as detailed instructions concerning the size of the forces to be sent to war under various circumstances. The *Scroll* imparts a definite impression that waging war was one of the main functions of the king. Regarding our subject, the *Scroll* states as follows: "He shall not go [to war] until he has presented himself before the High Priest who shall inquire on his behalf for a decision by the *Urim* and *Tummim*. It is at his word that he shall go out and at his word that he shall come, he and all the children of Israel who are with him. He shall not go following his heart's counsel until he [the High Priest] has inquired for a decision by the *Urim* and *Tummim*. He shall [then] succeed in all his ways on which he has set out according to the decision which . . ." *Temple Scroll*, 58 xviii–xxi (ed. Qimron, p. 83); English translation: G. Vermes, *The Complete Dead Sea Scrolls in English* [London, 1998], p. 214). It would appear that in rabbinic law, the Sanhedrin takes the place of "the law of the *Urim* and *Tummim*"; cf. Fraade, "The Torah of the King," p. 36. Fraade is correct in stating that the emphasis in the *Scroll* upon the sanctity of the royal camp that goes to war and the need to receive the approval of the priests, who take counsel with the *Urim* and *Tummim*, is based upon an exegesis of Deuteronomy 23:10, 15: "When you go forth against your enemies and are in camp, then you shall keep yourself from every unseemly thing. … Because the Lord your God walks in the midst of your camp, to save you and to give up your enemies before you, therefore your camp must be holy." Yigael Yadin thinks that, because of its relation to Deuteronomy 20:1 ("when you go out against a city"), this passage is referring to an optional war (see Yadin, *The Temple Scroll*, vol. I, p. 358; vol. II, p. 263). However, Wise and Fraade are correct in stating that this passage relates specifically to Deuteronomy 23, that is, to every war, including that referred to in rabbinic literature as a "commanded war." See M. O. Wise, *A Critical Study of the Temple Scroll from Qumran Cave 11* (Chicago, Ill., 1990), pp. 114–117; Fraade, "The Torah of the King," p. 36 n. 31.

2.6 Separation between Monarchy and Priesthood

A clear separation between the priesthood and the monarchy emerges from the Talmudic tradition. Thus, in the *Palestinian Talmud, Shekalim:*

> One does not anoint priests to be kings. R. Yudan 'Antondria said: According to "the scepter shall not depart from Judah."
>
> R. Hiyya bar Adda said: "So that he may continue long in his kingdom, he and his children, in Israel." What is written thereafter: "the priests and Levites [or the Levitical priests] shall not have ..."[113]

This section is evidently opened by a *beraita,* which states that the priests cannot be anointed as kings.[114] This "separation" is completed by the tradition (or halakhah) stating that kings cannot be appointed as priests (and certainly not as high priests), as the origin of the priests is from Aaron alone.

The reason for the statement that "One does not anoint priests as kings" is provided by two Palestinian amoraim. R. Yudan 'Antondria finds support for the principle of separation between the priesthood and the monarchy in Jacob's words to Judah in his final days: "The scepter shall not depart from Judah" (Genesis 49:10). This is interpreted in the Talmudic tradition as conveying rulership to the tribe of Judah, and particularly to the Davidic house; it follows that an Aaronide priest, from the tribe of Levi, cannot be anointed as King.[115] R. Hiyya bar Adda learns the same principle of separation from the adjacency of these passages (i.e. the Chapter of the King and the establishment of the status of the priests) in Deuteronomy. While the principle of separation is not mentioned in these chapters explicitly, it is consistent with the idea of the "separation

---

113 *Palestinian Shekalim* 6.1 (49d), *Palestinian Sotah* 8.3 (22c); *Palestinian Horayot* 3.2 (47c). In *Sotah* and in *Horayot* the passage begins: "One does not anoint priests as king." For alternative readings, see D. Goodblatt, "The Union of Priesthood and Kingship in Second Temple Judea" (in Hebrew), *Cathedra,* 102 (2001): 7–28; p. 15, n. 31.

114 Concerning the fact that the opening statement is a *beraita* and not an amoraic source, see D. R. Schwartz, "On Pharisaic Opposition to the Hasmonean Monarchy," *Studies in the Jewish Background of Christianity* (Tübingen, 1992), pp. 44–56; at pp. 49–51; Goodblatt, "Union of Priesthood and Kingship," p. 15. My remarks in this section are largely based on Goodblatt's study.

115 See also *Genesis Rabbah,* 97.8 (ed. Theodor and Albeck, pp. 1212–1213; 99.10 (ed. Theodor and Albeck, p. 1280): "'The scepter shall not depart from Judah' – this is the royal throne," and numerous parallels.

of powers" – courts, the High Court, the monarchy, the priesthood, and prophecy – implied in that section. But whatever the proof text for the separation, the *beraita* in the *Palestinian* rejects the approach appearing in the Book of Psalms – according to which the king is also a priest – and continues the approach of Deuteronomy, according to which there is an implied separation between the monarchy and the priesthood.[116]

David Goodblatt considers this *beraita* to be the earliest source in the Jewish tradition to explicitly state that there is a separation between monarchy and priesthood. Opposed to the approach widespread among historians of the Second Temple period, Goodblatt argues that one does not find in any sources from this period, nor in the Bible itself, an explicit and clear expression that rejects in principle the unification of these two institutions.[117] In his opinion, the opposition of the Pharisees to the Hasmoneans – who took upon themselves both crowns, "the crown of kingship" and "the crown of priesthood" – was not based upon a principled approach of the need for separation between these two offices.[118] The claim

116 See above, Chapter 1.2; See also *Genesis Rabbah*, 55.6 (ed. Theodor and Albeck, p. 589): "'And He said to him: Abraham; and he said: Here I am.' R. Joshua said: In two places Moses compared himself to Abraham. The Holy One blessed be He said to him: 'Do not put yourself forward in the king's presence, or stand in the place of the great' (Proverbs 25:6). Abraham said: 'Here I am.' Here I am for priesthood and here I am for kingship. He merited to priesthood: 'The Lord has sworn and will not change His mind: You are a priest for ever after the order of Melchizedek' (Psalms 110:4). And he merited kingship: 'You are a prince of God among us' (Genesis 23:5). Moses said: 'Here I am' (Exodus 3:4). Here I am for priesthood, here I am for kingship. The Holy One blessed be He said to him: 'Do not come near' (Exodus 3:5). "Draw close.' There is no drawing close save for priesthood, as is said: 'And anyone else who come near, he shall be put to death' (Numbers 1:51). 'To here' – there is no 'to here' except for royalty, as is said 'that you have brought me thus far' (2 Samuel 7:18)." According to this midrash, Moses sought both priesthood and kingship (which Abraham had merited), but he was not answered, and it is possible that this expresses a certain opposition to the unification of the two functions. Compare M. Kister, "Metamorphoses of Aggadic Traditions" (in Hebrew), *Tarbiz*, 60 (1991): 179–224; pp. 205–207; and cf. Goodblatt, "Union of Priesthood and Kingship," pp. 18–19, which note that this source in *Genesis Rabbah* does not express principled opposition to the unification of priesthood and kingship, as it follows from them that "Once in the days of Abraham, and perhaps in the days of Moses, one person bore both crowns" (Goodblatt, "Union of Priesthood and Kingship," p. 19).
117 Schwartz, "On Pharisaic Opposition."
118 On the factors and the historical background for the unification of these functions ("crowns") by the Hasmoneans, see Schwartz, "Priesthood and Monarchy," and the references there to research literature.

of the Pharisees, rather, was that the Hasmoneans were not fit to serve in the priesthood (by reason of their being ritually unfit, or for ethical and political reasons).[119] Goodblatt even points out sources from the period of the Temple that required the unification of the two institutions.[120]

According to Goodblatt, the *beraita* in the *Palestinian* does not reflect a polemic conducted by Pharisees against the Hasmoneans around the question of them having taken upon themselves both crowns; rather, it expresses a theoretical, "academic" approach.[121] Goodblatt's conjecture indicates a conscious rejection of the approach of royal theology on the part of the tannaim, in which the king plays a central role in ritual.

However, it seems to me that the *beraita* in the *Palestinian* does not contain anything not already implied in the Mishnah and in other tannaitic sources. As noted earlier, Chapter 2 of *Mishnah Sanhedrin* is deeply impressed by the separation between the status of the high priest and that of the king. Moreover, even if the principle of separation is not explicitly mentioned in the Torah, it is implied in the manner of editing of the Book of Deuteronomy, from where distinctions emerge between the various institutions of rule, including between the monarchy and the priesthood. As Daniel Schwartz has noted, the Chapter of the King in the Book of Deuteronomy concludes with the promise that the legitimate

---

119 Thus Goodblatt interprets the famous *beraita* in *Babylonian Kiddushin* 66a concerning King Yannai and the parallel story in Josephus, *Jewish Antiquities* 13.288–295 (ed. Shalit, pp. 99–100), which refers to John Hyrcanus. See Goodblatt, "Union of Priesthood and Kingship," pp. 11–13. Goodblatt argues that if the historical truth is that the problem of the Pharisees was that Yannai had taken the royal crown in addition to that of the priesthood that he already had (thereby unlawfully uniting the two crowns), as argued by Schwartz, "On Pharisaic Opposition," why, according to the story, did the Pharisees demand that he relinquish specifically the crown of priesthood?

120 Thus, for example, Philo, *Life of Moses*, 1.334; 2.3; in Philo, *Supplements*, II, trans. R. Marcus (Cambridge, Mass., 1953), pp. 271, 273; and cf. Goodblatt, "Union of Priesthood and Kingship," pp. 20–21; D. Goodblatt, *The Monarchic Principle: Studies in Jewish Self-Government in Antiquity* (Tübingen, 1994), pp. 50–51; and compare H. A. Wolfson, *Philo*, rev. edn (Cambridge, Mass., 1962), vol. II, pp. 339, 344.

121 Both Schwartz ("Pharasaic Opposition," pp. 54–55) and Goodblatt agree that the question of the unification of the kingship and the priesthood was not an actual one in the time of the rabbis and that the *beraita* in the *Palestinian* reflects a theoretical academic discussion. However, Schwartz thinks that the lack of the beraita's relevancy indicates that the tradition was an ancient one, whereas Goodblatt argues, quite rightly, that this conclusion is not necessary, for the rabbis frequently engaged in non-actual matters (see Goodblatt, "Union of Priesthood and Kingship," pp. 15–16).

king will rule "he and his children, in Israel" (Deuteronomy 17:20), while the following verse emphasizes that "the priests and Levites shall have no portion or inheritance with Israel" (Deuteronomy 18:1). It would appear that the Bible is clearly suggesting here that the priests and Levites are, inter alia, excluded from the kingship.[122] As we have seen, this approach is also implied in R. Hiyya's view in *Palestinian Shekalim*. The separation between the priesthood and the monarchy likewise follows from the priestly sources in the Torah; Israel Knohl has recently claimed that, just as the Book of Deuteronomy clearly separates the king from the priesthood, so too does the priestly source in Leviticus separate the priesthood from political authority and power.[123] "Although the sacred sphere contained within the holy enclosure," writes Knohl, "is a kind of independent kingdom headed by the anointed priesthood who wear the trappings of royalty, they in no way serve as a replacement for civil-political rule." He continues, "The Priestly Torah recognized non-priestly political leadership, whose representatives are the chieftains of the congregation. It seeks, however, to maintain an interior 'holy kingdom' alongside the broader political structure."[124]

While it is difficult to draw a direct analogy from the Book of Deuteronomy and from the priestly source in the Torah regarding the outlooks widespread among the Pharisees (and among other groups), Goodblatt is correct in stating that, in order to base this dispute on the issue of the "unification of the crowns" during the period of the Second Temple, one needs to point towards sources that state this explicitly.[125] Nevertheless, it is difficult to accept his claim that there are no sources in the ancient Jewish tradition indicating the existence of a viewpoint that

---

122 See Schwartz, "Priesthood and Monarchy," pp. 13–25, at p. 21.

123 See I. Knohl, *The Sanctuary of Silence: The Priestly Torah and the Holiness School* (Minneapolis, Minn., 1995), p. 155; I. Knohl, *The Divine Symphony: The Bible's Many Voices* (Philadelphia, Pa., 2003), pp. 93–94. Knohl argues, in the former book, that a clear expression of the separation between priesthood and kingship in the Torah is found, *inter alia*, in the story of the deaths of the 250 people who offered incense – see Numbers 16:35 – as well as in the story of King Uziahu, who sought to offer incense on the altar and leprosy appeared on his forehead (2 Chronicles 26:16–20).

124 Knohl, *Sanctuary of Silence,* p. 155.

125 My own argument pertains to the very existence of a dispute concerning this matter. However, the view that there is a distinction between priesthood and monarchy does not necessarily require an explicit source, and it suffices to point towards those sources that imply this view. The methodology used by Goodblatt in this matter is far too positivistic; see the next note.

separates between the two offices. Not only does such a viewpoint emerge from the law of Deuteronomy and from the priestly literature in the Torah (particularly from the priestly document), but a significant part of the biblical drama is based upon the division of the political leadership and the priesthood into two separate offices.[126]

Whether or not the tannaitic sources express a new viewpoint within the Jewish tradition or whether they repeat one inherent in the Bible and develop it further, it is clear that the idea of separation between the priesthood and the monarchy is a cornerstone of the political approach of the tannaim. As mentioned, this approach embodies rejection of the model of royal theology even in its sacral version.[127]

2.7 Anointing

That the king is lacking in any sacral standing and has no special relationship to God, according to the Mishnah, is expressed in the absence of any reference to the ceremony of him being anointed with oil. According to the biblical "history" (as distinct from biblical law), anointing was the ceremonial-ritual means of establishing a divine, or at least sacral, king.[128] On this point, *Mishnah Sanhedrin* is similar to the Chapter of the King in Deuteronomy (that details the law of the king), in which no mention is made of anointing; this point joins together with

---

126 Goodblatt cites numerous biblical precedents for such a "separation of powers": Moses and Aaron, Joshua and Eleazar, David and Zaddok and Eviatar, Joash and Jehoiada, Josiah and Hilkiah, Zerubavel and Joshua. See Goodblatt, "Unification of Kingship and Priesthood," p. 13. In this context, I wish to note a central methodological consideration. Guiding Goodblatt's research on this matter (and elsewhere) is that it is impossible to establish findings regarding outlooks or facts from the past except on the basis of explicit texts. This requirement seems to me not to be essential, as it is possible for a given approach to form an inseparable part of a literary body, even though it is not given explicit expression therein but only by implication. Thus, for example, the issue of separation between priesthood and kingship is not explicitly mentioned in the Bible nor in the Mishnah, although all of the data indicate that such separation was self-evident to the authors of these writings.

127 The separation between priesthood and monarchy is also connected to the separation between monarchy and judicial proceedings, as both in the Bible and in the Second Temple sources the priesthood not only served in the holy place but was also charged with the interpretation of the law and the performance of justice. See, for example, the remarks of Josephus, *Contra Apion*, II.184–187.

128 See above, Chapter 1.2.

several other similar points between the Mishnah and the Chapter of the King in Deuteronomy.

The omission of the anointing of the king in *Mishnah Sanhedrin* may be accidental, as the Mishnah does not at all discuss the means of appointing or installing a king – neither the method of appointment of the first king, with which the dynasty began, nor the method of appointing a king who is the son of the king. To recall, the Mishnah is lacking in many other laws relating to the king; apart from the first law in *Mishnah Sanhedrin* concerning the king – "The king does not judge nor is he judged" – brought as an aside to a discussion (in the previous chapter and in that which follows) of the court's authorities, it is difficult to provide an explanation for the principles of choice of the mishnaic editor regarding the laws of the king.[129] Nevertheless, the absence from the Mishnah of the subject of anointing – even though it does appear, as I shall show below, in other places in the Talmudic literature – integrates well with its tendency to negate (and certainly to limit) the sacral nature of the monarchy.

Anointing is also not mentioned at all in the collection of homilies about the king in *Sifrei Devarim*. The language appearing in a number of midrashim in *Sifrei* is *manui* ("appointment" and not "anointing").[130] While the editor of *Sifrei* gathers together homilies on the verses of the Chapter of the King in Deuteronomy – in which there is no mention of anointing – it seems likely that, if this editor were to see anointing as a fundamental element regarding the monarchy, he would have found a way of mentioning it in the collection of midrash that he gathered. It would therefore seem that, regarding this matter, the tendency of the editor of *Sifrei* is similar to that of the Mishnah's editor – as Epstein noted regarding other aspects of the Chapter of the King.[131]

But while neither the Mishnah nor *Sifrei Devarim* mention the subject of anointing the king, it is mentioned in several places in the Talmudic literature. As I shall show below, the laws pertaining to it indicate a substantive change as compared to the nature of anointing in the biblical history. This change is rooted in the fact that the function of anointing the king in the Talmudic sources ceased to be sacral and assumes a political character.

---

129 This phenomenon is not unique to the subject of the king but is widespread in the Mishnah. See, for example, the discussion of H. Albeck, *Introduction to the Mishnah* (in Hebrew) (Jerusalem and Tel Aviv, 1979), pp. 99ff.

130 See, for example, *Sifrei Devarim* 157 (ed. Finkelstein, p. 208): "You shall surely place' – If he dies appoint another in his place"; and cf. *Tosefta Sanhedrin* 4.11 (ed. Zuckermandel, p. 421); and see the discussion below

131 See Epstein, *Introduction to Tannaitic Literature,* pp. 72 and 732.

Tosefta Sanhedrin states that "the king requires anointing"; however, this halakhah is immediately qualified: "the son of a king does not require anointing."[132] In other words, only that king with whom a new dynasty begins needs to be anointed while a king who inherits the throne from his father is not anointed. These laws are preceded in the *Tosefta* by the following halakhah: "One does not anoint kings except because of controversy. Why did they anoint Solomon? Because of the controversy of Adonijah. And Jehu – because of Yoram; and Joash – because of Atalyah; and Jehoahaz – because of his brother Jehoiakim, who was two years older than him."[133] According to this halakhah, kings are anointed only when there is a struggle between rivals to the throne – at times between brothers, at times between the legitimate heir and a rebel. Under such circumstances, the function of anointing is to indicate the legitimate heir. Despite the order of editing of these halakhot in the *Tosefta*, it is clear that the halakhah, according to which one anoints kings because of controversy, does not qualify the rule according to which a new king requires anointing but is in addition to it. In other words, in addition to the king requiring anointing, the son of a king in times of controversy also requires anointing.[134]

Let us compare this halakhah to that relating to the high priest, brought in the adjacent *Tosefta*. Together with the statement that the king is anointed, it also states there that the high priest is anointed.[135] However, unlike the son of a king, who is not anointed, "The high priest who was the son of a high priest, even up to ten generations, requires anointing."[136] It would seem that the contrast between the rule regarding

---

132 *Tosefta Sanhedrin* 4.11 (ed. Zuckermandel, p. 422); cf. *Sifra, Mekhilta de-Miluim* 1 (ed. Weiss, 41b); *Palestinian Shekalim* 6.5 (49c); *Palestinian Horayot* 3.2 (47c); *Palestinian Sotah* 8.3 (22c); *Babylonian Keritut* 5b; *Babylonian Horayot* 11b; *Leviticus Rabbah,* 10.8 (Margaliot ed., pp. 213–214); *Tosefta Bava Kamma* 7.8 (ed. Zuckermandel, p. 358); *Midrash Tannaim* 17.20 (ed. Hoffman, p. 106); and cf. *Genesis Rabbah,* 71.35 (ed. Theodor and Albeck, p. 827); *Tosefta Sanhedrin,* 4.11.

133 *Tosefta Sanhedrin,* 4.11 and numerous parallels (see n. 132 above).

134 From the wording of the *Tosefta* it is clear that, in a time of dispute, the son of the king is also anointed. However, the order of the laws in the *Tosefta* suggests the conclusion that a new king is only anointed in time of controversy and that the son of the king is never anointed.

135 This statement is brought at the end of R. Judah's words in *Sifra 96, Mekhilta de-Miluim* 1.9: "Miraculous deeds were done with the anointing oil made by Moses in the wilderness ... From it were anointed Aaron and his sons all seven days of preparation; from it were anointed high priests and kings." See the parallels in *Babylonian Keritut* 5b, and in numerous other places (see n. 132 above).

136 *Tosefta Sanhedrin* 4.11, and many parallels (see n. 132 above).

the anointing of the priest and that regarding the king reflects a difference in the purpose of anointing in each of these offices. The anointing of the high priest appears to have a sacral function, whereas the anointing of the king serves a political purpose: "pointing out" the new king when it becomes necessary. The anointing of the priest, in contrast, doubtless serves a sacral and not a political purpose. This conclusion logically follows, of course, from the ritual function of the high priest. For that reason, evidently, is a need to anoint the "son of the high priest" "even to ten generations," whenever a new high priest is appointed. Had the purpose of anointing the king been similar to that of the high priest, the son of a king would also require anointing. And, indeed, as noted above, it is clear from the Bible that every king – including the son of a king, and even when there is no controversy – is anointed.[137] The departure of the tannaitic halakhah from biblical practice with regard to the king, particularly when compared with its attachment to the biblical practice regarding the anointing the high priest, suggests that the tannaim turned the anointing of the king away from its original purpose in the Bible – i.e. a sacral anointing intended to bring the spirit of God down upon the king and to turn him into the "anointed of God" – to a political purpose. The goal of anointing in tannaitic halakhah is to give the king sociopolitical authority, and no more.[138] If anointing fulfills a sacral purpose, why isn't the son of a king anointed as well? It is clear that the "spirit" is not drawn upon him by virtue of his father's anointing, as seen by the need for anointing of the son of the high priest. The political purpose of anointing the king is doubtless emphasized by the statement that "One does not anoint kings except because of controversy" – at a time of controversy anointing is intended to decide who is the legitimate king. If, however, the legitimacy of the heir is not controversial, and he ascends his father's throne peacefully, anointing is superfluous.

I now turn to the discussion of the issue of anointing in *Babylonian Keritut,* and in various passages in the *Palestinian.*[139] After bringing the

---

137 See above Chapter 1.2.

138 It may be that the tannaitic halakhah returns the anointing to its original purpose, which was political-legal, as is possibly implied from different biblical sources. See above Chapter 1.2; and cf. T. N. D. Mettinger, *King and Messiah: The Civil and Sacral Legitimation of Israelite Kings* (Lund, 1976), p. 208. However, everyone agrees that it is clear from the final redaction of the Bible that the anointing of kings had a sacral purpose and that this was doubtless how it was read by the tannaim.

139 There are numerous parallels to this *sugya*; see *Babylonian Horayot* 11b; for parallels in the *Palestinian*, see below.

beraita in the *Tosefta* relating to the anointing of high priests and kings and their sons, the discussion in *Babylonian Keritut* brings the reasons for these laws:

> It was said: Even a high priest son of a high priest requires anointing. From whence? As is written, "The priest from among Aaron's sons who is anointed . . ." (Leviticus 6:15). Scripture could have said, "the priest after him among his sons." Why does it say, "who is anointed"? We learn from this that even among his sons, the one who is anointed will be high priest, the one who is not anointed will not be high priest.
>
> It was said: One does not anoint a king son of a king. From whence? Rav Ahha bar Yaakov said: As is written, "that he may continue long in his kingdom, he and his children [all the days]" (Deuteronomy 17:20) – it is an inheritance.[140]

The law stating that the son of a high priest requires anointing is inferred by our *sugya* from the language of the verse in Leviticus 6:15 ("the priest who is anointed"). The *sugya* emphasizes that anointing is a necessary condition for being considered a high priest – a condition that does not exist in the case of the king. And, indeed, Rav Ahha bar Yaakov states that, unlike the high priest, one does not anoint the son of the king, because the monarchy passes directly via inheritance ("it is an inheritance"). It would appear that the reason for the distinction between them is the same as that suggested above: since the anointing of the king is a matter of his political status, if this status – like other matters related to status – is passed down in inheritance (which is the usual way to ascend the royal throne), anointing is superfluous. Such is not the case regarding the "sacral status" of the high priest; here is a need for a sanctifying ritual as inheritance alone cannot convey sanctity. The argument that the anointing of the high priest is a sanctifying ritual is rooted not only in the fact that every high priest requires anointing; in the final analysis (and as has been argued by scholars of ritual), there are rituals that are not "religious" but "secular," which are likewise similarly concerned with change in status or the acquisition of status.[141] However, the combination found here between the requirement for anointing on the part of every high priest and the fact that this anointing prepares him to serve in the realm of the holy, suggests that one is speaking here of a

140 *Babylonian Keritut* 5b.
141 See Mettinger, *King and Messiah*, p. 208, and the references there.

sanctifying anointment. This anointing is opposed, as we have said, to the anointing of the king.[142]

From here, our *sugya* turns to deal with the halakhah concerned with the anointing of the king because of controversy. Evidently, the Talmudic (amoraitic?) discussion of this law led to a certain change in relation to the tannaitic halakhah:

> For what reason did they anoint Solomon? Because of the controversy of Adonijah. From whence do we know that when there is controversy anointment is required, and not everyone whom the king wishes to inherit him, inherits? Rav Papa said: The verse says, "in the midst of Israel" (Deuteronomy 17:20) – at a time when there is peace within Israel.
>
> They taught: Jehu son of Nimshi was also only anointed because of the controversy of Yoram son of Ahab. Why? Might we not see [that it was because] he was the first king [in a new dynasty].
>
> Our text is lacking, and you should read it thus: Kings of the Davidic house are anointed, but kings of Israel are not anointed. And if you say: for what reason did they anoint Jehu son of Nimshi? Because of the controversy of Yoram son of Ahab. But it is said: Kings of the Davidic house are anointed, kings of Israel are not anointed. From whence? As is written, "Rise, anoint him, for this is he" (1 Samuel 16:12). This one requires anointing, another one does not require anointing.[143]

The tannaitic halakhah regarding a situation of political dispute, in which the son of the king is also anointed, was expounded by the amora Rav Pappa on the basis of the verse, "he and his children, within Israel"

---

142 Further on in this *sugya,* a distinction is drawn between the manner of anointment of the high priest and the king. See *Babylonian Keritut* 5b: "Our Rabbis taught: The kings are anointed with a kind of crown, and the priests with a kind of *k.* R. Manashe said: With a kind of Greek *k.*" See, however, *Genesis Rabbah,* 71.35 (ed. Theodor and Albeck, p. 827): "R. Levi said. Two tribes ascended from among them: a tribe of priests and a tribe of royalty. You find that everything that was written regarding one is written regarding the other: in this one there is anointing and in that one anointing; in this one there is a scepter and in that one a scepter; in this one a covenant of salt and in that one a covenant of salt; in this one a step and in that one a step; in this one a crown and in that one a crown; in this one drawing near and in that one drawing near; in this one a chain of relation and in that one a chain of relation; in this one a miter and in that one a miter."

143 *Babylonian Keritut* 5b.

– i.e. at a time when there is peace within Israel. Rashi explains this: "When there was peace within Israel the monarchy was an inheritance and did not require anointing, but when there is a dispute it is not regarded as an inheritance, and it requires anointing at its beginning."[144] In other words, it is the nature of kingship to be passed on by inheritance, in which case there is no need for anointing; however, when there are those who challenge the heir, the need arises for a decisive act to mark the new king – hence, the political act of anointing. The Talmud challenges this law from the continuation of this *beraita* itself: namely, why does the *beraita* state that Jehu son of Nimshi was anointed because of the challenge of Yoram son of Ahab? After all, one could explain his anointing in terms of his beginning a new royal line![145] This question evidently derives from the assumption that the need to anoint the first in a new line is more fundamental than the need to anoint in order to determine the rightful heir in case of dispute. In response to this question, the Talmud gives a surprising answer: it "corrects" the language of the *beraita* ("[Our text] is lacking") and introduces a new element: "The kings of the Davidic house are anointed; kings of Israel are not anointed."

Immediately thereafter in the *sugya* the question arises as to the source of this distinction: "It is said: Kings of the Davidic house are anointed, kings of Israel are not anointed. From whence? As is written, 'Rise, anoint him, for this is he' (1 Samuel 16:12). This one requires anointing, another one does not require anointing."[146] In the parallel *sugya* in the *Babylonian Horayot* (11b), this same homily is attributed to Rava. The amora concludes, from a homily interpreting the phrase used by God in addressing Samuel when David was anointed, that "this" (i.e. David) required anointing, but another king (i.e. from Israel) is not anointed. The conclusion of the "corrected" *beraita* is dramatic: that only kings of the Davidic house are

---

144 *Babylonian Keritut* 5b, s.v. *biz'man sheshalom be-Yisrael.*

145 Cf. 1 Kings 19:16; 2 Kings 10.

146 *Babylonian Keritut* 5b; *Babylonian Horayot* 11b. It is interesting to note that this homily is brought as a gloss to *Palestinian Shekalim* 6.5 (49c), as the reason why the son of a king does not require anointing: "The king initially requires anointing; a king who is the son of a king does not require anointing. What is the reason? 'Come, anoint him, for that is he' – this one requires anointing, and his son does not require anointing. But a high priest who is the son of a high priest, even to the tenth generation, requires anointing." Cf. J. Sussman, "Tradition of Learning and Tradition of Versions of the Jerusalem Talmud: To Clarify the Versions of the *Yerushalmi Shekalim*" (in Hebrew), in *Mehkarim be-Sifrut ha-Talmudit: Study Day in Honor of the 80th Birthday of Saul Lieberman* (Jerusalem, 1983), pp. 12–76; p. 72, notes to lines 54–55. However, in *Palestinian Sotah* 8.3 (22c), the homily is part of the body of the *Palestinian* text.

anointed – and not those of Israel. In practice, initially David alone was anointed, as his sons inherit the kingship from him without any [further] need of anointing; however, in the case of dispute both the kings of the Davidic house and those of Israel are anointed.[147]

It would seem that the distinction, with regard to anointing, between kings of Israel and kings of the Davidic line, does not appear in the tannaitic sources; like the subject of the king and justice, the distinction between them is integrated into the halakhic discussion by the amoraim. It is instructive to note that, unlike the discussion of the rule, "The king judges, but is not judged," in which the distinction between Davidic kings and those of Israel only appears in the Babylonian Talmud (by Rav Yosef), regarding the question of anointing it is presented in the *Palestinian* as well.[148] Even though it is briefer, the *sugya* in the *Palestinian* is on this point close to the *Babylonian*:

> One does not anoint kings, except because of controversy. Why, then, was Solomon anointed? Because of the controversy with Adonijah; and Johash because of Ataliah, and Jehu because of Yoram.
>
> Is it not written: "Rise, anoint him, for this is he"? This one requires anointing, but the kings of Israel do not require anointing?! . . .
>
> Jehoiahaz because of Jehoiakim his brother, who was two years older than him.[149]

147 Perhaps the inference "This one requires anointing and another one does not require anointing" is specific: the word *zeh* ("this") refers to David alone, and not even to his sons. Not only are the kings of Israel not anointed but, in the absence of controversy, even the kings of the Davidic house are not anointed, whereas in a case of controversy, even an Israelite king is anointed. Nevertheless, it is possible that at the time of renewing the monarchy and the ascent of a king from the Davidic house anointing would be required.

148 See below, Chapter 3.6.

149 *Palestinian Horayot* 3.2 (47c); and see *Palestinian Shekalim* 6.1 (49c); *Palestinian Sotah* 8.3 (22c). It is interesting to note that this homily is itself brought in these *sugyot* in the *Palestinian* only a few lines earlier (with the addition of a gloss) in support of the argument that the son of a king does not require anointing: "The king initially requires anointing; a king who is a son of a king does not require anointing. What is the reason? As is said, "Come, anoint him, for this is he" – this one requires anointing but his son does not require anointing; but a high priest son of a high priest, even after ten generations, requires anointing." It would seem that the redactor did not notice that the identical homily is brought immediately thereafter for a different purpose.

The discussion in the *Palestinian* incorporates within the *beraita* a question that is not part of the actual text of the *beraita*: "Is it not written … and the kings of Israel do not require anointing." The question is: Why did they anoint Jehu, who was a king of Israel, and as such did not require anointing? The discussion in the *Palestinian* does not relate to this question but immediately returns to the *beraita* and continues: "Jehoiahaz because of Jehoiakim …"[150] Are we to understand that the conclusion of the *sugya* is that the anointing of Jehu was superfluous? Or does this question have no normative significance? According to the latter possibility, the conclusion of the *Palestinian* would seem to be similar to that of *Babylonian*: initially only Davidic kings are anointed, but in a time of controversy both the Davidic kings and the kings of Israel are anointed. However, according to the former reading, the conclusion of the *Palestinian* is that the king of Israel is not anointed at all – neither as the first king in a new line, nor in case of dispute![151]

Let us return to the *sugya* of the *Babylonian*. To recall, the question was raised: Why was Jehu b. Nimshi anointed, when [we know that] kings of Israel are not ordinarily anointed! To this, our *sugya* responds: "Because of the controversy." This answer immediately raises a further question: "And because of the controversy of Yoram son of Ahab, the anointing oil was profaned?! [But it was] as Rav Pappa said: [He was anointed] with fine balsam-tree oil (*afarsemon*); here, too, with fine balsam-tree oil."[152] The assumption underlying this question is that the kings of Israel are not the chosen ones of God and therefore are not "His anointed." The kingship is intended for David and his sons alone or, in the language of Maimonides: "Once David was anointed, he merited to the crown of kingship, and the kingship was for him and his male children for ever, as it is said: 'Your throne shall be established for ever.'"[153] The answer in our *sugya* is based on the words of Rav Pappa in a different context,

---

150   It is a widespread phenomenon in *sugyot* of the *Palestinian* that a question is posed without an answer. See also those *sugyot* in *Palestinian Sanhedrin* 2.1 (5a), discussed in Chapter 2.6 above.

151   Compare Maimonides' *Yad, Hilkhot Melakhim* 1.7, 10, 11.

152   *Babylonian Keritut* 5b; *Babylonian Horayot* 11b; compare *Palestinian Shekalim* 6.1 (49c); *Palestinian Horayot* 3.2 (47c); and *Palestinian Sotah* 8.3 (22c).

153   See Maimonides' remarks in *Hilkhot Melakhim* 1.7; and compare also what he says there in 1.9: "Kings of the Davidic house reign forever, as is said, 'Your throne shall be established for ever' but if a king should arise from the rest of Israel, the monarchy will cease from his house, for it was said to Jeroboam, 'but not all the days'"; and see Rabad's gloss on that spot.

according to which the anointing of the kings of Israel was not with holy oil (i.e. the anointing oil) but with pure balsam oil.[154]

The distinction drawn by the amoraim, reflected in both the *Babylonian* and the *Palestinian*, between the Davidic kings who were anointed and those of Israel who are not anointed, does not appear in the tannaitic sources. However, a distinction between the Davidic kings and those of Israel with regard to anointing does appear in tannaitic sources, albeit in a different context. In *Tosefta Sanhedrin* the following passage appears: "One does not anoint kings except with a horn. Saul and Jehu were anointed from an [earthenware] vessel (*min ha-pah*), because their kingdom was to be broken in the future; David and Solomon were anointed from a horn, because their kingship was to be an eternal one."[155] The distinction between the "kings of Israel," Saul and Jehu, who were anointed from a vessel, and David and Solomon, who were anointed from a horn, is based upon scriptural verses in the books

154 A similar answer appears in the *sugyot* found in the *Palestinian Talmud* (*Shekalim, Horayot, Sotah;* see n. 152 above), which explain the type of oil used to anoint Jehu. Rav Pappa's remarks are brought further on in the *sugya* at *Babylonian Keritut* 5b: "And was it truly the anointing oil [i.e. were all of the kings mentioned in the *beraita* in fact anointed with the anointing oil]? And it has been taught: Once the ark was hidden away, there were also hidden the jar with the manna, and the vial of the anointing oil, and the staff of Aaron with almonds and flowers, and the chest in which the Philistines send a gift to the God of Israel, as is said, 'and the vessels of gold which they returned to me I shall place in a chest by my side' (1 Samuel 6:8). And who concealed them? Josiah king of Judah concealed them ... Rav Pappa said: [He was anointed] with balsam oil (*afarsemon*)." The conclusion of the *sugya* is thus that, because the oil was hidden away in the days of Josiah, even the Davidic kings who came thereafter were anointed with balsam oil. However, note the *beraita* at the beginning of this *sugya:* "And was there only one miracle done with the anointing oil? Many miracles were done with it from beginning to end: it began with no more than twelve *log*, and with it were anointed the sanctuary and its vessels, and Aaron and his sons all seven days of preparation, and with it were anointed high priests and kings; and all of it exists in the future, as is said 'this shall be my holy anointing oil throughout your generations' (Exodus 30:31). The numerical value (*gematria*) of the word 'this' (*zeh*) is twelve. Our Rabbis taught: 'And Moses took the anointing oil and anointed the Sanctuary' (Leviticus 8:10). R. Judah said: The anointing oil made by Moses in the wilderness, many miracles were done with it from beginning to end. In the beginning there were no more than twelve *log*, how much was absorbed by the coking vessel, how much was absorbed by the roots, how much was burned up by the fire – yet there were anointed with it the sanctuary and its vessels, Aaron and his own sons all seven days of preparation, and with it the high priests and kings were anointed."

155 *Tosefta Sanhedrin* 4.11 (ed. Zuckermandel, p. 422).

of Samuel and Kings.[156] The horn symbolizes continuity, and particularly power, as in the verses: "On that day I will cause a horn to spring forth to the house of Israel" (Ezekiel 29:21); "my strength [lit., horn] is exalted in the Lord" (1 Samuel 2:1), and many other such verses.[157] While the *Tosefta* does not explicitly distinguish between the kings of Israel and those of the Davidic line, it nevertheless would seem that the distinction between "a kingdom that is to shattered in the future" and "an eternal kingdom" implies a categorical distinction between the two monarchies; in the final analysis, in the Talmudic tradition an "eternal kingdom" cannot be other than the Davidic kingship.[158] Nevertheless, the *beraita* in the *Tosefta* seems to imply that the kings of Israel were also anointed. Moreover, it follows from the language of the *beraita* that all the kings, including the kings of Israel, were anointed from a horn.

And, indeed, there are tannaitic sources relating to the subject of anointing that do not make any distinction between Davidic kings and those of Israel. Thus, for example, the following *beraita*:

> Our Rabbis taught: One does not anoint kings except by a spring, so that their kingship may continue, as is said: "And the king said [to them: Take with you the servants of your lord, and cause Solomon my son to ride on my own mule], and bring him down to Gihon, and let [Zadok the priest and Nathan the prophet] anoint him there" (1 Kings 1:33–34).[159]

Even though the source of which this *beraita* speaks is based on Solomon, no discrimination is made in this *beraita* between the kings of Israel and the kings of Judah, making it plausible that the ceremony of anointing by the spring – the drawing of the spring's waters symbolizing continuity – pertains to all kings, including the kings of Israel.[160]

---

156 David (1 Samuel 16:13); Solomon (1 Kings 1:39); Saul (1 Samuel 10:1); Jehu (2 Kings 9:3).

157 See S. Morag, "On Horn, on Salvation, and on the Horn of Salvation" (in Hebrew), *Studies in Biblical Hebrew* (Jerusalem, 1995), pp. 218–224 (*Jerusalem Studies in Jewish Thought*, 4 [1985]: 345–351).

158 See the wording used by Maimonides in *Hilkhot Melakhim* 1.9; and see n. 153 above.

159 *Babylonian Keritut* 5b; the completions of the verse are my own. See also *Babylonian Horayot* 11b; *Palestinian Horayot* 3.2 (47c); *Palestinian Shekalim* 6.1 (49c); *Leviticus Rabbah* 10.8 (ed. Margaliot, pp. 213–214).

160 Compare Maimonides, *Hilkhot Melakhim* 1.11: "When one anoints kings of the Davidic house, they are only anointed by a spring"; and compare Rabad's gloss, *Hilkhot Melakhim*, 1.9.

The tendency in the amoraic sources – to distinguish between kings of the Davidic house and those of Israel, and to exclude the latter from the ceremony of anointing – reinforces the non-sacral nature of the kings of Israel. Their kingship is perceived as a worldly one, without any connection to the heavenly realms. The Mishnah and other tannaitic sources (*beraitot* and halakhic midrashim) relate, according to the amoraim, to the king of Israel. As we have seen, according to the *Babylonian*, a new king of Israel does not require anointing at all and, according to a plausible reading of the *Palestinian*, is not even anointed at a time of controversy. According to the *Babylonian*, even when an Israelite king requires anointing (i.e. in the case of dispute), he is not anointed with the holy oil but with balsam-wood oil. Insofar as anointing is an indication of sacralism, all of these signs indicate that the kingship of Israel was lacking in this component.

To the extent that the amoraim distance anointing from the kings of Israel and emphasize the distinction between the kings of Israel and the kings of the Davidic house, they are in practice emphasizing the sacral nature of the latter. This tendency is, of course, suitable to the "biblical tradition" – both that of the Deuteronomistic history and various chapters of prophecy and particularly to the royal hymns in the Book of Psalms – which emphasize the relation of the Davidic kings to God. It could be that underlying this tendency is a distinction between the eschatological king, whose status is sacral (and possible even divine), and the earthly monarchy, which has no holy element. In any event, this distinction also indicates that the Mishnah and the laws of the king found therein describe a limited earthly monarchy, without any sacred dimension.[161]

---

161 Maimonides follows a similar direction regarding the matter of anointing. See the discussion by G. J. Blidstein, *Political Concepts in Maimonidean Halakhah* (in Hebrew), 2nd edn (Ramat Gan, 2001), pp. 68–71.

THREE

Rabbinic Literature: The King and the Law

3.1 "The King Does Not Judge, Nor Is He Judged"

The Mishnah in *Sanhedrin* states as follows: "The king does not judge nor is he judged; he does not testify, nor is he testified about."[1] This halakhah, with which the Mishnah begins its discussion of the king, establishes a break between the king and the judicial system.[2] On the one hand, "the king does not judge" – that is to say, he does not sit as a judge in a juridical proceeding.[3] But, on the other hand, "he is not judged" – that is to say, the king has immunity from the judicial system: he cannot be placed on trial (in capital cases) nor sued (in a civil case). Against the background of the Bible, this statement is surprising in two respects:

1   *Mishnah Sanhedrin* 2.2; and cf. *Midrash Tannaim* 17.4 (ed. Hoffman addition, p. 104); *Mishnah Horayot* 2.5; *Palestinian Sanhedrin* 2.3 (20a); *Palestinian Horayot* 2.6 (46d); *Deuteronomy Rabbah* 5.8 (*Shoftim;* ed. Lieberman, p. 98); *Midrash Tehillim*, 10.2 (ed. Buber, p. 125); and see *Sifrei Zuta, Deuteronomy* 17.18 (ed. Kahana, p. 262); 19:17 (ed. Kahana, p. 282); 21.2 (ed. Kahana, p. 293).

2   It is no accident that the halakhot stating that the king does not judge and is not judged opens the laws concerning the king in *Mishnah Sanhedrin*; this follows from the fact that this tractate's opening chapters deal with the various kinds of courts (of 3, 23 and 71 – i.e. the Sanhedrin) and their prerogatives. During the course of discussion of these courts, with which Chapter 1 is concerned, laws are brought concerning the authority of these courts over the high priest (*Mishnah Sanhedrin* 2.1) and the king (*Mishnah Sanhedrin* 2). In this discussion, the Mishnah brings additional laws relating to the status of the high priest (*Mishnah Sanhedrin* 2) and to the status and prerogatives of the king (*Mishnah Sanhedrin* 2). However, it would seem that it is not merely chance that the editor of the Mishnah chose to present the subject of the king in this manner; see below.

3   There were those who found difficulty in this and suggested that the Mishnah's intention was that the king does not judge within the context of the Sanhedrin but that he does judge in the royal court. In this way they sought to resolve the seeming contradiction between this Mishnah and what is stated below (*Mishnah Sanhedrin* 2.4): "And he writes a Torah scroll for himself ... When he sits in judgment, it is with him." It would appear, however, that the sense of the Mishnah is that the king does not have any judicial function. On this contradiction within the Mishnah, see below.

on the one hand, according to the biblical tradition, the kings engaged in the practice of justice (like the kings of the Ancient Near East, who stood at the head of the judicial system of their kingdoms); on the other hand – and according to what is stated in the Chapter of the King in Deuteronomy – the king is subjugated to the Torah, from which one might infer that he is held accountable for his actions.[4] These difficulties (or part of them) underlie the discussions of this rule in both Talmuds. I shall begin with the *sugya* in the Babylonian Talmud:

> "The king does not judge," etc. Rav Pappa said: They only spoke here regarding the kings of Israel, but kings of the Davidic dynasty are judged and may be judged, as is written, "O House of David: Thus says the Lord, execute justice in the morning" (Jeremiah 21:12). And if we do not judge him – how can be judged? But Scripture says: "Come together and hold assembly" (Zephaniah 2:1). Resh Lakish said: Adorn yourself, and then adorn others.[5]

The amora Rav Pappa limits our mishnah to the kings of Israel, while the kings of the Davidic house "judge and are judged."[6] This distinction is based on the biblical tradition (here, in the version of the Book of Jeremiah), according to which the prophet commands the Davidic house to do justice.[7] The Talmud bases the law according to which a Davidic king may be judged on the principle of mutuality, attributed to Resh Lakish: "Adorn yourself and then adorn others" – in other words, a person cannot judge unless he himself is subject to being judged. It follows from this that the (Davidic) king "is judged." It is interesting to note that both the law in the Babylonian Talmud regarding the kings

---

4   According to the Book of Deuteronomy, it is indeed not clear whether the king judges. See *Deuteronomy and the Hermeneutics,* by Levinson, who thinks that according to Deuteronomy the king does not judge. In any event, as we shall see below, the Talmuds do not think that it follows from Deuteronomy that the king does not judge; this was inferred from another source.

5   *Babylonian Sanhedrin* 19a.

6   In a Yemenite manuscript of *Tractate Sanhedrin* (ed. Fisch, p. 394), these words are ascribed to Rav Pappa. However, in the other textual witnesses they are ascribed to Rav Yosef. See Kahana, *Sifrei Zuta le-Devarim,* p. 285 and n. 13 there.

7   As we shall see below, the *sugya* in the *Palestinian* (that goes in a different direction) learns from a different, "historical" tradition that David practiced justice and righteousness. In any event, one may point towards numerous biblical sources indicating that the kings of Israel and Judah sat in judgment; see Albeck's remarks in his edition of the Mishnah, "Completions and Supplements" to *Sanhedrin,* 2.2 (p. 443).

of Israel and that regarding the kings of the Davidic house refrain from
attributing to the king any sort of superior status, certainly not one which
would suit the king in terms of the approach of royal theology. Insofar
as the legal system is concerned, Davidic kings are like ordinary judges:
they may judge and are judged. In contrast, the kings of Israel are not
judged nor may they judge. Why? This question is discussed further on
in the same *sugya*:

> But regarding the kings of Israel, for what reason are they not
> [judged]? Because of a certain incident, when a certain servant
> of King Yannai killed a person. Shimon ben Shetah said to the
> Sages: Look at him, and we shall judge him. They sent for him
> [to Yannai]: Your servant has killed someone. He sent him to
> them. They sent [a message] to him: You should come as well,
> for it is written: "and its owner had been warned" [Exodus
> 21:29]. The Torah says: let the owner of the ox come and stand
> together with his ox. He came and sat. Shimon ben Shetah said
> to him: Yannai the King! Stand on your feet, and they shall give
> testimony about you. For it is not before us that you stand, but
> you stand before He who spoke and created the world, as is
> said "then the two parties to the dispute shall appear before the
> Lord" [Deuteronomy 19:17]. He said to him: It is not as you say,
> but as his colleagues say. He turned to the right – they buried
> their faces in the ground; he turned to the left – they buried
> their faces in the ground. He said to them: You are masters of
> thought; let the master of thoughts come and take recompense
> from you. Immediately the angel Gabriel came and beat them all
> into the ground. At that same time they made an edict: the king
> does not judge nor is he judged.[8]

This story is discussed extensively by Talmudic researchers and among
historians, the predominant view in research being that, despite its
fantastic components, it contains a core of historical truth.[9] Scholars

8   *Babylonian Sanhedrin* 19a–b, according to the Yemenite manuscript as brought by
    Kahana, *Sifrei Zuta le-Devarim*, pp. 283–284.
9   See G. Alon, *Toldot ha-Yehudim be-Eretz Yisrael be-tequfat ha-Mishnah veha-Talmud*
    (*History of the Jews in Palestine*) (Tel Aviv, 1953), vol. I, pp. 35–38; J. N. Epstein,
    Mevo'ot le-Sifrut ha-Tanna'im (*Introductions to Tannaitic Literature*) (Jerusalem,
    1957), p. 55; Kahana, *Sifrei Zuta le-Devarim*, pp. 284–285; H. D. Mantel, "Herod's
    Trial," in his *Studies in the History of the Sanhedrin* (in Hebrew) (Tel Aviv, 1969),
    pp. 357–365. For a summary of the research literature on this subject, see Y. Ben-

base this argument primarily on a story containing similar components that appears in Josephus' *Antiquity of the Jews*.[10] Josephus tells there of John Hyrcanus and Shamaya (or perhaps Shammai, who substitutes for Shimon ben Shetah in our story), who murdered, according to his story, Herod himself (and not Yannai's servant), who was accused of killing Hezekiah and his cohorts.[11] Even though this story is without parallel in

Shalom, *The School of Shammai and the Zealots' Struggle Against Rome* (in Hebrew) (Jerusalem, 1994), p. 289. Compare J. Efron, "Shimon ben Shetah and King Yannai" (in Hebrew), in his *Studies of the Hasmonean Period* (Tel Aviv, 1980), pp. 131–194 (and see especially "Yannai and His Servant before the Court of Ben Shetah," pp. 158–162). Efron ("Shimon ben Shetah and King Yannai," p. 158) surveys the approach of the scholars to the aggadah and to the words of Josephus ("Shimon ben Shetah and King Yannai," nn. 249–250). In his opinion, Yannai explicitly represents the type of the rebellious Hasmonean king, and the entire incident is intended to illustrate and to explain why the king was stripped of authority over the judiciary. Shimon ben Shetah, Yannai's famous opponent, fulfills the function of Samias (mentioned by Josephus) and chastises the judges. The story is interwoven with incidents involving the Sanhedrin (see *Palestinian Sanhedrin* 1.18 [7a]). Samias' warning was fulfilled, according to Josephus, after a number of years – while the curse of Ben Shetah occurred, according to the story in the *Babylonian*, immediately (on Gabriel who struck the Earth, see *Babylonian Sotah* 12b). Efron notes that there is no echo of this story in the *Palestinian* (see the discussion below), and that in its present form the story was fashioned by the Babylonian amoraim. Because of these defects he thinks that this aggadah is bereft of all historical importance. Cf. Z. Kfir, "King Yannai and Shimon ben Shetah: An Amoraic Legend in Historical Disguise" (in Hebrew), *Tura* (1994): 85–97; and see Kahana's critique, *Sifrei Zuta le-Devarim*, pp. 284–285, n. 11.

10   Josephus, *Antiquities*, XIV.4.168–176.

11   It is interesting to note that Josephus writes that Hyrcanus was both priest and prophet: "Now he [Hyrcanus] was accounted by God as worthy of three of the greatest privileges: the rule of the nation, the office of high priest, and the gift of prophecy" (*Antiquities* XIII.299–300). It is important to emphasize, however, that according to Josephus, "On Pharisaic Opposition to the Hasmonean Monarchy," in his *Studies in the Jewish Background of Christianity* (Tübingen, 1992), pp. 44–56, Hyrcanus did not attribute the monarchy to himself, but it was first sought by Aristobulus: "And he was the first to put a diadem on his head, four hundred and eighty-one years and three months after the time when the people were released freed from the Babylonian captivity and returned to their own country" (*Antiquities* XIII.301). On the relation of the Pharisees (and following them, that of the sages) to the unification of priesthood and monarchy, see D. R. Schwartz, "On Pharisaic Opposition to the Hasmonean Monarchy," in his *Studies in the Jewish Background of Christianity* (Tübingen, 1992), pp. 44–56; D. Goodblatt, "The Union of Priesthood and Kingship in Second Temple Judea" (in Hebrew), *Cathedra*, 102 (2001): 7–28; and see below.

the tannaitic literature (nor is it presented in the *Babylonian* as a *beraita*), many scholars assume that it is ancient and that, as the *Babylonian* claims, it bears relation to the Mishnah, "The king does not judge nor is he judged."[12] For our purposes, the question of the antiquity of the story is, in any event, of secondary importance.

The story brought in *Babylonian Sanhedrin* is thus fashioned according to the tannaitic halakhah. According to the Talmudic version of the story, the "servant" of King Yannai – evidently one of his military commanders – killed a certain person, and Shimon ben Shetah initiates his trial. Shimon ben Shetah does not suffice with trying the "servant"; he also wishes to try the master who sent him, as he suspects that the servant acted on the order of Yannai.[13] Ben Shetah infers Yannai's responsibility from the biblical verse, "and its owner has been warned" (Exodus 21:29): "Let the owner of the ox come and stand [in judgment] with his ox."[14] The Torah states that, unlike the "innocent" ox – who surprised his

---

12   See Epstein, *Introduction to Tannaitic Literature*, p. 55, where he writes: "The main part of Chapter 2 is ancient. 'The king does not judge and is not judged' (§2) is an early edict, from the time of Yannai and Shimon ben Shetah according to the *Babylonian* (19a–b) or, according to Josephus in the *Antiquities*, from the time of John Hyrcanus and Shemaya (or Shammai)." Epstein notes further that: "Even more ancient [than the above edict] is Mishnah 4: 'When he goes to war it goes out with him; he comes in, he brings it in with him; he sits in judgment (thus in the original) it is with him; he reclines [to a feast] it is opposite him, as is said "And it shall be with him" etc.' – this passage was therefore taught prior to that same edict, before the time of Herod, at the time when the king still engaged in judgment" (*Introduction to Tannaitic Literature*, pp. 418–419). According to Epstein, "When he sits in judgment it is with him" is thus an ancient mishnah, that preceded the edict that "the king does not judge ..." That is, the Mishnah concludes that the king (whether of Israel or of the Davidic line) does not judge at all, not even in his own tribunal. See E. E. Urbach, "The Biblical Monarchy as Viewed by the Sages" (in Hebrew), in A. Rofé and Y. Zakovitch (eds.), *Isaac Leo Seeligmann Volume: Essays on the Bible and the Ancient World* (Jerusalem, 1983), pp. 439–451; p. 441. A similar story, albeit different from it in a number of important details, appears in *Tanhuma, Shoftim* (ed. Buber, p. 30) (and compare the [standard] printed editions of *Tanhuma*, ibid., 7); however, this midrash is even later. For a possible indication of the tannaitic source of the story, based upon the testimony of the Karaite Yeshu'ah ben Yehudah, see Kahana, *Sifrei Zuta la-Devarim*, p. 284.

13   In the Talmudic literature, Herod is referred to as "a slave of the Hasmonean House" (*Babylonian Bava Batra* 3b), and possibly for that reason the story in the *Babylonian* alludes to the story as brought by Josephus.

14   See also *Sifrei Devarim* 190 (ed. Finkelstein, p. 230): "'who have the dispute' – let the owner of the ox come and stand over his ox"; and in *Babylonian Bava Kamma* 112b.

masters by killing someone, his owner thus being free of responsibility – in the case of an ox who "was wont to gore since yesterday and the day before, and whose owners had been warned and did not guard it," the law is that "the ox shall be stoned, and its owner shall also be put to death" (Exodus 21:29–30). From the law concerning the ox, Shimon ben Shetah draws an analogy to the case of a servant or messenger for whose actions his master is also responsible. This law corresponds to the opinion attributed to Shammai in *Babylonian Kiddushin*: "One who tells his messenger: Go and kill a certain person … the one who sent him is culpable" (43a). It also corresponds to that of the Sadducee in the dispute with the Pharisees in *Mishnah Yadaim*:

> The Sadducees say: We complain against you, O Pharisees, for you say that my ox and donkey that caused damage are held accountable, but my manservant and maidservant are exempt. But if my ox or donkey, about whom I am not obligated in commandments, I am yet culpable for the damage they cause, my manservant and maidservant, about whom I am responsible that they perform mitzvot, is it not logical that I be responsible for their damages?
>
> He said to them. No! If you say, regarding an ox and a donkey that they have no mind of their own, can you say regarding my manservant for my maidservant, who have minds of their own? If I insult him, he will go and light the fodder of another person, should I be obligated to pay?[15]

This syllogism is not consistent with the well-known halakhah that "There is no messenger for a sinful act," and there are those who wish to infer from this the antiquity of this story, which is based upon "ancient *halakhot*."[16]

When Yannai arrived at the court, he sat down in order to demonstrate that he did not recognize its authority or that it does not have the power to judge him; however, in order to emphasize that Yannai nevertheless stands in judgment, Shimon commanded him, in accordance with the halakhah, to stand up, emphasizing that, "It is not before us that you stand, for you

---

15   *Mishnah Yadayim* 4.7.

16   *Babylonian Kiddushin* 42b; and also in *Mishnah Bava Kamma* 6.4: "'He who sends the fire' … in the hands of a competent person, the one who is competent is accountable." Mantel, "Herod's Trial," pp. 361–362; but this is not a substantive proof of the antiquity of the story.

stand before none other than He who spoke and created the world."[17] It is as if to say: You may be the king, but opposite the Creator you are like any other human being. Shimon's solemn language, emphasizing the king's subjugation to the Torah, is directed not only to Yannai but also to his fellows in the court; however, these words make no impression on Yannai, and the sages are more afraid of him than they are of the Creator. God's reaction comes soon enough: the sages, the members of the court – who are the tragic heroes of this story – are pressed down to the ground by the angel Gabriel.[18] Despite the obvious criticism of the court, the conclusion of this *sugya* is that one is not to place human beings – even if they are judges – in such a situation of conflict, and that therefore "That same hour they decreed: the king does not judge, nor is he judged."[19] In this context, it is interesting to take note of a passage in the *Midrash on Psalms* that expounds a verse from Psalm 17:

> "Before You may my judgment go forth."
>
> Rabbi Levi said: The Holy One blessed be He said to David: Is it for naught that I have made for you a Sanhedrin? Go and be judged before them.
>
> David said to him: Master of the Universe. You have written in Your Torah, "and you shall take no bribe" (Exodus 23:8), and they fear before me to take bribery or to judge me. But it is Your will to take bribery, [as is said]: "Before You my judgment shall go forth."
>
> And from whence do we know that the Holy One blessed be He takes bribery? [As is said]: "You take bribery from the bosom of the evildoers" (Proverbs 17:23). And what is the bribery that He takes from evildoers in this world? Repentance and prayer and charity. Therefore it is written, "Before You may my judgment go forth." The Holy One blessed be He says: My sons, so long as the gates of prayer are open, repent, for I take bribes in this world. But once I sit in judgment in the Future to Come, I do not take bribes, as is said: "He will not accept compensation [nor be appeased though you multiply gifts]" (Proverbs 6:35).[20]

---

17   See *Sifrei Devarim* 190 (ed. Finkelstein, p. 230): "'and they shall stand' – it is a *mitzvah* that those being judged should stand." See *Sifrei Devarim*, 190 (ed. Finkelstein, p. 230): "'Before the Lord' – they think that they are standing before flesh and blood, but they are standing before none other than the Omnipresent."

18   On this motif see *Avot de-Rabbi Nathan*, Version A, 8 (ed. Schechter, p. 37); and cf. M. Kister, *Studies in Avot de-Rabbi Nathan: Text, Redaction and Interpretation* (in Hebrew) (Jerusalem, 1998), pp. 148–149 and n. 158.

19   See M. Lorberbaum, *Politics and the Limits of Law*, pp. 8–9.

20   *Midrash Tehillim* 17.5 (ed. Buber, p. 127).

This midrash, which characterizes repentance, prayer, and charity as a form of bribery (sic!) that God takes from man, is particularly interesting in light of the understanding of repentance implicit therein. It may be that the anonymous author indirectly criticizes the pretense of human beings to think of judgment as an objective process in which the judges are without ulterior motives. The term "bribery" has a double meaning in this section: the payment given to the judges for sitting in judgment (such is the meaning of the term in Deuteronomy 16:19); and payment given them in order to distort or slant the judgment. This passage is important for our purpose because of the claim that the Sanhedrin refuses to judge the king because of the salary that he pays them, which is liable to cause bias in their judgment; therefore, according to this midrash, "the king ... is not judged."

The story concerning Yannai exemplifies that approach, according to which in a monarchic system – even when the king's authorities or prerogatives are limited – it is inappropriate to apply the law to the king and, by extension, to make the king subject to the authority of the court. This aspect of the mishnaic halakhah concerning the king embodies an astute and sensible approach: a royal system, which, according to the sages, is a kind of lesser of two evils, requires of necessity (that is, in terms of its inherent political logic) the king's immunity from the law. To recall, the law stating that the king does not judge is explained by the Babylonian Talmud in terms of the principle of mutuality ("Adorn yourself and thereafter adorn others"): if the king is not judged, he has no authority to judge. At first glance, this claim is likely to be impressive. However, it seems doubtful whether it in fact lies at the basis of the mishnaic halakhah. The custom in the ancient world was that the kings stood at the head of the legal system – but were not themselves subject to it.[21] As I shall show below, this approach is expressed in the *sugya* in the *Palestinian*.

What is surprising in the discussion in the *Babylonian* is the mixture of political realism with ethical-value considerations, ignoring built-in social power relations. It would seem that the mishnaic halakhah is guided by the wish to separate the king from the system of justice and law. The sages may have thought that they would be able to "compensate" for granting the king immunity before the law by denying him judicial and legislative powers; that is to say, in "exchange" for elevating him above the law, the king would "forgo" powers in the realm of judgment and law. Is such an expectation realistic? I will again mention that the laws governing the

21   See note 75 below.

king in the Mishnah were never subjected to the test of reality. Regarding the king, as in many other matters in *Mishnah Sanhedrin* (such as, for example, regarding "capital law," the main subject of the tractate), the Mishnah does not depict a political-judicial reality, either from its own time nor from an earlier time.[22] As mentioned, the laws of the king in the Mishnah and in the tannaitic and Talmudic sources reflect a mixture of political realism, which takes into consideration the exigencies imposed by the powers embodied in the institution of the monarchy that it itself establishes, with a "normative" approach, which seeks to shape this institution according to theological-value outlooks. I shall return to this point later.

The law in the Mishnah corresponds to what is said in *Tosefta Sanhedrin*: "The king does not sit in the Sanhedrin, and neither the king nor the high priest sit in the intercalation of the year."[23] This *beraita* appears at the end of Chapter 2 of the *Tosefta*, in which the laws of sanctifying the new month and intercalating (i.e. adding an extra month to) the year are discussed. In the context of detailing the procedures for fixing new moons and intercalated years, the law is also mentioned that the king does not sit with the court (of three) that "intercalates the year";[24] this law is brought in connection with the general statement, according to which "the king does not sit in the Sanhedrin." Sitting in the Sanhedrin, in this context, means a formal appointment. According to the *Tosefta*, the king does not participate in the discussions of the Sanhedrin – neither in those discussions of a "legislative" character, nor in matters of rulings and deciding the law. The reason given in the *Tosefta*, which is brought as law in the *sugya* of the *Babylonian*, differs from the reason given by the *sugya* of the *Babylonian* for the law of the Mishnah:

> One does not place the king in the Sanhedrin, nor a king or a
> high priest in the intercalation of the year.

---

22 On this quality of *Tractate Sanhedrin* regarding other matters, see Y. Lorberbaum, "The Image of God: In Rabbinic Literature, Maimonides and Nahmanides" (in Hebrew), Doctoral Dissertation, Hebrew University of Jerusalem, 1997, pp. 224–225.

23 *Tosefta, Sanhedrin* 2.1 (ed. Zuckermandel, p. 418); and compare to the version cited in *Babylonian Sanhedrin* 18b: "One does not seat the king in the Sanhedrin." On the use of the term יושב ("to seat") to signify an appointment, see I. Gafni, "*Yeshiva* and *Metivta*" (in Hebrew), *Zion*, 43 (1978): 12–37.

24 See *Tosefta Sanhedrin* 2.1 (ed. Zuckermandel, p. 419) – the opinion of Rabbi Meir as against the dissenting opinion of the sages; and see *Mishnah Sanhedrin* 1.2 (the dispute between Rabbi Meir and Rabban Shimon ben Gamaliel).

> The king in the Sanhedrin – as is written, "You shall not answer to a quarrel" (Exodus 23:2) – does not answer before one who is great.
>
> Nor a king or a high priest in the intercalation of the year; a king – because of his storehouses; a high priest – because of chill.[25]

The political realism implied in the discussion of the *Babylonian* regarding the case of Yannai is translated here into a normative prohibition: "One does not place the king in the Sanhedrin" – not because of a desire to avoid mishap but because it is forbidden to disagree with him. As in Rashi's words, "One is not allowed to contradict the words of the outstanding one among the judges; and if you the king says 'Guilty,' thereafter no one will be willing to learn merit on his behalf."[26] There is no mention here of the "incident which happened"; according to this passage, "the king does not judge" because of the political logic inherent in the two institutions – the monarchy and the Sanhedrin – and the relations between them. The discussions of the members of the Sanhedrin need to be conducted free of any extraneous considerations. Moreover, the participation of the king in these discussions is likely to harm his own status, as his arguments are likely to be confuted and rejected ("you shall not answer a great one").[27] The source in the Babylonian *sugya* emphasizes the opposite reason: that the king's presence in the court is liable to incline the balance of views towards his own opinion. It should be noted that the reason for the prohibition against the king sitting in the deliberations about the intercalation of the year is different – conflict of interests; that is to say, the fear that he will be guided by irrelevant considerations (Rashi, s.v. *mishum afsanya*: "because he distributes money to his soldiers, so-and-so much per annum; and it is convenient to him that all years should be leap years"). Although this reason is not mentioned in connection with the

---

25 *Babylonian Sanhedrin* 18b.

26 *Babylonian Sanhedrin,* 18b, s.v. *lo ta'aneh 'al riv;* and cf. *Mishnah Sanhedrin* 4.2.

27 It should be noted that the relation between the law of the Mishnah and that of the *beraita* in the *Tosefta* is not clear, also with regard to the law that the king is not judged. This law is not mentioned in the *Tosefta,* and it is possible that this tradition specifically thought, as did other traditions, that the king is judged; and see further below. Nevertheless, one ought not to conclude from silence in this case, as the *Tosefta* brings this law in connection with the discussion relating to procedures for intercalating the month, so that the question as to whether or not the king may be judged does not at all arise in this context.

prohibition against the king sitting in the Sanhedrin, the *sugya* may allude to the idea that it is also relevant to that.[28]

The claim that "the king does not judge and is not judged" contradicts what is stated further on in this chapter of the Mishnah, where it is stated that:

> He writes a Torah scroll for its own sake. When he goes out to war, it goes out with him. When he comes back, he brings it in with him. When he sits in judgment, it is with him. When he reclines [to feast], it is opposite him. As is said: "And it shall be with him, and he shall read in it all the days of his life" (Deuteronomy 17:19).[29]

It is surprising that this apparent contradiction is not discussed at all in the Talmudic *sugya* and hardly by the classic commentators to the Mishnah. The author of *Tosafot Yom Tov* explained, in line with the *Babylonian* (and evidently in wake of Maimonides' *Commentary to the Mishnah*), that "sit in judgment" refers to kings of the Davidic dynasty or to kings of Israel "before the edict" (i.e. that "the king does not judge . . ."). However, it is difficult to accept this solution since, as noted earlier, there is no mention in the Mishnah of the distinction between the kings of Israel and the Davidic kings regarding the matter of sitting in judgment, nor does it appear in any other tannaitic sources. Louis Finkelstein mentions a commentator who suggested that the king "sitting in judgment" refers to royal judgment and not to the Sanhedrin. But this conjecture is also difficult to accept as there is no hint in any of the sources that the king has a separate judicial system of his own.[30]

---

28   The king is likewise limited with regard to administrative procedures relating to the judicial system. Thus, for example, the Mishnah states that: "One does not make a Sanhedrin for the tribes except in a court of seventy-one" (*Mishnah Sanhedrin* 1.5). Another administrative matter appearing in the same mishnah pertains to extending the Temple courtyards or the boundaries of the city of Jerusalem. Here, too, the permission of the Sanhedrin is required: "One does not add to the city or to the courtyards except by a court of seventy-one" (*Mishnah Sanhedrin* 1.5), because the extension of the city has implications for matters of sacred things and purity. See *Mishnah Shevu'ot* 2.2.

29   *Mishnah Sanhedrin* 2.4 (as per MS Kaufmann); and cf. *Tosefta Sanhedrin* 4.7 (ed. Zuckermandel, p. 421), where the text is as follows: "He goes out to war and it is with him; he comes in and it is with him; he sits in the court and it is with him; he enters the bath house, it waits for him at the entrance."

30   See the comments of L. Finkelstein in his edition of *Sifrei Devarim*, pp. 211–212, n. 13, which refers to *Mitzpeh Eitan*. Cf. Maimonides, *Hilkhot Sanhedrin* 2.4–5; and cf. G.

From other tannaitic sources it follows that the king is judged by the
Sanhedrin. Thus, in *Tosefta Sanhedrin* 3.4: "And one does not appoint a
king or high priest save in a court of seventy-one people."[31] From the
context there it is clear that "place" (מעמידין) means to place on trial.
Jacob Nahum Epstein has commented that the Mishnah regarding the
king who "sits in judgment" is ancient and precedes the law that "the king
does not judge," which in his opinion is an ancient edict, from the time of
Yannai and Shimon ben Shetah, or perhaps from that of John Hyrcanus
and Shemaya. Other scholars and historians think along similar lines.[32]
According to this approach, following the "edict," the king – whether
from Israel or from the Davidic line – is not allowed to judge at all.[33]
However, as we have seen, Rav Pappa (according to the reading of the
Yemenite manuscript, or Rav Yosef according to the other manuscripts)
distinguishes between them and applies the edict to the kings of Israel
alone.[34] The halakhah found at the beginning of the chapter ("the king

J. Blidstein, *Eqronot medini'in be-mishnat ha-Rambam* (*Political Concepts in Maimonidean Halakha*) (Ramat-Gan, 2001), pp. 128–152.

31 Zuckermandel edition, p. 418. In this, the king is unlike every other person, who is judged before a court of three or before a court of twenty-three; see *Mishnah Sanhedrin* 1.1–4. A similar tradition follows also from the words of R. Yosef in *Babylonian Sanhedrin* 18b, in which the high priest testifies regarding the king. The *Babylonian* (*Babylonian Sanhedrin* 18b) attempts to harmonize its words with the law in the Mishnah that "The king does not judge and is not judged" by stating that the high priest testifies before the king; out of respect to the high priest the king is present in the Sanhedrin when he gives testimony but leaves immediately after the high priest concludes. It is clear, however, that R. Yosef's statement reflects a different tradition than that of the Mishnah – one that originates evidently in the Tosefta. Kahana states that this law is also evidently implied by the story in *Tanhuma*, *Shoftim* 6 (ed. Buber, p. 30) and by the homily of the *Sifrei Zuta Devarim*: "'And the two people shall stand' – even a king and an ordinary person"; Kahana, *Sifrei Zuta le-Devarim*, p. 285. Also regarding the issue of whether the king may serve as judge *Sifrei Zuta Devarim* differs from the Mishnah, as it expounds (21.2; ed. Kahana, p. 293): "'And your judges' – this refers to the king and the high priest"; and cf. Kahana, *Sifrei Zuta le-Devarim*, p. 286 n. 14.

32 See Epstein, *Introduction to Tannaitic Literature*, pp. 55, 418, 419; and cf. Urbach, "The Biblical Monarchy," p. 441; Kahana, *Sifrei Zuta le-Devarim*, p. 285.

33 Presumably, Epstein thinks that *Tosefta Sanhedrin* 2.14 – "The king does not sit in the Sanhedrin, nor do the king or the high priest sit on the intercalation of the year" – is also part of this edict.

34 There is no support in tannaitic halakhah for the possibility that there are certain matters in which the king has judicial authority. Compare *Guide for the Perplexed* 3.40; Rambam, *Hilkhot Melakhim* 3.10; *Hilkhot Rotzeah* 2.2–5; and cf. Blidstein,

does not judge nor is he judged") applies to the kings of Israel, whereas the halakhah at its end ("he sits in judgment") refers to the Davidic kings, who both judge and are judged.

It seems to me that there is no need to make either the homily regarding the king sitting in judgment or the "edict" stating that "the king does not judge" so early. Another possibility, no less likely, is that there were two different viewpoints among the tannaim: one – that the king judges, which was also evidently related to the tradition that the king is judged; and the other – that the king neither judges nor is judged.[35] These traditions embody two different legal-political outlooks: one closer to the spirit of the Bible, according to which the king is like any other person; and the other, reflecting, as we said, political realism. There is thus no proof to the claim that the tradition that "the king does not judge nor is he judged" is an ancient "edict," certainly not in the formal sense of that term. This tradition was not necessarily created immediately after the "incident of Yannai" (or Herod) but it may have taken shape under the impact of that event (or a similar one) that was left as a distant historical memory.

This suggestion, like that of Epstein, does not of course explain the contradiction in the Mishnah. In the final analysis, did the redactor not notice that he was combining, in the short unit about the king in Chapter 2 of *Mishnah Sanhedrin* (which consists of only four *mishnayot*) two contradictory traditions? It should be noted that, unlike the conclusive,

---

Political Principles, pp. 128–146. It is nevertheless possible that this possibility is implied in *Tosefta Sanhedrin* 4.6 (ed. Zuckermandel, p. 421): "Those executed by the court: their property goes to their heirs; those executed by the king: their property goes to the king; but the Sages say: Those executed by the king, their property goes to their heirs. Rabbi Judah said to them: It says, 'Behold, it is in the vineyard of Naboth, where he went down to inherit' [2 Kings 21:18]." It is possible that "those executed by the king" refers to those tried in a special royal judicial forum; however, it is likewise possible that the phrase alludes to rebels whom the king killed in war and not in a judicial procedure.

35 I tend to associate both these laws with the same tradition – even though it is possible that they reflect two different, independent traditions. Thus, for example, it is possible that the tradition appearing in the Mishnah and in *Sifrei Devarim* – i.e. that the king judges ("sits in judgment") – is unrelated to that found in *Tosefta Sanhedrin* 3.4, according to which the king is judged (i.e. before a court of seventy-one). Such a tradition appears in the *sugya* of the *Palestinian* – see below; on the other hand, in *Tosefta Sanhedrin* are two laws: that the king does not judge ("one does not seat the king in the Sanhedrin") and that the king is judged (but only before the Sanhedrin, and not before a "lower" court). However, these two traditions are not necessarily connected with one another.

legalistic-halakhic formulation – "The king does not judge … nor does he testify … nor does he perform *halitzah*" – the Mishnah continues with midrashic exegesis of biblical verses. The tradition that "the king sits in judgment" is incorporated within a homily dealing with the transcendent status of the Torah, which guides the king and is with him wherever he turns. This homily is of an aggadic-ethical character: more than it determines the exact halakhah, it expresses the king's intimate relationship to the Torah and his submission to it, all by way of a homily based on the verse: "And it shall be with him, and he shall read in it all the days of his life" (Deuteronomy 17:19).[36] It is possible that the editor wished to incorporate this ethical-conceptual homily further along in this chapter of the Mishnah in order to express the king's relation to the Torah and, because he did not wish to interrupt the flow of the homily, did not delete that part that contradicts the law, which appears several *mishnayot* earlier.

From our examination of the tannaitic sources in the Mishnah, the *Tosefta* and in the *beraitot,* as well as in Babylonian amoraic sources, it follows that there were a number of traditions concerning the king's relationship to the legal proceedings. According to the Mishnah and the *sugya* in the *Babylonian,* the king has nothing to do with the judiciary: he does not judge, nor is he judged. According to the *beraita* quoted in the *Tosefta* (*Sanhedrin* 2.3), the king does not sit in the Sanhedrin; in contrast, according to another source in the *Tosefta* (*Sanhedrin* 3.4), and according to the Babylonian amoraic tradition (Rav Yosef in *Babylonian Sanhedrin* 18b), the king is judged (before the Sanhedrin). The only tannaitic source according to which the king judges is, as mentioned previously, the Mishnah at the end of Sanhedrin 2 ("he sits in judgment"). It is possible that these sources reflect development and change in the tannaitic understanding: the first halakhah understood the king as any other person, who can judge and is judged; but because of the "incident that happened," or because of political realism, they "decreed" that the king does not judge nor is he judged. There may also have been an intermediate stage, in which it was stated that the king does not judge (because of the reasons mentioned above) but he may be judged. Another possibility is that a number of different views existed simultaneously: that the king judges and is judged ("sits in judgment" in the Mishnah; "one does not appoint a king except by a Sanhedrin of seventy-one" in the *Tosefta*); that the king does not judge but is judged (an alternative interpretation of the *Tosefta* mentioned); and that the king neither judges nor is judged.

36 This is similar to the homily in *Tosefta Berakhot* 6.25 and at the end of Chapter 9, concerning how the commandments surround a person.

The common denominator between all these possibilities and traditions is that the king is not above the judicial system and that, in particular, he is not responsible for it. Even according to the (Mishnaic) tradition that the king judges ("he sits in judgment"), there is no allusion to the view that the king guides the legal system and is the supreme legislator, for which reason he is not subject to it. This point is important for our discussion, because implied therein is a certain reservation from or even exception to royal theology, a striking characteristic of which is the king's leading role in the judicial system.

Moreover, as has been demonstrated by Haim Shapira, in continuing the biblical approach, the sages also stress God's presence in the court.[37] A clear expression of this is found in a passage in *Tosefta Sanhedrin* that appears (with slight changes) also in the *beraitot* in both the *Babylonian* and *Palestinian Sanhedrin:*

> The judges must know whom they are judging, and before whom they are judging, and who judges with them.
>
> And the witnesses should know concerning whom they are giving testimony, and before whom they are giving testimony, and with whom they are testifying, and who is testifying with them, as is said, "then both parties to the dispute shall appear before the Lord" [Deuteronomy 19:17] and it says, "God stands in the divine council, in the midst of the judges he holds judgment" [Psalms 82:1].[38]
>
> And it also says concerning Jehoshaphat: "And he said to the judges: See what you are doing, for it is not for man [alone] that you judge."[39]

This *beraita* emphasizes God's presence in all aspects of the legal adjudication. God judges together with the judges; the proceedings are conducted before Him (or in His presence), and He is even judged by

---

37 See H. Shapira, "For the Judgment is God's: On the Relation Between God and Human Judgment in Jewish Legal Tradition," *Bar-Ilan Law Review,* 26 (2009): 51–89. On the biblical approach, see above, Chapter 1.2–3.

38 The *Palestinian* adds here the phrase: "before He who spoke and the world came into being"; see *Palestinian Sanhedrin* 1.1 (18a).

39 *Tosefta Sanhedrin* 1.9 (ed. Zuckermandel, p. 416). Further along in this passage the tanna confronts the fear that this reality arouses among the judges: "Lest the judge might say: What have I to do with this difficulty? Does it not already say, 'And He is with you with the word of judgment' – you have naught but what your eyes see"; and cf. Shapira, "For the Judgment is God's."

them![40] According to the *beraita* in the *Tosefta,* God is present not only with the judges but also amongst the witnesses: they testify before God, God gives testimony together with them, and they even take testimony from Him! The emphasis on God's presence among the witnesses is intended to express the view that God envelops all aspects of the judgment, as derived from the unique status of the witnesses according to tannaitic halakhah.[41] The significance of the sharp claim in the *Tosefta* – that God too is judged by the judges ("Let the judges know Whom they are judging"), and that the witnesses also testify concerning Him ("and the witnesses should know about Whom they are giving testimony") – is that the activity of the witnesses and the judges bears implications relating to God himself; for, if their activity is in fact also His activity, then an error or oversight on their part is tantamount to an error that emanates from God Himself. For that reason, their acts also have cause to "judge" Him.[42]

Similar to that proposed above concerning the Book of Deuteronomy (and other sources in the Torah), also the statement in the Talmudic sources that God is present in the court emphasizes the inferior status of the king. In this respect, the relation between God and the court emphasizes the separation between God and the king generally and between the king and the judicial process in particular. One is hard put to exaggerate the distance between the status of the king in the Mishnaic law and the call of the Psalmist, "O God, give Your justice to the king, and Your

---

40 Cf. *Sifrei Devarim* 190 (ed. Finkelstein, p. 230): "'Before the Lord.' They think that they are standing before flesh and blood, but they are only standing before the Omnipresent."

41 The witnesses have a decisive stature in all stages of the procedure: in the initiative to place the people on trial (in capital cases), in the determination of guilt, and even in the execution of the punishment. According to the tannaim, the witnesses are the plaintiffs, they provide the evidence, in a certain sense they are also the judges, and finally they are those who execute the punishment. See Y. Lorberbaum, "Murder, Capital Punishment and Imago Dei: Man as the Image of God in Early Rabbinic Literature" (in Hebrew), *Pelilim,* 7 (Tel Aviv, 1998), pp. 223–272, at p. 235 and n. 45.

42 Shapira, "For the Judgment is God's." Shapira notes there that the *Palestinian* evidently takes exception to this daring approach and modified it: "For is it possible for flesh and blood to judge its Creator? Rather, the Holy One blessed be He said: It was I who said that Reuben shall receive 100 dinar and that Shimon will have nothing, and you take it from this one and give it to that one not according to law. I need to pay him and to render account with that same man" (*Palestinian Sanhedrin* 1.1 [18a]). The court does not judge the Almighty but simply holds him accountable because of his responsibility to perform justice, to become involved. However, this does not seem to be the literal meaning of the *beraita.*

righteousness to the royal son" (Psalms 72:1). Against the background of the royal theology, according to which there is a mixture between the king and God – and in its course between both of them and the performance of justice and law – the Torah, and in its wake the sages, move the presence of God from the king to the court and to the Temple and distinguish in a sharp and clear manner between these and the king.

3.2 "Before You My Judgment Shall Come Forth"

Unlike the sources discussed above, according to which "the king does not judge and is not judged," the *sugya* in the Palestinian Talmud differs from the tannaitic sources and the *sugya* in the Babylonian both in its conclusions and in its rhetoric:

> "The king does not judge nor is he judged," etc. "Does not judge." And it is written: "And David administered justice and equity to all his people" (2 Samuel 8:15), and you say thus!?
>
> We may say from this: He judged the judgment, and merited the one who merited and held accountable the one who is accountable. If the one accountable was poor, he gives him [the other] from his own [money]. We thus find that he does justice to this one, and righteousness to the other.
>
> Rabbi [i.e. R. Judah] said: If he judged, and found innocent the one who is innocent and guilty the one who is guilty, the Omnipresent considers it as if he has done righteousness with the one culpable, in that he removed stolen [property] from his hands.
>
> "And he is not judged." According to the phrase, "Before You may my judgment come" (Psalms 17:2).
>
> Rabbi Yitzhak said in the name of Rabbi: The king and the public are judged before him every day, as is said, "to maintain the judgment of his servant, and the judgment of his people Israel, each day" (1 Kings 8:59).
>
> Rabbi Yudan said: If he wished to perform *halitzah* or *yibbum* [levirate marriage or release therefrom], he is remembered for good. They said to him: If you say thus, you detract from the honor of the king.[43]

The *sugya* in the *Palestinian* questions the mishnaic law that "the king does not judge" on the basis of what is related in the Book of Samuel

---

concerning David: namely, that he performed justice and righteousness for all his people. As is its way in many other places, the *Palestinian* does not answer the question and, in a somewhat associative manner, turns to an interpretation of the biblical idiom *mishpat u-zedaka* ("justice and righteousness") in light of the tannaitic sources found in the *Tosefta*.[44] The verse from 2 Samuel is cited in *Tosefta Sanhedrin* in the course of its discussion of the issue of compromise:[45]

> Rabbi Joshua b. Korhah said: It is a mitzvah for [the judge] to "cut" [i.e. to bring the parties to compromise], as is said, "Render judgments that are true and make for peace in your gates" (Zechariah 8:16).
>
> But is it not the case that wherever there is a judgment of truth there is no peace, and wherever there is peace there is no judgment of truth? What, then, is true judgment in which there is also peace? Let us say: this refers to compromise. As it says regarding David: "And David administered justice and equity to all his people."
>
> But is it not that wherever there is justice there is no righteousness, and wherever there is righteousness there is no justice? Rather, what judgment is it in which there is righteousness? Let us say: this is compromise.[46]

The contrast between "true judgment" and "peace" is identified by Rabbi Joshua with that between "justice" and "righteousness," which he sees as resolved by means of compromise, described as "true judgment in which there is peace."[47] Further along in this chapter in the *Tosefta* other opinions are brought, which resolve the tension between "judgment" and "righteousness" in a different manner:

> If he judged the judgment, merited the one who was deserving and held accountable the one who is accountable: if he held a poor person accountable, he takes his own [money] and gives it; thereby, he performs righteousness [i.e. charity] with this one, and judgment with that.

44   Compare Finkelstein's comment in his edition of *Sifrei Devarim*, p. 211 and n. 13.
45   See on this, recently, the paper by H. Shapira, "The Debate Over Compromise and the Goals of the Judicial Process," *Dinei Yisrael*, 26 (2009): 183–228.
46   *Tosefta Sanhedrin* 1.3 (ed. Zuckermandel, p. 415); and cf. *Babylonian Sanhedrin* 6b.
47   On what might be described as the "paradox of compromise," see A. Hassid, "Ethical Compromise: Two Justifications" (in Hebrew), *Iyyun*, 50 (2001): 107–130.

> Rabbi said: If he judged the judgment, and merited the one deserving and found accountable the one who is accountable, we find that he has done righteousness with the one accountable, in that he removed stolen [property] from his hand, and judged the one deserving, in that he returned to him that which is his.[48]

These two solutions reject compromise as the aim of the legal procedure. The first opinion combines "judgment" – that is, reparation of the one deserving by the one accountable under law (a kind of corrective justice) – with "righteousness" – i.e. helping a poor person who is accountable from the judge's own pocket (a kind of distributive justice)! Rabbi rejects this solution, as for him "justice" means ruling according to the proper righteous rules, which give the entitled one that which is coming to him; while "righteousness" is a kind of parallel term, in that it prevents the one who is accountable from sinning.[49]

Neither of these opinions have anything to do with the juridical authority of the king, their only concern being the judicial conduct of the judge per se. They are brought in this *sugya* of the *Palestinian* in the context of a verse that portrays King David practicing justice and righteousness. The absence of an answer in this *sugya* to the question: "'and he does not judge' – but is it not written" is likely to lead one to contradictory conclusions. One possible conclusion is that, notwithstanding this question, one nevertheless adheres to the mishnaic law, according to which the king does not judge; but another conclusion is that, in light of the biblical source cited, the *sugya* in the *Palestinian* rejects the mishnaic law and adopts the opposite halakhic conclusion, according to which the king does in fact act as judge. It would appear that the continuation of the *sugya* suggests that the latter possibility is more likely – a point to which I shall return later.

After posing the question ("and does he not judge?"), to which as mentioned no answer is given, the *sugya* in the *Palestinian* then turns to discuss the second half of this law: "the king ... is not judged." The law that the king is not judged is based here upon a verse in Psalms: "Before You let my judgment come forth," which the midrash in the *Palestinian* interprets in a non-literal way. Rashi interpreted this as follows: "'Before you let my judgment come forth' – those sins I have done for which I am deserving to be judged with sufferings, will go before you, and will not go before you in judgment."[50] But according to the *Palestinian*, this

---

48   *Tosefta Sanhedrin* 1.4–5.

49   See *Babylonian Sanhedrin* 6b.

50   Rashi's Commentary to Psalm 17:2, s.v. *milfanekha mishpati yetze.*

verse (including the word אצי, "will come forth") is not intended as an exemption from judgment and punishment but, on the contrary, as a judgment that is conducted specifically before God. According to the *sugya*, the king – because of his special relationship to God – is not judged by the court; the king is not treated like an ordinary human being and is not judged by an earthly tribunal.[51] Here the *Palestinian* resorts to a widespread motif in royal theology, according to which the king does not render an accounting to human beings but to God alone. This motif is emphasized in the words of Rabbi Yitzhak in the name of Rabbi: "The king and the public are judged before him [i.e. before God] every day": the king is tantamount to the entire public. To use Mowinckel's term, the king is a kind of collective personality, who embodies within himself the entire people.[52] The idiom, "king and public," refers to one entity: the king, who embodies the public and is directly judged by God "every day"; as if to say, his relationship to God – and thereby the relation of the people to God through the mediation of the king – is a constant one.

In light of this, one reaches the conclusion that in the first part of the *sugya* of the *Palestinian* the Mishnaic law is rejected. The *sugya* of the Palestinian Talmud is based upon royal theology or sacral theology, according to which the king is not judged and certainly does not judge. The *sugya* in the *Palestinian* is thus the contrary of that in the *Babylonian*, both on the halakhic-normative plane and in terms of the conceptual basis for that halakhah. The *Babylonian*'s (ideological) point of departure is that the king is not judged "because of something which happened" – i.e. the incident of Yannai (or Herod) and the structural problems that it indicates; and because of the principle of reciprocity ("adorn yourself and adorn others" – Zephaniah 2:1; lit.: "Come together and hold assembly"), the king also does not judge. These laws are applied by the Babylonian Talmud (in the name of Rav Pappa) to the Israelite

51 See *Deuteronomy Rabbah, Shoftim* (ed. Lieberman, p. 98); and see *Midrash Tehillim* 17:2 (ed. Buber, p. 125): "Our Rabbis taught: 'The king does not judge and is not judged.' [R. Yohanan said:] David said before the Holy One blessed be He: Master of the World, You are a king and I am a king. It is fitting for a king to judge a king, as is written there: 'Before You my judgment shall go out.'"

52 See S. Mowinkel, *The Psalms in Israel's Worship*, trans. D. R. Ap-Thomas (Oxford, 1967), p. 57. Likewise the opinion appearing in the *Palestinian*, according to which the function of the king is to do justice and simultaneously also to help the poor ("justice and righteousness") is a widespread motif in royal theology. Cf. Mowinkel, *The Psalms in Israel's Worship*, pp. 69–71, who interprets thus Psalm 72:4: "He shall judge the poor people and save the downtrodden and exploited."

monarchy alone, whereas the kings of the Davidic dynasty "judge and are judged." In contrast, the *Palestinian* rejects the Mishnaic law and concludes from the biblical evidence that the king does in fact judge. The *Palestinian* does not distinguish between the kings of Israel and the Davidic kings: all kings sit in judgment. And, indeed, in *Palestinian Horayot* there is a *beraita* that explicitly identifies between the two: "The king of Israel and the king of Judah are equal: this one is not greater than that, nor is that one greater than this."[53] The king of Judah here evidently refers to a king of the Davidic line.[54] Moreover, unlike the Babylonian Talmud, the *Palestinian* rejects the principle of reciprocity: the king judges but is not judged.[55] The basic difference between them is rooted in the different explanations they give for the halakhah that the king is not judged: the *Babylonian* bases it upon political realism while the Yerushalmi bases it upon the king's special relationship with God (and evidently also the fact that he embodies in his personality the public as a whole).

The *Babylonian* expresses the law of the Mishnah and provides a reason for it while the *Palestinian* significantly departs from it. The basic difference is rooted in different understandings of monarchy: the *Palestinian* bases its laws upon some version of royal theology whereas the Mishnah – and in its wake the *Babylonian* – rejects this approach and adopts laws that reflect a limited understanding of monarchy: they distance the king from the judicial system ("the king does not judge") and, in order to avoid mishaps (and perhaps based on past experience), they also distance judgment from the king ("and he is not judged").

As noted above, the Mishnah opens the brief group of laws about the king specifically with the halakhah that the king does not judge and is not judged; it would appear that by so doing it alludes to the idea that the status of the king is shaped thereby. The "lip service" paid by the

---

53 *Palestinian Horayot* 3 (47c); and see *Tosefta Horayot* 2.8 (ed. Zuckermandel, p. 476): "The Sage takes priority over the king, for if a sage dies there is none like him, but if the king dies, all Israel are fitting for kingship" (on this source see also below); and see *Babylonian Horayot* 13a; *Palestinian Horayot* 3 (48a); and see Alon, *Studies in Jewish History*, p. 17; Urbach, "Biblical Monarchy," p. 447.

54 But in a different context (regarding the subject of anointing), the *Palestinian* distinguishes between the kings of Israel and the Davidic kings; see above, Chapter 2.7.

55 Compare S. Atlas, "The King does not Judge and is not Judged" (in Hebrew), in his *Paths in Hebrew Law* (New York, 1970), p. 163. Atlas thinks that the distinction made in the *sugya* of the *Babylonian* between Davidic kings and those of Israel is based upon the *sugya* of the *Palestinian*; but see what he wrote there, p. 164.

Babylonian to the biblical sources (which are closer to royal theology) is seen in the distinction made between the Davidic kings' house and that of Israel; but here too its outlook is not suitable to the royal theology (and evidently also not to the biblical approach), as kings of the Davidic line are in fact judged in court.

It is interesting to compare the different approaches, widespread in Talmudic law, concerning the king and judgment (or, to be more precise, regarding the question as to whether or not the king may sit as judge) with the sectarian law in this matter, as it emerges from the *Temple Scroll*. In the *Scroll* it states regarding the king, among other things:

> the twelve princes of his people shall be with him, and twelve from among the priests, and from among the Levites twelve. They shall sit together with him to (proclaim) judgment and the law, so that his heart shall not be lifted above them, and he should do nothing without them, concerning any affair.[56]

The scroll describes here a court or council in which the king sits (evidently at its head), where he is joined by twelve leaders of Israel (*nesiei*, i.e. princes), twelve priests and twelve Levites. The phrase, "they shall sit together with him to (proclaim) judgment and the law," suggests that the purpose of the court is to judge and to decide those cases brought before it, and evidently also to serve as the authorized forum to interpret the Torah, that is, to legislate ("and the law"). The *Temple Scroll* admonishes the king that he should not impose his will upon the court but should take heed of the decisions of the priests and the Levites. The language of the Book of Deuteronomy, "that his heart not be lifted above his brethren" (Deuteronomy 17:20) – which in its simple meaning warns the king not to impose himself improperly over the citizens as a whole – is explained here as referring to the king's sitting in judgment and the nature of his relationship with his fellow judges.[57]

---

56   *Temple Scroll*, 57, xii–xv (ed. Qimron, p. 82); English: Vermes, 213.

57   See S. T. Fraade, "The Torah of the King (Deuteronomy 17:14–20) in the Temple Scroll and Early Rabbinic Law," in J. R. Davila (ed.), *The Dead Sea Scrolls as Background to Postbiblical Judaism and Early Christianity: Papers from an International Conference at St. Andrews in 2001* (Leiden, 2003), pp. 25–60; p. 35, n. 28. From an analysis of the language of the doctrine of the king in the *Temple Scroll*, Yoav Barzilay conjectures that there was an earlier version of the *Scroll*, according to which the king was the supreme judge, and twelve princes of the congregation sat alongside him as advisers. In his opinion, a later editor changed the picture: he expanded the

Further on, the *Temple Scroll* returns to this matter: "He shall not twist judgment; he shall take no bribe to twist a just judgment and shall not covet a field or vineyard or a vineyard, any riches or house, or anything desirable in Israel. He shall (not) rob."[58] In this passage as well it is clear that the king judges because, just as the Torah warns the judges, so too the king is warned not to take bribery nor to pervert the law. It would seem that the *Scroll* also places limits here upon the power of the king to take property from the people, in accordance with the view according to which everything stated in the chapter of the king (i.e. in Samuel) – the king is forbidden to do.

Unlike the Mishnaic law and the *sugya* of the *Babylonian*, according to the *Temple Scroll* the king judges (albeit it is not clear whether he is judged, as the *Scroll* is silent on this matter); while, unlike the *sugya* in the *Palestinian*, the king not only judges but is also a member of equal status in the court, in which the priests and Levites set the tone and evidently also direct and dictate the results of its discussions.[59]

3.3 The King's Subjugation to the Torah

Included within the framework of the limitations placed upon the king is, of course, his subjugation to the Torah and, as I shall show below, also to its accepted exegetes. To recall, this subjugation is emphasized in Deuteronomy 17:18–20:

> And when he sits upon the throne of his kingdom, he shall write for himself in a book a copy of this Law, from that which is in charge of the Levitical priests. And it shall be with him, and he shall read in it all the days of his life, that he may learn to fear the Lord his God, by keeping all the words of this Torah and these statutes, and doing them. That his heart not be lifted up above his brethren, and that he may not turn aside from the commandment, either to the right hand or the left, so that he may continue long in his kingdom, he and his children in Israel.

---

council, altered its composition, and made the king subordinate to its rule. See Y. Barzilay, "The Law of the King in the Temple Scroll: Its Original Characteristics and Later Redaction" (in Hebrew), *Tarbiz*, 72 (2003): 59–84, pp. 73–74. However, this suggestion is no more than conjecture.

58   *Temple Scroll*, 57, xix–xxi (ed. Qimron, p. 82); English, p. 213.

59   As noted by Fraade, "The Torah of the King," p. 35 n. 29, the structure of the court in the Temple Scroll is influenced by what is stated in Deuteronomy 17:9, where the "judge" is mentioned after the "Levitical priests."

The obligation to write a scroll of the Law is an inseparable part of the special commandments imposed upon the king by the Chapter of the King in the Book of Deuteronomy. As will be recalled, these commandments relate to matters of women, horses or gold and silver. The obligation to write a Torah scroll symbolizes the subjugation of the king to the law in general and is intended to strengthen this subjugation; in a certain sense, it is a direct sequel to the other laws mentioned that also imply his subjugation to the Torah. The verses emphasize that the king's subjugation to the Torah is a precondition of his continued rule and the rule of the dynasty that will emerge from him, and it expresses the principled equality between his status and that of his "brethren" ("that he shall not lift up his heart above his brethren"). In that respect, these verses embody a rejection of the approach of royal theology, in all variations of which the king is not a regular person. Here, too, the tannaitic halakhah as found in the Mishnah and in the tannaitic midrashim is directly derived from the approach of Deuteronomy. The following is the language of the Mishnah in Sanhedrin:

> "And he shall write for himself in a book a copy of this Law" – for his own sake. When he goes out to war it is with him; he comes in, it is with him; he sits in judgment, and it is with him; he reclines [for a meal] and it is opposite him. As is said, "and it shall be with him, and he shall read in it all the days of his life" (Deuteronomy 17:19).[60]

The tannaitic halakhah requires the king to write a scroll of the Torah for himself (*Sifrei Devarim* even emphasizes that it does not suffice that he have a scroll written by his ancestors), and the scroll accompanies him wherever he goes.[61] Regarding the biblical idiom, *mishneh torah* ("a copy of the Torah"), which seemingly suggests that the king does not have to write the entire Torah for himself, the tannaim comment: "*Mishneh.* You might think that this refers only to the 'repetition of the Torah' [i.e. Deuteronomy]. From whence [do we know that he must write] the rest of the words of the Torah? Scripture says: 'to observe all the words of this Torah and the laws, to do them.'" The king's subjugation is thus

---

60   *Mishnah Sanhedrin* 2.4 (based on MS Kaufmann); and cf. *Sifrei Devarim* 160–162 (ed. Finkelstein, pp. 211–213); *Tosefta Sanhedrin* 4.7 (ed. Zuckermandel, p. 421).

61   *Sifrei Devarim* 160 (ed. Finkelstein, p. 211): "'And he shall write for himself' – for his own sake, for the one of his fathers is not sufficient."

to the entire Torah, and not only to portions thereof – and certainly not only to those laws that pertain specifically to him.[62]

The Torah emphasizes that the king writes his Torah scroll "before the Levitical priests" (Deuteronomy 17:18) – evidently in order to emphasize that the king is also subjugated to its authorized interpreters, who are (according to the adjacent section in the Torah) the priests and the Levites.[63] For the tannaim, who distanced the king from the judiciary, this subjugation is self-evident; hence, they add, "'[and he shall write it …] before the Levitical priests' – that it be proofed before the Levitic priests."[64]

An explicit expression of the king's subjugation to the Torah appears in the description of the *Hakhel* ceremony in *Mishnah Sotah*. At the beginning of Chapter 7, the Mishnah differentiates between subjects (or sections) of the Torah read on ceremonial occasions in every language (for example, the passage of Sotah, the "confession" [i.e. declaration] of tithes, the recitation of Shema, prayer, oaths), and those things read specifically in the holy language. One of those matters "said in the holy language" is the "Chapter of the King" (*Mishnah Sotah* 7.2). Further on in the chapter, the Mishnah explains thus:

> "The Chapter of the King." How so? At the end of the last festival day of Sukkot, in the eighth year which concludes the seventh year, they make a platform of wood in the Temple courtyard, and he sits

---

62   Compare *Sifrei Devarim* 161 (ed. Finkelstein, p. 212): "'And these laws' – this refers to the laws of the monarchy"; and compare also the alternative readings there at the beginning of 160 (p. 211). Concerning the idiom *mishneh torah*, see *Tosefta Sanhedrin* 4.8 (ed. Zuckermandel, p. 422): "If so, why does it say: 'And he shall write a copy of this Torah.' This teaches that he writes two Torah scrolls, one which comes in and goes out with him, and one which stays in his house. That which comes in and goes out with him does not enter with him into the bathhouse nor into the House of Water, as is said, 'And it shall be with him and he shall read therein all the days of his life' – in a place suitable for reading. And are not matters *a fortiori*? If regarding the king of Israel, who only engages in the needs of the public, it says, 'And it shall be with him and he shall read it all the days of his life,' Other people all the more so!"

63   See Deuteronomy 17:8–13; and see above, Chapter 1.3. The subjugation of the king to the priests is alluded to in the language, "that his heart not turn aside from the mitzvah either right or left" (Deuteronomy 17:20), which reiterates the language of the warning to hearken to the voice of the Levitical priests in the previous passage: "You shall not depart from the word which they tell you, right or left" (Deuteronomy 17:11). It should be noted that the status of the king in Deuteronomy 17:20 is like that of "his brethren," who are subjected to the Sanhedrin.

64   *Sifrei Devarim*, 161 (ed. Finkelstein, p. 212).

upon it, as is said: "at the end of seven years," etc. (Deuteronomy 31:10) "when all Israel come" (Deuteronomy 31:10).

The *Hazan* of the *Knesset* takes a Torah scroll and gives it to the head of the *Knesset,* and the head of the *Knesset* gives it to the Vice [*segan,* High Priest], and the Vice gives it to the High Priest, and the High Priest gives it to the king, and the king stands and receives it, and reads it sitting down.[65]

The Mishnah describes here the gathering of *Hakhel* that occurs once every seven years, at the end of the last festival day of Sukkot following the sabbatical year.[66] The central role in the ceremony is set aside for the king; the ceremony is fashioned in such a way that the various officeholders, in ascending order according to rank, receive the Torah scroll from one another and give it to the next one, while the king – who has the highest rank of all – is the last one to receive it, and he is also the one to read the Torah. According to the continuation of the Mishnah, all of those sections read by the king are taken from the Book of Deuteronomy: "And he reads from the beginning of 'These are the words' until *Shema,* [including] *Shema* [Deuteronomy 1:1–6:9], *Ve-haya im shamo'a* ['And if you will surely hearken': Deuteronomy 11:13–21], 'You shall surely tithe' [Deuteronomy 14:22–26], 'when you have finished paying all the tithes' [Deuteronomy 21:12–15], blessings and curses [Deuteronomy 27:11–26; 28:1–69], until he completes all of them."[67] The focus on Deuteronomy is evidently based upon the language of Scripture: "You shall read this Law before all Israel in their hearing" (Deuteronomy 31:11). According to the view of the tanna cited in the Mishnah, the "Chapter of the King" in Deuteronomy is not included among those things that the king reads.[68]

---

65 *Mishnah Sotah* 7.8, according to MS Kaufmann; and cf. Albeck's discussion in his edition of the *Mishnah Sotah,* "Completions and Supplements," pp. 288–289; for alternative readings, see D. Henshke, "How 'The King's Portion'? On Methods of Editing the Mishna" (in Hebrew), *Sidra,* 16 (2000): 21–32, at pp. 21–22, nn. 1–16.

66 On alternative readings here, see D. Henshke, "When is the Time of *Hakhel*?" (in Hebrew), *Tarbiz,* 71 (1992): 177–194; p. 177.

67 *Mishnah Sotah,* 7.8 according to MS Kaufmann.

68 According to the manuscript of the Mishnah of the *Babylonian* and the printed editions, the king also reads the "Chapter of the King" in Deuteronomy. However, according to most manuscripts, this chapter is not included in what the king reads on the occasion of the *Hakhel.* See Lieberman, *Tosefta ki-feshutah: Zera'im–Nashim: Sotah,* 684, where he comments that the Chapter of the King is an addition to the original mishnah.

The ceremony of *Hakhel* is referred to in the Mishnah as "the Chapter of the King" not because of the contents of the chapter but because of the identity of the one doing the reading.[69]

According to what is stated in the Book of Deuteronomy, the priests are those commanded to read in the Torah on the occasion of *Hakhel*.[70] Indeed, Josephus identified the reader as the high priest.[71] But not so, as we have noted here, according to the Mishnah. It is not clear whether the fashioning of the ceremony in which the king is the one to read the Torah is an innovation of the sages or whether the Mishnah takes the model of the ceremony as it was already practiced at the time of the Temple.[72] This issue depends upon the authenticity of the story that appears further on in the Mishnah, regarding King Agrippas:

---

69   See Lieberman, *Tosefta ki-feshutah, Zera'im–Nashim: Sotah,* p. 684. According to R. Judah, quoted in *Tosefta Sotah,* the Chapter of the King is included among those chapters that the king reads: "Rabbi Judah says: He did not need to begin from the beginning of the book, but only to read *Shema, Vehaya im shamo'a,* 'You shall surely tithe,' 'When you complete to tithe,' and the Chapter of the King until he completes it all and those expounded therein, and he concludes 'til the end": *Tosefta Sotah* 7.17 (ed. Lieberman, pp. 196–197). However, Rabbi Judah does not refer to the occasion of the *Hakhel* as the "Chapter of the King." On the dispute between the tanna and R. Judah in the Mishnah, see Henshke, "When Is the Time of *Hakhel?*" pp. 26–30.

70   In Deuteronomy Moses commands the priests to read "this Torah before all Israel" (Deuteronomy 31:9).

71   *Antiquities* IV.208–210 (Loeb Classical Library IV.574–577): "When the multitude hath assembled in the holy city for the sacrifices, every seven years at the season of the feast of tabernacles, let the high priest, standing upon a raised platform from which he may be heard, recite the laws to the whole assembly; let neither women nor children be excluded from this audience, nay nor yet the slaves." In light of the story of Agrippas further on in the Mishnah (see immediately below), Hanoch Albeck thinks that the custom did not participate in the ceremony of *Hakhel;* see in his edition of the Mishnah, *Seder Nashim,* "Completions and Supplements," p. 389. However, it would seem that Josephus's words do not necessarily reflect a historical occasion but rather describe the event as described in Scripture. It should be noted that already Hecataeus of Abdera, writing in the last quarter of the fourth century BCE, states that: "It is he [the high priest] who in their assemblies and other gatherings announces what is ordained, and the Jews are so docile in such matters that straightaway they fall to the ground and do reverence to the high priest when he expounds the commandments to them." See Stern, *Greek and Latin Authors,* vol. I, pp. 27–28.

72   In his commentary to the Mishnah, ad loc., Albeck explains that there is no textual evidence for the law that the king reads the Torah on the occasion of the

King Agrippas stood and received [the scroll] and read it standing up, and he was praised by the sages. And when he came to [the verse], "You may not put a foreigner over you, who is not your brother" (Deuteronomy 17:15), he wept tears. They said to him: Do not fear, Agrippas, you are our brother, you are our brother.[73]

In any event, the fashioning of the *Hakhel* ceremony expresses the subjugation to the Torah of the entire polis, whose most explicit representative is he who stands at its head: the king. The ceremony of the *Hakhel*, in which the king declares the subjugation of the public, and thereby his own subjugation, to the Torah, embodies in a ceremonial way what is stated in the Chapter of the King in Deuteronomy: "And it shall be with him, and he shall read in it all the days of his life, that he may learn to fear the Lord his God, by keeping all the words of this Law and these statutes, and doing them" – as well as the interpretation that these words received in the laws of the king in *Mishnah Sanhedrin*.

The tannaitic halakhah, according to which king is subject to the Torah, does not fit the approach widespread in the Greco-Roman world, which found expression in the saying, *para basileos nomos agraphos* ("the

Hakhel. However, he quotes *Sefer Yera'im* (289), which quotes 2 Kings 23:2–3, that relates concerning Josiah: "And he shall read in their ears all the words of the Book of the Covenant found in the house of the Lord, and the king stood upon the platform, and he made the covenant before the Lord, that they would go after the Lord."

73   *Mishnah Sotah* 7.8, according to MS Kaufmann. Compare the opposite reaction that appears in *Tosefta Sotah* 7.9 (ed. Lieberman, p. 196): "It was said in the name of Rabbi Nathan: Israel [ought to have been] subject to destruction, because they pandered to Agrippas" (cf. *Babylonian Sotah* 41b); and *Palestinian Sotah,* end of Chapter 7 (22a): "They taught: Rabbi Hanina b. Gamaliel said: Many were slaughtered on that day because they flattered him." And see D. Schwartz, *Agrippa I: The Last King of Judaea* (in Hebrew) (Jerusalem, 1987), pp. 173–175. The scholars deliberate as to whether this *mishnah* refers to Agrippas I or Agrippas II. In wake of other scholars, Schwartz raises the possibility that it was the high priest who generally read the Torah on the occasion of the *Hakhel* but that Agrippas I was the one who read when Josephus was young; however, in the days of Agrippas II the custom was as described by Josephus (see above, n. 72); cf. Schwartz, *Agrippa I*, p. 174 and nn. 57–60, where he also raises contrary considerations, according to which one was speaking specifically of Agrippas II; and compare D. Trifon, "A Mishnaic Fragment as Evidence of the Status of King Agrippa II" (in Hebrew), *Cathedra*, 53 (1990): 27.

king has no written law").[74] And, indeed, according to that approach commonly held in the Hellenistic and Roman world, the king is not subject to the law – not even to his own laws.[75] This aphorism and the approach it expresses were known to the sages, as may be shown by the following midrash:

> Rabbi 'Lazar said: *Para basileos nomos agraphos.* In what is customary in the world, [if] a king of flesh and blood declares an edict, if he wishes [to do so] he fulfills it, if others wish, they fulfill it. But the Holy One blessed be He is not so, but issues an edict and He fulfills it first. What is the reason? "They shall keep my charge, I am the Lord" [Leviticus 22:9]. I am He who observed the mitzvot of the Torah first.[76]

74   See S. Lieberman, *Greek in Jewish Palestine,* p. 38, n. 51; and see Halevi, "The Authority of Kingship," p. 226. Halevi notes a proclamation that was posted in the courtyards of Rome on a bronze tablet in 69 CE, which read as follows: "The emperor Caesar Aspanius is free of the laws and decisions of the Roman people."

75   Scholars have demonstrated that the approach that the king is subject to his own laws only took shape in the late Middle Ages (i.e. during the twelfth century). This approach was a theoretical development of Roman law as reflected in the Justinian Codex; however, Roman law itself (in the above-mentioned codex and in other sources) did not subjugate the king to its laws (certainly not explicitly). On the contrary: there is support for the theory that, according to the Roman legal approach, while it is fitting from an ethical and political viewpoint that the king obey his own laws, from a strictly "juridical" viewpoint the laws do not obligate him. See H. J. Berman, *Law and Revolution: The Formation of the Western Legal Tradition* (Cambridge, Mass., 1983), pp. 145 and 585 n. 58, and the references in the note mentioned. It should be noted that this approach (according to the Justinian Codex [Institutes 1.2] and according to a number of Roman thinkers, primarily Stoics, such as Cicero [*De republica* III.22] and Marcus Aurelius [*Meditations,* Book IV, §4]), pertains to the civil law but not to the natural law (which is immutable and which applies to all).

76   *Palestinian Rosh Hashanah* 1.2 (57b). A slightly different version appears in *Leviticus Rabbah* 35.3 (ed. Margaliot, pp. 820–821): "Rabbi 'Lazer said: *Para basileos nomos agraphos.* It is customary in the world that, when a king of flesh and blood makes a decree, if he wishes, he fulfills it, and if not, in the end he is made to fulfill it by others. But the Holy One blessed be He is not so." In any event, the sense of the two passages is identical. In both places an illustrative homily is brought further on: "You shall stand up before old age and honor the face of the elder, and you shall fear your God, I am the Lord' [Leviticus 19:32]. I am He who first performed the mitzvah of standing before the elderly"; in the *Palestinian* the language is slightly different.

As opposed to the literal meaning of the biblical text, Rabbi Eleazar ['Lazar] interprets the word "my guarding" not only as referring to those commandments which God commands Israel but also those commandments which God Himself fulfills ("first").[77] This statement includes the view that God and Israel are equal "before the law," and the idea that God gives Israel a kind of personal example.[78] If God behaves thus, then the king of Israel, according to their approach, should all the more so! The king of Israel is diametrically opposed to a foreign king, whose laws do not obligate himself, and who, in the words of the *beraita* in *Babylonian Pesahim* concerning the kings of the nations: "the king does what he wishes."[79]

There are, of course, distinctions between the king and his subjects, as noted by the midrash in *Sifrei Devarim* immediately thereafter:

> As we have seen a layman is equal to a king in matters of Torah; is he so in other matters? The Scripture says: "to observe all the words of this Torah" – as he is equal to him regarding words of Torah, but not regarding other matters. From this they said: The king may break through to make a road, and one cannot protest against this, to widen a thoroughfare and one cannot protest this. The King's highway has no set limits, and all the people take loot and place it before him, and he takes a portion at the head.[80]

One should note that those things in which the king is not equal to the layman are limited to his prerogatives within the administrative realm, to matters of appropriating property ("he breaks through to make himself a highway") and to matters of military and warfare.[81] However, as we shall

---

77 This exegetical move in relation to God is very common in the midrash. See Lorberbaum, "The Image of God," p. 244, n. 74.

78 The view that God performs commandments is related to a pattern of thinking that is widespread in rabbinic literature. I elaborated on this in my as-yet-unpublished lecture, "*Imago Dei – Imitatio Dei:* 'Precious Is Man Who Was Created in the [Divine] Image ... Precious Is Israel, Who Were Called Sons of the Omnipresent:' On *Tzelem* and *Ben* in Tannatic Literature" (in Hebrew), delivered at the Thirteenth World Congress of Jewish Studies, 23–28 Av 5761, Jerusalem, 2001.

79 *Babylonian Pesahim* 110 a.

80 *Sifrei Devarim* 161 (ed. Finkelstein, p. 212); and see *Mishnah Sanhedrin* 2.4: "And he goes out to a voluntary war according to [the instruction of] the court of seventy-one, and he breaks through to make a road, and none can protest. And the royal highway has no limit, and all the people give before him and he takes a portion at the head."

81 See *Mishnah Bava Batra* 6.7.

see below, even regarding going out to war the king's authority is limited
as he is only allowed to launch a "permitted" war with the approval of the
Sanhedrin (of which, as we recall from the Mishnah, he is not a member);
it is only in the case of a commanded war that he does not require their
approval. These "extraordinary privileges" of the king fit the "law of the
king" in the Book of Samuel, which focuses upon the king's prerogative
to seize the property of the people ("and your fields and vineyards and
good olive trees he shall take," 1 Samuel 8:14) and to go to war ("and he
shall fight our wars": 1 Samuel 8:20).[82] However, in comparison to what
is stated in the Book of Samuel, the tannaim restrict his powers even in
matters of foreign policy and security as the king is not free to conduct an
independent policy.

As we have seen in Chapters 2 and 3, from the Mishnaic laws of the king
emerges a picture of a monarchy with rather limited authority. Most of the
tannaim think that a royal form of rule is necessary in order to assure law
and order, for administrative matters and, primarily, for needs of defense
– both internal and against external enemies – and therefore one is
commanded to anoint a king; nevertheless, the "constitution" that emerges
from the Mishnah and from parallel tannaitic sources is that of a limited
monarchy. First and foremost, this limitation derives from the subjugation
of the king to the Torah, and this – in the laws that are unique to the king –
limits his prerogatives within the personal realm (i.e. the number of women
whom he is allowed to marry) and in the areas of property and the military.
As we have seen, the tannaim modified those limitations that the Torah
places upon the king in several of these areas, but, even so, according to
its approach, his power is quite limited – certainly in comparison to other
kings in the ancient Near East and in later Antiquity. The limitations upon
the king are not restricted to these areas alone; no less significant is his
separation from the sacral cult in the Temple and from the judicial arena.

The status of the king may also be inferred from the editorial model
of *Mishnah Sanhedrin*, which opens with the structure of the courts and
their authorities, including that of the Sanhedrin (Chapter 1). Thereafter

---

82 It is possible that, according to the Mishnah, the king is only allowed to break
through a road, etc., in time of war. However, he does not enjoy any general
authority of appropriation. The matter of breaking through to make roads is
mentioned in the Mishnah in the context of an optional war. From *Sifrei Devarim*
it follows that his authority in these matters is general. According to what is
stated in the halakhic midrashim and in the Mishnah, the king is not required
to compensate those whose property he has appropriated; cf. Rambam, *Hilkhot
Melakhim*, p. 4; and Blidstein, *Political Principles*, pp. 177–178 and n. 11 there.

it describes the status of the high priest (beginning of Chapter 2), and only then does it turn to those laws pertaining to the king, which are likewise few in number, as if to say: the authority of the king is what is left of those authorities that have already been divided among the other realms. The first part of *Mishnah Sanhedrin* (Chapters 1–2) is thus arranged along the model of Chapters 16–18 of the Book of Deuteronomy, in which the various institutions are also presented alongside one another, and from which one likewise gains the impression of division of authorities: the king is granted (or left with) rather limited political prerogatives.[83] While there are differences between the Mishnah and the Book of Deuteronomy, a clear line nevertheless connects between them. This continuity is both programmatic and structural and indicates that the Mishnah (and other tannaitic sources) adopted the Deuteronomic model of limited monarchy – admittedly through a refashioning of its details – and rejected the other approaches to monarchy: royal theology (or sacral monarchy), on the one hand, and direct theocracy, on the other.

83   This does not suffice to claim that the parallel between Deuteronomy and the Mishnah holds true in all details. There also differences; thus, for example, the matter of the "rebellious elder" (*zaken mamre*), incorporated in Deuteronomy 17:8–13 in the description of the High Court, is discussed in the Mishnah in the context of the chapter entitled *Elo ha-Nehnakim* (*Sanhedrin* 11). The editorial consideration is quite clear: the Mishnah enumerates those transgressions for which the punishment is judicial execution, within the editorial framework of cataloging the four different categories of death penalties imposed by the court.

FOUR

Limited Monarchy in Tannaitic Halakhah:
Reasons and Context

Why did most of the tannaim adopt the view that advocated limited
monarchy and rejected the other two models – namely, direct theocracy, on
the one hand, and royal theology, on the other?[1] At first glance, the answer
to this question appears to be simple: the tannaim accepted the underlying
approach of the "Chapter of the King" in the Book of Deuteronomy. In the
final analysis, as against direct theocracy – sourced primarily in the Book of
Judges; and royal theology – which appears in the Books of Psalms, Samuel,
Kings, and Chronicles – the approach of limited monarchy appears in the
Torah itself. Thus, unlike the other two approaches, whose sources are found
in "non-obligatory" psalms and historical narratives, limited monarchy
appears in the Book of Deuteronomy as a normative, binding law.[2]

While this "naive" and formalistic explanation does carry a certain
weight, it is incomplete; considerations of methodology and content reveal
that the picture is more complex. To begin with, the above explanation is
based on the assumption that rabbinic literature is limited primarily to what
it declares itself to be: namely, biblical exegesis, and particularly exegesis
of the Torah. But while scriptural exegesis is clearly an essential aspect
of rabbinic literature, it is not its be all and end all. Theories of exegesis
(hermeneutics) developed over recent decades have put forward weighty
claims, according to which, behind the "traditional" interpretations that
allegedly humbly submit to the primacy of the sanctified canonical text, a
new agenda is concealed. Even if we do not accept the full range of radical
claims made by theoreticians of the last generation, we cannot ignore
the fact that rabbinic literature departs significantly from the Bible with
regard to many areas – not only in its details but also in general.[3] While the

---

1   It is important to remember that the minority opinion of Rabbi Nehorai (see
    above, Chapter 2.1) also exists, totally rejecting the institution of the monarchy. R.
    Nehorai's words evidently imply a preference for direct theocracy. This, however,
    as mentioned earlier, is a minority opinion. Most of the tannaim think that there
    is an obligation to appoint a king, as also ensues from the Mishnah.

2   In many respects, the rabbinic tradition continues Deuteronomic theology and
    halakhah. Nevertheless, the rabbis borrowed more than a little from the Holiness
    School in the Bible – and we cannot elaborate here.

3   See, for example, M. Halbertal, *Interpretative Revolutions in the Making: Values as
    Interpretative Considerations in Halakhic Midrash* (in Hebrew) (Jerusalem, 1997).

sages indeed engaged in exegesis, this was not only with the intention of unraveling or harmonizing the meaning of the written text. Underlying their exegetical activity lay an independent world view and structures of thought, by whose means they reshaped the biblical text.[4] The existence of rival models of monarchy (which were doubtless familiar to the rabbis) – whether in the Bible or in the political reality surrounding them – only served to strengthen this consideration. In other words, even when the sages adopted the approach towards monarchy found in the Book of Deuteronomy, they did not do so exclusively out of subjugation to the authority of Scripture. It is worth remembering in this context that the discussion of the concept of kingship in rabbinic literature cannot be isolated from the traditions of political thinking and practice among the Jews generally. As we have seen in the above discussions, Deuteronomy was not the model for the political order in Jewish society of the Second Temple period; rather, this claim would seem to apply more to the political approach that lay at the basis of the Roman Empire, which was a version of royal theology.

Moreover, the Davidic monarchy – and particularly the kingdoms of David and Solomon – were understood within the Jewish tradition, including that of rabbinic literature, as the ideal model for monarchic rule. It was not for naught that, in rabbinic literature, the messianic era is strongly connected with the Davidic kingdom.[5] As demonstrated earlier, such a model of monarchy is extremely far from the limited monarchy of the Book of Deuteronomy and far closer (and in the case of Solomon literally identical) to royal theology or, at the very least, to sacral monarchy.

In addition, further sources in rabbinic literature, not directly connected to the Deuteronomic Chapter of the King, shed light on the political view of the sages and the monarchic rule that they fashioned. These sources provide us with a broad and "richer" context, both with regard to the rabbis' attitude toward other approaches to monarchy and to the manner in which they fashioned the Deuteronomic model of kingship. And, indeed, in several matters the rabbis departed from the biblical sources (both the Chapter of the King in Deuteronomy and the law of the king in Samuel), which served as a kind of platform for their own approach to monarchy. One such matter was their decision

---

4   For our purposes, it does not matter whether these structures of thought are original or whether they are rooted in cultural influences of one sort or another.

5   See E. E. Urbach, *The Sages: Their Concepts and Beliefs* (Jersualem, 1969), vol. I, pp. 659, 677–678. I discussed the centrality of the Davidic dynasty in the rabbis' world view above, Chapter 2.1–2.

– as opposed to the literal meaning of Scripture – that the appointment of the king is a mitzvah, an obligation.

4.1 "That His Fear Shall Be Upon You"

Unlike the case in Deuteronomy, which seems to imply that there is no actual commandment or obligation to appoint a king (albeit there is an obligation to establish other institutions, such as the court and the priesthood), according to the majority of tannaim and evidently also according to the Mishnah, the appointment of a king is a mitzvah.[6] This move seems to be rooted in the political view of the sages, according to which the presence of a king is vital for imposing law and order. The demand that the king must impose fear appears repeatedly in the Talmudic sources. Thus, for example, in *Sifrei Devarim,* in its exegesis of the repetition of the verb *sim,* "to set" – "You shall indeed set a king over you" (*som tashim alekha melekh*; Deuteronomy 17:15) – we read: "And does it not already say, 'you shall indeed set a king over you' (Deuteronomy 17:15)? Why does Scripture say, 'you shall set a king over you'? That his fear shall be upon you." As we may remember, Samuel's speech is interpreted by Rabbi Judah in a similar spirit: "This chapter was only said in order to frighten them, as is said, 'You shall indeed set a king upon you.'"[7] According to R. Judah, Samuel's speech does not present a statute of the king; his words were simply meant to prepare the ground for the appointment of the king. By means of this speech, Samuel prepares a society, which, according to the biblical account, had until that point conducted itself as a direct theocracy (that is, a society in a state of anarchy), for monarchic rule. According to Rabbi Judah, then, the basis of monarchy is the imposition of fear. This element is a precondition for attaining the goal that the elders had presented to Samuel: security in the face of external enemies and a proper system of internal law.

According to the *Sifrei* (and following *Mishnah Sanhedrin*), the normative implication of the principle "'you shall indeed set a king upon you' – that his fear shall be upon you" is that: "From this they inferred: one does not ride upon the king's horse, nor does one sit upon his throne, nor does one use his scepter, nor may one see him nude, nor when he is having his hair cut, nor when he is in the bathhouse."[8] The honor and awe of the king are expressed in other Mishnaic laws as well:

---

6   See above, Chapter 2.1.

7   *Tosefta Sanhedrin* 4.5 (ed. Zuckermandel, p. 421).

8   *Sifrei Devarim* 157 (ed. Finkelstein, p. 209); and *Mishnah Sanhedrin* 2.5; *Babylonian Sanhedrin* 22a.

The king ... does not perform *halitzah* nor is *halitzah* performed for his wife; does not perform levirate marriage nor is his wife subject to levirate marriage. Rabbi Judah said: If he wished to perform *halitzah* or *yibbum,* good for him [lit.: may he be remembered well]. They replied to him: One does not hearken to him, and one does not marry his widow. Rabbi Judah said: A king may marry the widow of the king ... [9]

The king's "honor" also underlies the words of the amora Rav Ashi: "A *nasi* who [chose to] forgo his honor – his honor is excused.[10] A king who forgoes his honor, his honor is not excused, as is said, 'You shall indeed put a king upon you' – that his fear shall be upon you."[11] This saying, like the other laws mentioned above, combines honor and fear and would seem to embody the view that the two terms belong to the same continuum. The

9   *Mishnah Sanhedrin* 2.2; and compare the wording of *Tosefta Sanhedrin* 4.2 (ed. Zuckermandel, p. 421): "He does not perform *halitzah,* nor does one perform *halitzah* for his wife. He does not perform levirate marriage, nor does one do levirate marriage to his wife. Rabbi Judah said: If he wished to perform *halitzah* he may do so. They replied: [If so,] you are injuring the honor of the king. And one does not marry his widow, as is said. 'They were shut up until the day of their death, as if in living widowhood' (2 Samuel 20:3) ... And one does not ride upon his horse, nor sit upon his throne, nor does one use his crown or scepter, nor any of the articles he uses. When he dies all these are burned on his account, as is said. 'You shall die in peace, and as [spices] were burned were your fathers, the former kings who were before you ... ' [Jeremiah 34:5]." And compare the laws pertaining to the high priest: "He performs *halitzah* and *halitzah* is done for his wife, and one performs levirate marriage to his wife. But he does not perform levirate marriage, for he is forbidden to marry a widow" (*Mishnah Sanhedrin* 2.1).

10   *Nasi:* usually translated "prince"; the term used in the Bible for leaders of the individual tribes, and in some places possibly as synonym for the king; also title of leader in the late Second Temple and Mishnaic period.

11   *Babylonian Ketubot* 17a. One must draw a distinction between the fear imposed by the king by virtue of his status and the fear imposed by every human being by virtue of his being alive. Thus, for example, in *Babylonian Shabbat* 151b: "Rabbi Shimon b. Eleazar said: A one-day old infant need not be guarded against rats and mice; but Og king of Bashan, once he died, needed to be guarded against rats and mice. As is said 'The fear of you and the dread of you shall be ...' (Genesis 9:2). So long as a person is alive – his fear is felt by other living creatures. Once he dies – his fear is nullified." Cf. *Babylonian Kiddushin* 71a. However, this saying may also be interpreted in a Hobbesian spirit: that the basic "state of nature" is such that "man is a wolf to man": Every man, even the weakest, constitutes a danger to his environment, and only upon his death does the fear of him disappear.

connection between honor and fear follows likewise from the proximity in the Mishnah of the law, "the king does not judge nor is he judged" (rooted in the notion of the fear of the king) and the laws that "he does not perform *halitzah* nor is *halitzah* performed for his wife; he does not perform levirate marriage," which pertain to his honor.[12]

Indeed, one finds in the tannaitic sources a widespread, conservative, almost Hobbesian view regarding the necessity for strong and stable rule.[13] Thus, for example, the well-known mishnah in Avot states: "Rabbi Hannaniah the vice high priest said: One should pray for the welfare of the kingship, for without the fear thereof, each person would swallow up his neighbor."[14] In *Babylonian Avodah Zarah* the words of R. Hannaniah are accompanied by the following remark:

> Just as among the fish in the sea, whoever is greater than his neighbor swallows him up, so too with human beings: were it not for the fear of the kingship, whoever is greater than his neighbor would swallow him up. Concerning this we taught: "Rabbi Hannaniah the vice high priest said: One ought to pray."[15]

12   Fear and honor are also combined in the following midrash: "'Let them stand there with you' [Numbers 11:16]. They came in with you into the Tent of Meeting, and all of Israel behaved towards them with awe and honor as they behave towards you, and they will say: Beloved are these who entered with Moses to hear the word of the Holy One blessed be He." *Sifrei Bamidbar* 92 (ed. Horowitz, p. 93).

13   The need for stability also explains why the sages interpreted the words "'You shall indeed put' – appoint another in his place" and "'He and his sons' – if he dies, his son reigns in his stead" (*Sifrei Devarim,* 157 [ed. Finkelstein, pp. 208, 162]; at p. 216).

14   *Mishnah Avot* 3.2 (according to MS Kaufmann); compare the text in *Avot de-Rabbi Nathan,* Version B, 31 (ed. Schechter, p. 68): "Rabbi Nehunya, the deputy high priest, said: Pray for the welfare of the kingdom that rules over us all the days, for were it not for its fear, each person would swallow his neighbor alive." On this aphorism and others similar to it, see M. D. Herr, "Roman Rule in Tannaitic Literature (Its Image and Valuation)" (in Hebrew), doctoral dissertation, Hebrew University of Jerusalem, 1970, pp. 109–114.

15   *Babylonian Avodah Zarah* 4a. This conservative viewpoint is also appears in the Talmudic sources regarding more fundamental human units, such as the home and the family. Thus, for example, in *Babylonian Gittin* 6b: "Rav Hisda said: A person should never impose excessive fear within his house, for the concubine at Gibeah suffered excessive fear of her husband, and [as a result] many thousands and tens of thousands in Israel fell. Rav Yehudah said in the name of Rav: Whoever imposes excessive fear within his house in the end comes to three transgressions: sexual licentiousness, bloodshed, and violating the Sabbath"; and cf. *Babylonian Gittin* 7a.

These sayings were doubtless uttered in the context of the *Pax Romana*.[16] However, the sages do not seem to have drawn a distinction on this point between a foreign kingdom and what they perceived as the main purpose of the Israelite king.[17]

The demand that the king impose fear is repeated several times among the tannaim and elicits a certain sense of surprise: is it not self-evident that fear is a basic component of a monarchic regime? To require the appointment of a king implies, *ipso facto,* the creation of a regime that imposes fear on the people. What reason is there, then, to command the appointment of a king and then to go back

This warning from three amoraim came, of course, against the background of the view that the head of the household ought to impose fear within his own home. On the family and the home as the core of society, see Aristotle, *Politics,* Book I.2, 1252b.

16 See Herr, "Roman Rule," pp. 107–108. It is in this manner that one also ought to understand the demand appearing in tannaitic sources – namely, to honor the kingship. See, for example, *Mekhilta de-Rabbi Yishmael, Pisha* 13 (ed. Horowitz and Rabin, p. 45); and the blessing instituted upon seeing kings of the Gentile nations: "Blessed is He who has shared His honor with flesh and blood" (*Babylonian Berakhot* 58a). Herr comments that this tendency was strengthened during the amoraic period; see "Roman Rule," p. 205. In Talmudic literature one finds criticism of the excessive violence entailed in such peace. See, for example, *Mekhilta de-Rabbi Ishmael, Beshalah,* 1 (ed. Horowitz and Rabin, p. 89): "Rabbi Shimon b. Gamaliel said: Come and see the wealth and greatness of this guilty kingdom, that it has not a single *numerus* [i.e. military unit] that sits idle, but all of them run day and night. And against them those of Egypt sit idle." Cf. *Mekhilta de-Rashbi,* 14.7 (ed. Epstein-Melamed, p. 51). For further Talmudic sources concerning the violent manner of activity of the Roman legions, see Herr, "Roman Rule," pp. 113–114.

17 According to the sages, the leaders of the community also need to impose fear. This follows from *Babylonian Rosh Hashanah* 17a: "'They spread their terror in the land of the living [Ezekiel 32:23].' Rav Hisda said: This refers to a *parnas* who imposes excessive fear upon the public not for the sake of Heaven. Rav Yehudah said in the name of Rav: Any *parnas* who imposes excessive fear upon the public not for the sake of Heaven, will not have a son who is a scholar, as is said, 'Therefore men fear him; he does not regard any who are wise in their own conceit' (Job 37:24)." On the connection between the king and the *parnas,* see *Sifrei Devarim* 162 (ed. Finkelstein, pp. 212–213). The sober political view, concerned with the need for strong rule, is also related to a sober perception of the motivations of the ruler: "You shall be careful regarding rule, for the rulers do not draw close to a person except for their own interest; they appear as if they love him when it is to their benefit, but do not stand at the time of his trouble" (*Mishnah Avot* 2.3). Here, too, the saying refers to the Roman rule. However, a complaint against rulers in general, including Israelite rulers, seems implied therein; see Herr, "Roman Rule," pp. 107–108.

and specifically point out that the king must impose his fear upon the people? Moreover, the midrash in *Sifrei Devarim* and the Mishnah concerning fear is not addressed to the king but rather to his subjects: it does not say that "your fear shall be upon them" but rather, "that his fear should be upon you," which is as if to say that each individual is commanded to "fear" the king. An instruction or suggestion of this type is even stranger: is it possible to command a person to be afraid? And what justification is there for such a thing? A king by his very nature imposes fear – and, if he does not do so, what will the person fear? The answer to this quandary would seem to lie in the fact that the appeal to the subjects that they should "be afraid" – rather than to the king that he should "impose fear" – expresses a certain acceptance of a royal regime and recognition of the fact that it is a necessary evil. When the midrash emphasizes, "'You shall indeed put' – that his fear shall be upon you," it does not refer to the subjects' sensation of fear but rather to the recognition that, despite its obvious structural faults, the monarchy is a form of rule that is necessary for imposing law and order. This recognition is intended to create an acceptance of the existence of the king, as a kind of lesser of two evils, purposing to create an attitude of respect towards his authority.[18]

The redirection of the imperative from the king (who by his very nature imposes fear) to the individual (who is "commanded" to fear the king) may thus be interpreted as a demand to each individual to recognize the authority of monarchy as a social institution. To use the terminology of Max Weber, by the instruction "that his [the king's] fear shall be upon you," the sages emphasize the need to establish a "routine" political institution, which has a certain continuity and is not based upon the charisma of the individual holding the office.[19] This approach is,

---

18   A similar formula – "imposing obligation" upon the public in order to cause fear, that is, to cause the public to recognize his authority – is found in the following homily that relates to the status of the court: "It is written: 'And I charged your judges at that time' (Deuteronomy 1:16), and it is written, 'And I commanded you at that time' (Deuteronomy, 1:18). Rabbi Eleazar said in the name of Rabbi Simlai: This is a warning to the public that the fear of the judge should be upon them, and a warning to the judge that he should tolerate the public. To what extent? Rav Hanan said, and some said Rav Shabbtai said: 'As a nurse carries the sucking child' (Numbers 11:12)" (*Babylonian Sanhedrin* 8a).

19   See M. Weber, *On Charisma and Institution Building: Selected Papers*, ed. S. N. Eisenstadt (Chicago, Ill., 1968). According to his view, charisma is "a certain quality of an individual personality, by virtue of which he is set apart from ordinary men and treated as if endowed with supernatural, superhuman, or specifically exceptional powers or qualities" (*On Charisma*, p. 48). "By its very nature, the existence of

on the one hand, the negation of direct theocracy, which periodically requires the emergence of a charismatic judge (upon whom the "spirit of the Lord" rests) and, on the other, of royal theology, based upon the supernatural charisma of God that is emanated upon the king (as is told, for example, regarding Solomon: "and bestowed upon him royal majesty," 1 Chronicles 29:25).[20]

The rejection of direct theocracy is thus related to the view that the social order requires routine, ongoing formal frameworks, and authority. This approach is clearly implied by the following *beraita* in *Tosefta Rosh Hashanah:*

> Why did [Scripture] not tell us the names of the righteous ones? So that each person will not come along and say: I wish to compare Rabbi so-and-so to Eldad and Medad; I wish to compare Rabbi such-and-such to Nadav and Avihu.
>
> Therefore it says: "the Lord, who appointed Moses and Aaron." And it says: "And the Lord sent Jerubaal and Bedan, and Jephthah and Samuel" [1 Samuel 12:6, 11] Jerubaal is Gideon, Bedan is Samson, Jephthah as given.
>
> And it says: "Moses and Aaron were among his priests" [Psalms 99:6]. Scripture compared three of the lightest people in the world to three of the greatest ones of the world, to teach us that the court of Jerubaal was considered as great before the

charismatic authority," writes Weber, "is specifically unstable ... The charismatic hero does not deduce his authority from codes and statutes, as is the case with jurisdiction of office" (*On Charisma*, p. 22). Charisma is not an "'institutionalized' or permanent structure, but a place where its 'pure' type functions. It is the exact opposite of the permanent in the institutional sense" (*On Charisma*, p. 22).

20   On charismatic monarchy, see Weber, *On Charisma*, pp. 33–34. Weber thinks that "These forms in which a ruler's charismatic legitimation may express itself vary according to the relation of the original charismatic powerholder with the supernatural powers ... Normally, this can only be hierocratic power. This holds expressly for the sovereign who represents a divine incarnation, and who thus possesses the highest 'personal charisma.' Unless it is supported and proved by personal deeds, his claim of charisma requires the acknowledgement of professional experts in divinity" (*On Charisma*, p. 40). Concerning the charismatic king, Weber comments that, due to his charismatic qualities, and because the charismatic leader always stands before the test of success (*On Charisma*, p. 32), he needs a different personality, one that can bear responsibility for the activities of the government – particularly for its failures and for practices that are not accepted by the people (*On Charisma*, p. 43).

Omnipresent as the court of Moses, and the court of Jephthah was as great before the Omnipresent as the court of Samuel.

This teaches you, that whoever is appointed as a leader over the public, even if he is the lightest of the light, is considered like the most noble of the noble.

And thus it also says: "You shall come to the priests and the Levites, and to the judge [who is in office in those days]" [Deuteronomy 17:9]. You have naught but the judge who is in your own generation. As it says, "Say not: 'Why were the former days [better than these?]" [Ecclesiastes 7:10].[21]

Implicit in this passage is the view that political frameworks – of the court and of the community leaders generally – are based upon structural authorities independent of the personalities of those who fill those positions. Political frameworks cannot be based upon charisma (in the Weberian sense) – i.e. upon the wisdom or unusual talent of leaders and those holding authority. Social order is rooted in impersonal, institutionalized and formal social structures, whose continuity and permanence are separate from the qualities of those who hold office. Our *beraita* begins by discussing judges but then goes on, for good reason, to apply this principle to all public officeholders: "to teach you that whoever is appointed as leader over the public, even if he is the lightest of the light, is considered like the most noble of the noble." This principle is the exact opposite of charisma, upon which the anarchic "rule" in the Book of Judges was based.[22] It is also diametrically opposed to royal theology, which is based upon the supernatural status of God rather than upon earthly social structures – formal, routine, and impersonal.[23]

The element of fear that the king needs to impose, and the social need to establish such authority – both of which are emphasized in tannaitic literature – are not mentioned in the Torah. The homily on the repetition of the words *som tasim* – "'You shall surely place' – that his fear may be upon you" – is far from the literal meaning of Scripture;

---

21   *Tosefta, Rosh Hashanah* 1.18 (ed. Lieberman, pp. 311–312); and see S. A. Cohen, *The Three Crowns: Structures of Communal Politics in Early Rabbinic Jewry* (Cambridge, 1990), p. 191.

22   Buber presents the approach of the Book of Judges as involving confrontation with the problem of charisma, and particularly with the "permanence of charismatic authority, which by its very nature is unstable"; see M. Buber, *The Kingship of God*, trans. R. Scheimann (New York, 1967), pp. 139–141.

23   Cf. *Mishnah Rosh Hashanah* 2.9.

likewise, Rabbi Judah's claim that the prophet Samuel's words are only intended "to frighten them." As noted earlier in Chapter 2.3, Samuel's speech may be interpreted as an attempt to discourage the elders from their request or as a proposed charter for the monarchy. It may be that, in the eyes of the biblical author, the element of fear inherent in the institution of the monarchy is self-evident, for which reason he did not mention it; but it is also possible that, unlike the tannaim, the biblical author did not see this element as substantive to royal rule, for which reason he did not mention it.[24] In either case, the fundamental difference between the Bible and the tannaim relates to the question of whether monarchy is a necessary evil. According to the tannaim, the obligation to appoint a king exists specifically because of the fear that he imposes, which in their view was essential to any political order. In contrast, the Bible does not specifically command the establishment of the monarchy, and one even detects therein a certain reservation regarding the subject – perhaps specifically because of its inherent power and fear.[25]

24 It may be that on this point there is a difference between the Chapter of the King in Deuteronomy – in which the element of fear and awe does not exist at all – and the "law of the king" in Samuel, in which it is implied in Samuel's speech, and possibly also in the request of the elders.

25 It is instructive to compare the political approach of the sages regarding the qualities of the king to the theological approach reflected in *Exodus Rabbah* 8.1 (ed. Shinan, p. 200): "'Who is the King of Glory' [Psalms 24:8]. Why do they call the Holy One blessed be He the King of Glory? Because He shares His glory with those who fear Him. How so? [In the case of] a king of flesh and blood, one does not ride upon his steed and one does not sit upon his throne. But the Holy One blessed be He placed Solomon upon His throne, as is said, 'And Solomon sat on the throne of the Lord as king' (1 Chronicles 29:23), and He made Elijah ride upon his steed. And what is the steed of the Holy One blessed be He? Storm and whirlwind, as is said, 'His way is in whirlwind and storm' (Nahum 1:3), and it is written of Elijah, 'And Elijah went up by a whirlwind into heaven' (2 Kings 2:11). One does not use the scepter of a king of flesh and blood, but the Holy One blessed be He gave his scepter to Moses, as is said 'And in his hand Moses took the rod of God' (Exodus 4:20). One does not wear the crown of a king of flesh and blood, but the Holy One blessed be He shall in the future place His crown upon the King Messiah. And what is the crown of the Holy One blessed be He? A crown of gold, as is said, 'His head is the finest gold' (Songs 5:11), and it is written, 'You set a crown of fine gold upon his head' (Psalms 21:4). One does not wear the garment of a king of flesh and blood, but Israel wears the garment of the Holy One blessed be He. And what is his garment? Strength, as is said, 'The Lord is robed, He is girded with strength' (Psalms 93:1). And he gave it Israel,

The tannaim's conservative outlook, rooted in a somewhat pessimistic view of humanity, explains why they rejected direct theocracy. The irrational nature of man and of society are not suitable to rule (or better: absence of rule) of this type. This explains why, as opposed to the Book of Deuteronomy and the overall mood of the Book of Samuel, the tannaim saw the appointment of a king as obligatory.

It is against the background of this viewpoint that one may explain why the tannaim expanded the prerogatives of the king relative to those granted him in Deuteronomy. As we observed earlier, unlike the case in Deuteronomy, according to the tannaim the king is allowed to marry a large number of women (eighteen) and, more important for our purposes, there is no practical limitation on his possibilities to accumulate

---

as is said, 'The Lord gives strength to His people' (Psalms 29:11). One may not be called by the name of a king of flesh and blood – Caesar, Augustus – and if one is called by his name one is put to death. But the Holy One blessed be He called Moses by His own name, as is said, "See, I make you as god to Pharaoh' [Exodus 7:1]." This interesting midrash draws a contrast between the behavior of a mortal king and that of the Almighty. A mortal king rules by means of honor and imposing fear, whereas God honors those who fear Him. The motifs used here by the author – the king's steed, his throne, his scepter – are, not by chance, motifs that appeared in *Mishnah Sanhedrin*. According to our author, the gap is not only between a foreign ruler (for example, the Roman emperor) and God, nor even between the king of Israel and God, but also between the laws of the king as they appear in the Mishnah (which refer to the fear and honor one ought to display towards him – honor that the Mishnah prohibits sharing with him) and the manner of God's behavior and His attitude toward human beings. Is this midrash purely "theological," or does it also, perhaps, allude to the manner of behavior of the ideal human king? If it is purely theological, why does the King of Kings not maintain a proper distance between Himself and His creations? And if it is ethical-political, is there not a certain tension or contrast between this aggadic midrash and the halakhah in the Mishnah? A discussion of these issues goes beyond the framework of the present work; they need to be clarified within a broader framework, concerned with the relationship between the political approach of the sages, as reflected in the laws of the king in Mishnah (and in other halakhic sources), and the political-theological approach implied in these aggadic sources, in which God is posed opposite a mortal king, whether by way of contrast or by way of analogy. Within the framework of this study, we also need to examine the political approach (or approaches) implied in those parables that begin, "a parable involving a king," which is, as is known, a widely used form of parable in rabbinic literature, particularly in that of the amoraim. On the parables of the king, see I. Ziegler, *Die Königsleichnisse des Midrasch* (Breslau, 1903); and see the comments of D. Stern, *Parables in Midrash: Narrative and Exegesis in Rabbinic Literature* (in Hebrew) (Tel Aviv, 1995), pp. 30–31, and the bibliography there.

wealth and property ("'he shall not multiply for himself' – for himself he does not multiply, but he may multiply in order to place in storage"), nor is there any limitation on the size of his army ("'for himself' – for himself he does not multiply, but he multiplies for his chariot and his horsemen").[26] These means are essential for the establishment of royal rule (limited in authority, but efficient). Nevertheless, it is important to note that the demand that the king impose fear, as well as the expansion of his authorities, are moderated in the tannaitic halakhah, as these are "balanced" by laws that limit his power in numerous areas.[27]

It would appear that we need to consider the biblical sources, the conservative view, and possibly also their historical context, in light of the statements regarding the fear imposed by the king. As we noted, the tannaim's words regarding the king's imposition of fear express a pessimistic view regarding human nature and the nature of society; they also imply a rejection of direct theocracy (that is, of anarchic rule) as implied by a number of biblical sources, particularly those in the Book of Judges. The laws of the king took shape under historical circumstances in which Israel did not have any sovereign authority and possibly also in light of the historical memory from the period of the Great Rebellion and the Destruction of the Temple, during which central rule in Jewish society was disbanded.[28] These words of the sages also express anxiety concerning the situation of Jewish society in Palestine during their own period, when it was lacking in any real authority. It is also important to remember that the laws of the king were formed during a period in which the sages were struggling for power, leadership, and status within Palestinian Jewish society. The laws of the king took shape within the framework of the Study House, in a kind of "ivory tower," and under circumstances in

26   See above, Chapter 2.4

27   It is interesting to note, regarding the verse in Deuteronomy, "that his heart may not be lifted up above his brethren" [Deuteronomy 17:20] in which the king is given the status of first among equals, the *Sifrei* expounds: "and not above the holy things" (*Sifrei Devarim* 162 [ed. Finkelstein, p. 212]). There would appear to be a certain departure here from the literal meaning of the text – among other reasons because, unlike the Torah, which did not at all mention the obligation to fear or to honor the king and emphasized his equal status, the tannaim specifically emphasize his superiority and the fear he imposes. See Finkelstein's note, *Sifrei Devarim* 162 (ed. Finkelstein, p. 212., n. 10).

28   See A. Kasher, "Introduction: The Causal and Circumstantial Background of the War of the Jews Against the Romans" (in Hebrew), in A. Kasher (ed.), *The Great Rebellion: The Reasons and Circumstances for its Outbreak* (in Hebrew) (Jerusalem, 1983), pp. 9–90.

which they were not implemented in practice. Against this background, one might have expected the sages to limit the status and power of the "royal crown" and to strengthen that of the "crown of Torah." That this was not in fact the tendency reflected in their discussions of monarchy indicates that the political approach, which we have reconstructed from the sources, is not only the result of local historical-social circumstances but is also of a principled and more general outlook. I shall discuss this point in greater detail below.

The tannaim rejected not only direct theocracy; in the Mishnaic laws of the king, in the halakhic midrashim, and in the discussions found in the Babylonian Talmud, a clear rejection of royal theology is implied. The rejection of direct theocracy follows explicitly from the words of the tannaim (thus in the dicta brought above), while royal theology is only rejected by implication – through the limitations placed upon the king. However, it should be noted here that several midrashim concerning the commandment to appoint a king relate specifically to biblical sources that express royal theology, or at least sacral monarchy. Concealed here may be a longing for a "real" monarchy that was not realized in the halakhic realm.

It is nevertheless possible that a more direct criticism of royal theology is to be found in the words of Resh Lakish, in the *sugya* of the king in *Sanhedrin:*

> Resh Lakish said: Initially, Solomon ruled over the upper realms, as is said: "Then Solomon sat on the throne of the Lord" (1 Chronicles 29:23).
>
> Thereafter he reigned [only] over the lower realms, as is said: "For he had dominion over all [the region] across [west of] the river [Euphrates], from Tiphsah to Gaza" (1 Kings 5:4). ... [29]
>
> Thereafter he reigned only over Israel, as is said, "I, Koheleth, have been king over Israel" (Ecclesiastes 1:12).
> Thereafter he only reigned over Jerusalem, as is said, "The words of Koheleth, the son of David, king in Jerusalem" (Ecclesiastes 1:1).
>
> Thereafter he only reigned over his own couch, as is said, "Behold, this is the litter of Solomon" (Songs 3:7).

---

29   The deletion indicated here by an ellipsis is of a homily by Resh Lakish: "Rav and Shmuel [dissented on this]. One said: Tifsah is at one end of the world and Gaza is at the other; and one said: Tifsah and Gaza are adjacent to one another. Just as he ruled over Tifsah and Gaza, so did he rule over the entire world," *Babylonian Sanhedrin* 20b.

In the very end, he only reigned over his staff, as is said, "This was my reward for all my toil" (Ecclesiastes 2:10).[30]

In this colorful homily, Resh Lakish portrays Solomon as one who began by ruling over both the heavenly and earthly realms and who gradually lost all his power until, in the end, he was left only with his walking stick.[31] This homily may be read not only as a criticism of Solomon's personality but also, primarily, as a criticism of the theological-political outlook underlying his monarchy, marked by the seal of royal theology.[32] In Resh Lakish's homily, Solomon serves as an example of a ruler with a quasi-divine self-image – as one who sought to rule according to the model of royal theology. Solomon's sin, according to Resh Lakish, was rooted in his pretension in thinking that he ruled over the entire cosmos, both the upper and lower realms – a pretense that could only end with his fall to the opposite pole, as if to say that anyone who dares to imagine that he can rule over the upper realms ends up ruling only over his own stick.

The description of Solomon as one who desired to rule over the entire cosmos corresponds to the descriptions of the king-gods in the ancient Near East, from whom the author of the biblical Book of Kings derived his inspiration when describing Solomon's monarchy.[33] And, indeed, the description of Solomon as one who imagined himself as ruling over the upper realms bears a clear allusion to royal theology, which perceives the king as a kind of god whose rule extends far beyond the boundaries of his earthly kingdom. Resh Lakish's homily may thus be read as a criticism of the hubris implicit in royal theology – a hubris that it attributes to Solomon, who, according to the biblical sources, was the Israelite "divine king" par excellence. It was seemingly not by chance that the editor of the Babylonian Talmud incorporated the homily of Resh Lakish within this *sugya,* as it was particularly fitting to his own outlook, which takes exception to royal theology.[34]

---

30 *Babylonian Sanhedrin* 20b; and cf. *Babylonian Gittin* 68b; *Babylonian Megillah* 11a.

31 Concerning this last phrase in the words of Resh Lakish, the discussion of the Bavli brings the following dispute: "Rav and Shmuel [discussed it]. One said: his walking stick; and one said: his robe (*gondo*)" Cf. *Babylonian Gittin* 68b; and *Babylonian Sanhedrin* 20b. On the term *gondo* see the entries גונדא and גונדא in M. Sokoloff, *A Dictionary of Jewish Babylonian Aramaic* (Ramat Gan, 2002), pp. 266, 270. The translation there is "a kind of garment," the sense being a robe.

32 But compare *Exodus Rabbah* 15.26 (ed. Vilna, 31 a).

33 See above, Chapter 1.2.

34 See also another interesting midrash, attributed to Resh Lakish, in *Genesis Rabbah* 9.13 (ed. Theodor and Albeck, pp. 73–74): "Rabbi Shimon ben Lakish said, 'and

This reading of Resh Lakish's homily fits well with numerous of his sayings, spread throughout the Talmudic literature, in which he expresses principled opposition to the authority of the political ruler, as distinct from that of the sages. In scholarly research focused upon the polemic that emerges from the Talmudic sources between Resh Lakish and Rabbi Yohanan regarding the status of the *nasi* as opposed to that of the sages, Reuben Kimelman demonstrates that Resh Lakish based his objection to the supremacy of the house of the *nasi* on a political viewpoint that diminished the figure of the "civilian" ruler.[35] An interesting example representing the approach of Resh Lakish is found in *Babylonian Sanhedrin*:

> Rabbi Shimon ben Lakish said: What is the meaning of the Scripture, "From the wicked their light is withheld, and their uplifted arm is broken" (Job 38:15). Why is the letter *'ayin* in [the word] evildoers *(resha'im)* suspended? That once a person become poor below – he becomes poor from above.
> And let [the verse] not be written at all! Rabbi Yohanan ... said: Because of the honor of David.[36]

Resh Lakish explains that the letter *'ayin* in the word *resha'im* in Job 38:15 was "suspended" – i.e. written above the line of the other letters – in order to suggest that the word ought to be read without that letter: rather than reading, "From the wicked their light is withheld" it should be read "From the poor ... light is withheld." As explained by Kimelman, *rashim* (רשים) is actually the Aramaic spelling or equivalent to the Hebrew term ראשים, meaning "heads" – i.e. political leaders.[37] Thus, according to Resh Lakish,

behold, it was very good' [Genesis 1:31] – this alludes to the Kingdom of Heaven. 'And behold it was very good' – this refers to the kingship of earth. Is the kingship of the earth 'very good'? This is astounding!? Rather, that it imposes justice on the people." In MS München and in MS Paris the reading is: "'good' is the kingdom of heaven; 'very good' is the kingdom of earth." According to Resh Lakish, an earthly kingdom is preferable to the heavenly one, as it performs justice (for the Greek source of this term see *Genesis Rabbah*, ed. Albeck, p. 73, n. 11). In this homily as well Resh Lakish rejects the approach regarding the kingship of heaven, whether in the "anarchic" sense or in that of royal theology, preferring a concrete earthly kingship that imposes law and order. On this saying, see Herr, "Roman Rule," p. 136.

35   R. Kimelman, "The Conflict Between R. Yohanan and Resh Laqish on the Supremacy of the Patriarchate," *Proceedings of the Seventh World Congress of Jewish Studies: Studies in the Talmud, Halakhah Midrash* (Jerusalem, 1981), pp. 1–20.

36   *Babylonian Sanhedrin* 103b.

37   See Kimelman, "The Conflict," p. 5, n. 16, cf. n. 15. Among other sources, Kimelman bases himself upon G. Alon, *Studies in Jewish History: In the Time of the Second Temple*

the political leadership as such is identified as evil – in other words, as illegitimate. As Kimelman shows, this midrash of Resh Lakish ought to be read together with numerous other sayings of his, in which this amora expresses his opposition to the political authority of the *nasi*.

Resh Lakish's principled and systematic view in relation to the status of the *nasi* and his authority opposed that of his friend, Rabbi Yohanan, who supported the *nasi* and attempted with all his strength to buttress the latter's political standing.[38] Rabbi Yohanan's political viewpoint is formulated in numerous places, not merely as specific, localized support of the *nasi* but as an overall political outlook. In the way of the sages, Rabbi Yohanan also expresses his view through midrashic exposition of Scripture.[39] An outstanding example of this approach appears in the following passage:

> It is written, "For you shall go ..." (Deuteronomy 31:7) and it is written, "for you shall bring" (Deuteronomy 31:23).
>
> Rabbi Yohanan said: Moses said thus to Joshua: [This refers to] yourself, and the elders of the generation who are with you. The Holy One blessed be He said to him: Take your staff, and hit them upon their heads – there is one leader for each generation, and not two leaders of a generation.[40]

the Mishna and the Talmud (in Hebrew), 2 vols. (Tel Aviv, 1967–1970), vol. II. p. 52, n. 145; and cf. Urbach, *The Sages*, vol. II, p. 963, n. 77, who brings the reading of a manuscript that appears also among the *rishonim* and in *Dikdukei Sofrim:* "R. Shimon ben Lakish said: ... Once a person becomes a head from below, he becomes evil from above."

38   See Kimelman, "The Conflict," p. 5, nn. 15, 16; R. Kimelman, "R. Yohanan and the Professionalization of the Rabbinate" (in Hebrew), *Shenaton ha-Mishpat ha-'Ivri*, 9–10 (1982–1983): 329–358. It should be noted that R. Yohanan was evidently a scion of the family of the *nasi*: see *b Sotah* 21a ("R Yohanan of the House of the *Nasi*"). A clear expression of their differing approaches appears in the following passage: "['The God before whom my fathers walked,' Genesis 48:15]. Rabbi Yohanan and Resh Lakish [discussed this verse]. R. Yohanan said: Like a shepherd who stands and watches his flock. Resh Lakish said: Like a prince who walks with the elders before him. According to R. Yohanan, we need his honor; according to Resh Laakish he needs our honor" (*Genesis Rabbah*, MS Vatican, 98, ed. Theodor and Albeck, p. 1245).

39   Since the beginning of modern Jewish scholarship, scholars are accustomed to reading the homilies of sages (both tannaim and amoraim) as relating indirectly to concrete events or to principled positions. See on this S. Lieberman, "Some Aspects of After Life in Early Rabbinic Literature," in American Academy for Jewish Research (ed.), *Harry Austyn Wolfson Jubilee Volume* (Jerusalem, 1965), vol. I, p. 518, n. 35.

40   *Babylonian Sanhedrin* 8a.

Rabbi Yohanan explains the duplication of the language stated to Joshua in Deuteronomy 31: "you shall come," "you shall bring" (אתה תבוא ... אתה תביא) as meaning that Moses places the elders with Joshua as if of equal status and authority in the leadership ("you shall come" – i.e. with others, namely, the elders). In contrast, God emphasizes Joshua's supreme and exclusive authority: "there is one leader for each generation, and not two leaders of a generation."[41] Thus, Rabbi Yohanan gives preference to a single political leader (in his historical context, the *nasi*) over the status of the sages, who are portrayed as secondary leaders, subject to a secular political leadership superior to their own.

It would therefore appear that, in light of the analysis proposed by Kimelman, both Resh Lakish and Rabbi Yohanan in this *sugya* adhere to outlooks that (in comparison to those opinions that preceded them in the Talmudic literature) entail continuity, on the one hand, and innovation, on the other. Insofar as the matters pertain to criticism of the house of the *nasi* and the sages' struggle for power against it, Resh Lakish is the heir to that viewpoint prevalent among the sages of the generations preceding him.[42] However, his view regarding the lack of legitimacy of the political leadership, separate from the status of the sages (the "secular" realm), seems to be an innovation, as the sages specifically emphasize its necessity in order to preserve the rule of law and order. In contrast, the viewpoint of R. Yohanan regarding the political authority of the house of the *nasi* (which represents the authority of the "secular" political leader, distinct from the status of the sages) continues a viewpoint that was widespread among the sages. However, as Kimelman has demonstrated, the approach of Rabbi Yohanan regarding the absolute supremacy of the *nasi*, as opposed the status of the sages, comprises a real innovation in Talmudic literature.[43]

4.2 Royal Theology and the Image of God

The rejection, in tannaitic literature, of royal theology is consistent with the idea of the creation of man in the image of God and the view that the people of Israel are "sons of the Omnipresent." These approaches are

41   See Kimelman, "The Conflict," p. 2, n. 6.
42   See Kimelman, "The Conflict," p. 1.
43   See Kimelman, "R. Yohanan and the Status of the Rabbinate," where he explains Rabbi Yohanan's view regarding the political-socioeconomic crisis that befell the Roman Empire and, by extension, the Jewish community in Palestine, during the third century CE.

interrelated and play a central role both in biblical thought and in the world of the sages.

Biblical scholars have emphasized that the biblical view regarding the creation of man in the image of God originated in ancient Near Eastern literature, in those sources relating to the status of the king in Mesopotamia or in Egypt. An echo of the view that the Mesopotamian king was made in the image of God appears in the harsh polemics directed against the Babylonian king in Isaiah 14:13–14: "You said in your heart, 'I will ascend to heaven; above the stars of God I will set my throne ... I will ascend above the heights of the clouds, I will make myself like the Most High.'"[44] Samuel Loewenstamm has shown that, in contrast to the Mesopotamian sources, which identify the king alone (and his offspring) as being made in the image of God, the Torah, in Genesis 1, emphasizes that man – every man – is made in the image of God.[45] In his wake, Moshe Weinfeld writes of that same passage that "In Israel there was a 'democratization' of an idea that had previously been applied to the king alone."[46] This approach, which provided the basis for the "metaphysical" political status of the king, and therefore related to him alone, is transformed in the opening chapter of the Bible, according to Loewenstamm, to "the glory of the human race."[47]

Chapter 1 of Genesis describes man as created in the image of God and in His likeness, for which reason he is given dominion over the earth ("And fill the earth and subdue it," Genesis 1:28; cf. Genesis 9:2). The Bible utilizes the motif of the divine image, not only to describe the unique relationship that exists between man (every man) and

---

44   An additional polemical reference to this matter may appear in Psalm 89:7. See T. N. D. Mettinger, *King and Messiah: The Civil and Sacral Legitimation of the Israelite Kings* (Lund, 1976), pp. 268–275. Mettinger raises the possibility that the Bible contains an echo of the fact that the king of Israel was also perceived as in the image of God; see *King and Messiah*, p. 274.

45   S. E. Loewenstamm, "Man as Image and Son of God" (in Hebrew), *Tarbiz*, 27 (1957): 1–2; p. 1.

46   M. Weinfeld, "God the Creator in Gen. I and in the Prophecy of Second Isaiah" (in Hebrew), *Tarbiz*, 37 (1967): 105–132; p. 114; cf. C. Westermann, *Genesis 1–11: A Continental Commentary* (Minneapolis, Minn., 1992), pp. 151–154, where he summarizes all the views on this subject. Regarding the son as the image of his father, who in the context of the royal theology of ancient Egypt is himself in the image of God, see the comments of M. Schneider, "*Joseph and Onat* and Early Jewish Mysticism" (in Hebrew), *Kabbalah*, 3 (1998): 303–344; p. 341 and n. 156; and see H. Frankfort, *Kingship and the Gods: A Study of Ancient Near Eastern Religion as the Integration of Society and Nature* (Chicago, Ill., 1971), pp. 44–45.

47   Loewenstamm, "Man as Image."

God but also in order to establish man's status as ruling over the lower realms. These two elements – image and rule – are different sides of the same coin: because of man's relationship to God, he serves as a kind of extension of Him upon the earth; from this derives his power and "right" to have dominion over "the fish of the sea and over the birds of the air, and over every living thing that moves upon the earth" (Genesis 1:28). This move implies the rejection of royal theology: if not only the king, but the entire human race, is made in the image of God, the ground is pulled out from the basis upon which this approach to monarchy rests (at least in its Mesopotamian version). From this point on, it is no longer possible to base the authority of the king on any special relationship to God as this relationship is the heritage of every human being, From here on, his political authority must be based on a different approach.

The Mesopotamian sources see the king not only as "the image of God" but also as bearing the title, "son of God." Scholars of ancient Near Eastern literature have noted the common source of these two motifs – i.e. the image of God and the son of God – "in the language of the court, which attributes to the king a special relationship to the Divine."[48] But the term, "son of God," also has an echo in the Torah, and it too undergoes a process of generalization. Thus, in Deuteronomy, Moses says to the Israelites, "You are sons of the Lord your God" (Deuteronomy 14:1). Loewenstamm thinks that these things are also drawn from Mesopotamian royal theology: whereas the term, "the image of God," is removed from its original context and applied to humankind as a whole, that of the "son of God" is set aside to refer to "an entire people, who enjoyed special closeness to God by virtue of the covenant between them and God."[49]

This finding strengthens the argument that there is a connection between the democratization of the idea of being created in the divine

---

48   See Loewenstamm, "Man as Image," p. 2. The connection between the relationship of a "son" and that of "image" already appears in the Book of Genesis, as the "image of God" is transmitted from father to son: see Genesis 5:1–3; and cf. Y. Lorberbaum, *The Image of God: Halakhah and Aggadah* (in Hebrew) (Jerusalem, 2004), Chapter 8. The view that the king is the son of God was also widespread in many of the psalms: see, for example, Psalm 2:7; and cf. Loewenstamm, "Man as Image"; and, especially, S. Mowinkel, *The Psalms in Israel's Worship*, trans. D. R. Ap-Thomas (Oxford, 1967), pp. 54ff. Weinfeld holds that that the view that the king is in the image of God is also alluded to in the Psalms: see Weinfeld, "God the Creator," p. 132. In his opinion, this approach is evidently incorporated within those verses that speak of the king as the son of God.

49   See Loewenstamm, "Man as Image," p. 2.

image and the rejection, in Deuteronomy, of royal theology as a basis for establishing royal rule. Deuteronomy attributes the title "son of God" to every individual within Israel (even if only as a rhetorical device indicative of greater closeness); it ought not be surprising that it refrains from basing the monarchic system of rule on royal theology as, according to the latter, the title "son of God," with all it implies, is unique to the king.[50]

Both these approaches – according to which humankind is created in the divine image and the people of Israel are "sons of the Omnipresent" – play a central role in the world of the rabbis and in tannaitic literature. I have devoted a separate monograph to the idea of the image of God in rabbinic literature, in which I note the radical meaning attributed to this idea by the sages and the manner in which they applied it to various halakhic areas.[51] The idea that the people of Israel are sons of

---

50 See also B. M. Levinson, "The Reconceptualization of Kingship in Deuteronomy and the Deuteronomistic History's Transformation of Torah," *Vetus Testamentum,* 61 (2001): 511–534; pp. 530–531. Certain bible scholars went so far as to argue that the central motivation of the prohibition against the cult of images in Israelite religion – that is, the prohibition to represent foreign gods, or even the God of Israel, by means of statues for cultic purposes – is rooted in the opposition, widespread in Israelite religion from its earliest origins, to the institution of kingship in general and to royal theology in particular. See R. S. Hendel, "The Social Origins of the Aniconic Tradition in Early Israel," *The Catholic Biblical Quarterly,* 50 (1988): 365–382, p. 378. Hendel thinks that, alongside the rejection of the cult of the king and his images, the cult of images of the god were also rejected (as opposed to the cult of the god himself). This was so because in the ancient Near East the image of God was none other than a mirror image of the king, making the cult of the one tantamount to the cult of the other. See Frankfort, *Kingship and the Gods.* Hendel uses a sociological methodology of the school of Marx, Weber, and Durkheim, according to which structures of thought and religious practices are external manifestations of social structures (see Hendel, "The Social Origins," p. 381.) In his opinion, the Israelite prohibition against the cult of images (the theology of aniconism) was a religious expression of the early opposition in Israel to royal theology. However, Hendel's approach is not convincing, as it is difficult to make the introduction of aniconism within Israel dependent specifically on an anti-monarchic political view. It nevertheless seems that there is a close connection between the prohibition against representing God by means of images and statues and the opposition to royal theology in certain circles in ancient Israel. This matter requires further clarification, beyond the scope of this study.

51 See Lorberbaum, *Image of God.*

the Almighty is likewise a central theme in this literature.[52] I have shown elsewhere that the tannaim drew an explicit connection between these two approaches.[53] The connection between the view that man is created in the image of God and that Israel are sons of the Almighty appears in a famous saying of Rabbi Akiva in *Mishnah Avot*:

> He [Rabbi Akiva] used to say: Beloved is man who was created in the [divine] image. There was an extra measure of love that it was made known to him that he was created in the image, as is said: "for God made man in His own image" [Genesis 9:6].[54] Beloved are Israel, who were called Sons of the Omnipresent; they are especially beloved in that it was made known to them that they are called "Sons of the Almighty," as is said, "You are the sons of the Lord your God" (Deuteronomy 14:1).[55]

In the first part of this saying, Rabbi Akiva infers that man (every man!) is precious to God because he was created in the divine image. In the second part, the *tanna* infers that the people of Israel are particularly precious to God because they are called "sons of the Almighty." It would seem that these two parts of the saying are not isolated from one another; the structure and sequence of the words creates the clear impression of a relation between them.[56] Indeed, Samuel Loewenstamm noted this relation between these two motifs in Rabbi Akiva's saying and even speculated that both entered the saying through the inspiration of the

52   See A. Goshen-Gottstein, "God and Israel as Father and Son in Tannaitic Literature" (in Hebrew), doctoral dissertation, Hebrew University of Jerusalem, 1987, and the bibliography there.

53   See my unpublished lecture, "Imago Dei – Imitiatio Dei" (above, Chapter 3, n. 78); cf. Lorberbaum, *Image of God*, Afterword.

54   "As is said, 'For in the image of God,' etc." is added in the Kaufmann manuscript at the margin of the page; however, it appears in all the other manuscripts.

55   *Mishnah Avot* 3.14 (according to MS Kaufmann): "as is said, 'for you our sons' etc." was added in the Kaufmann manuscript at the margin of the page; however, it appears in all the other manuscripts.

56   Compare A. Goshen-Gottstein, "God and Israel as Father and Son in Tannaitic Literature" (in Hebrew), doctoral dissertation, Hebrew University of Jerusalem, 1987, pp. 52–53. I devoted my above-mentioned lecture to clarifying this relationship; see Y. Lorberbaum, "*Imago Dei – Imitatio Dei*: 'Precious Is Man Who Was Created in the [divine] Image ... Precious Is Israel, Who Were Called Sons of the Omnipresent': On *Tzelem* and *Ben* in Tannatic Literature" (in Hebrew), unpublished lecture, delivered at the Thirteenth World Congress of Jewish Studies, 23–28 Av 5761 Jerusalem.

"courtly language that attributes to the king a special relationship to God" – a relationship of image and of son.[57] Rabbi Akiva thus follows in the footsteps of the Bible: he applies the idea of the divine image to humankind as a whole while applying the title of "son" to an entire people, who are precious to God.[58]

Regarding Rabbi Akiva's saying and other similar sayings in tannaitic literature, one need not resort to royal theology in its specifically Mesopotamian version: the sages were exposed to this approach in their immediate surroundings as well. The royal system with which they were familiar was a version, at times exacerbated, of royal theology. As is well known, from the time of Augustus Caesar, the Roman emperor introduced throughout the empire, including Palestine, the cult of their statues, including, among other things, an approach which perceived the empire as a divinity, at times in the emperor's lifetime and generally speaking after his death.[59] The sages (like all of Palestinian Jewish society) were exposed to this cult, which they naturally opposed decisively. They nevertheless used it extensively for their own ideological needs.[60]

---

57 Loewenstamm, "Man as Image," p. 2.

58 It is possible that the following tradition in *Babylonian Shabbat* 128a may also be understood in light of the above-mentioned ideas: "Abaye Said: Rabban Shimon ben Gamaliel and Rabbi Shimon and Rabbi Ishmael and Rabbi Akiva all thought 'All Israel are children of kings'"; and cf. *Babylonian Bava Metzi'a* 113b.

59 The research concerning this phenomenon is very extensive; however, the fundamental work on the subject remains *The Divinity of the Roman Emperor*. On the cult of the emperors in Talmudic literature, see S. Spiegel, "Divination of the Emperors" (in Hebrew), in his *The Fathers of Piyyut: Texts and Studies Toward a History of the Piyyut in Eretz Yisrael* (Jerusalem and New York, 1992), pp. 294–302; Herr, "Roman Rule," p. 148; and cf. E. E. Urbach, "Laws of Idolatry in the Archaeological and Historical Reality of the Second and Third Centuries" (in Hebrew), in his *From the World of the Sages: Collected Studies* (Jerusalem, 1988), pp. 125–178.

60 Morton Smith thinks that the cult of images of the emperors influenced the sages' understanding of the Divinity, as well as Hillel's understanding, and in his wake the tannaim's, of the creation of man in the divine image. See M. Smith, "The Image of God: Notes on the Hellenization of Judaism with Especial Reference to Goodenough's Work on Jewish Symbols," *The John Ryland Library*, 40 (1958): 473–512; and see my critique of this view in Lorberbaum, "The Image of God in Rabbinic Literature: Maimonides and Nahmanides" (in Hebrew), doctoral dissertation, Hebrew University of Jerusalem, 1997. On the rabbis' use of the cult of images of the emperors, see Lorberbaum, "The Image of God" (dissertation version), Chapter 6. Israel Knohl has recently suggested that the cult of images of the emperors exerted a direct influence on the views of the Judean desert sect. He suggests that the hymns from Qumran, which in his view portray a "Messiah–God

In midrashic sources, references to the cult of the kings' statues expressing the idea of man's creation in the divine image are already attributed to Hillel the Elder. In *Avot de-Rabbi Nathan* the following story appears:

> "Let all your deeds be for the sake of Heaven" – like Hillel.[61]
>
> When Hillel would go out to a certain place, they would ask him: "Where are you going?" [He would answer:] "I am going to perform a mitzvah." "What mitzvah, Hillel?" I am going to the toilet." "And is this a mitzvah?" He said to them: "Yes, so as not to spoil my body."
>
> [On another occasion they would ask:] "Where are you going, Hillel." "I am going to perform a mitzvah." "What mitzvah, Hillel?" "I am going to the bathhouse." "And is this a mitzvah?" He said to them: "Yes, in order to clean my body." And you should know that it is thus: Just as the images that stand in the palaces of the kings, the one appointed over them polishes them and scours them, and the king pays him *salera* [salary] every year; moreover, he is elevated among the great ones of the kingdom; we, who were created in the image and likeness [of God], as is said "for God made man in His own image" (Genesis 9:6), how much more so![62]

Hillel's words clearly reflect the cult of statues of the Roman emperors. Augustus (30 BCE–4 CE), who referred to himself as "the son of God" (*divi filius*) – a title that also appears upon his coins – established the cult of the emperor and imposed it, particularly in the eastern provinces of the empire.[63] Hillel lived in the time of Herod (37–34 BCE), who was the ward

---

of flesh and blood" who was active among the members of the cult at the end of the first century BCE, are a reaction to the cult established by the Emperor Augustus; Knohl describes the Jewish "Messiah–son of God" along the lines of the Roman "emperor–son of God." See I. Knohl, *In Wake of the Messiah* (in Hebrew) (Jerusalem, 2000).

61 The words of Rabbi Yossi in *Mishnah Avot* 2.12: "And may all your deeds be for the sake of Heaven."

62 *Avot de-Rabbi Nathan*, Version B, 30 (ed. Schechter), p. 66. For a similar story, in a slightly different version, see *Leviticus Rabbah* 34.3 (ed. Margaliot, pp. 776–777); and cf. *She'iltot*, vol. I (ed. Mirski, p. 13); *Yalkut Shim'oni*, Proverbs 11; and the version preserved by R. Yitzhak Arama, *Akedat Yitzhak, Vayikra* (Pressburg, 1849), p. 141.

63 On Augustus Caesar as the son of God and his cult, see L. R. Taylor, *The Divinity of the Roman Emperor* (Middletown Conn., 1931), p. 177; K. Galinsky, *Augustan*

of Augustus and spread the cult of the emperor throughout Palestine.[64] For obvious reasons, Hillel refers to the "images [of the king] that stand in the palaces of the kings" (or "in their theaters and circuses"); however, scholars have shown that there was no clear, unequivocal distinction between the statues of the emperors, placed in public places for political reasons – i.e. for recognition and honor (*agalma*) – and those placed in the temples for cultic purposes (*eikon*).[65] In any event, Hillel clearly utilized the cult of the Emperor to express an explicitly religious idea. The persuasive power of the story is rooted, among other things, in its religious dimension.

The use of the example of the icon or image of the kings does not, of course, imply any acknowledgment of the divinity of the Roman emperor; it only assumes that the emperors (in their lives or after the deaths) are present in their images.[66] Hillel's parable is intended to express the iconic relationship (the relationship of "making present") that exists between an object and its image and likeness; one nevertheless cannot ignore its political-theological context. It is no coincidence that Hillel

Culture: An Interpretive Introduction (Princeton, NJ, 1996); D. Fishwick, *The Imperial Cult in the Latin West* (Leiden, 1987), vol. I, p. 1; S. F. R. Price, *Rituals and Power: The Roman Imperial Cult in Asia Minor* (Cambridge, 1984).

64   M. Stern, "The Reign of Herod and the Herodian Dynasty," in S. Safrai and M. Stern (eds.), *The Jewish People in the First Century* (Assen, 1974), pp. 216–283, especially pp. 240–241. Stern notes that Herod built elaborate temples for the cult of the emperor in Gentile cities, but in order to avoid offense to the feeling of the Jews refrained from doing so in their cities.

65   Price, *Rituals and Power,* pp. 178–179. This phenomenon may be echoed in the words of R. Meir in *Mishnah Avodah Zarah* 3.1. The Roman bathhouse was an inseparable part of the Palestinian Jewish city. Icons of the emperors were usually present in the bathhouses, but despite this the sages did not have a negative attitude toward them. There is no reason to assume that the story concerning Hillel does not contain a grain of truth, as this institution penetrated the life of the Jews with the Roman conquest. See J. Goldin, *Hillel the Elder: The Emergence of Classical Judaism* (New York, 1956), pp. 36–37.

66   Compare S. Lieberman, *Hellenism in Jewish Palestine* (New York, 1950), pp. 124–126. It is worth noting that Urbach – who claims that the belief in paganism declined during the tannaitic period, and that therefore the sages were more lenient regarding arts involving imagery – likewise thinks that the sages were strict involving matters of idolatry connected with the cult of the emperors. Cf. *Mishnah Avodah Zarah* 3.1; and Shmuel's words in *Babylonian Avodah Zarah* 40b. See Urbach, "Laws of Idolatry"; but cf. Z. Weiss, "The Jews of Ancient Palestine and the Roman Games: Rabbinic Dicta vs. Communal Practice" (in Hebrew), *Zion*, 66 (2001): 427–450; p. 439, n. 59.

uses a metaphor that expresses the most explicit form of royal theology of his time.[67] By using of this metaphor, Hillel would seem to have been implying a certain political-theological move, one similar to that found in the Bible: just as the creation of man in the divine image in the first chapter of Genesis, written against the background of Mesopotamian (or Egyptian) royal theology, implies a democratization of the idea of the image, similarly Hillel, who explicitly relates to Roman royal theology, implies a similar theological-political move.[68] Thus, a direct line connects the biblical understanding of the divine image with that understanding of the image attributed to Hillel. As I have conjectured elsewhere, Rabbi Akiva and many other tannaim accepted Hillel's approach and developed it in similar directions.[69]

The sages thus continued the line delineated in the Bible and even deepened and extended it: they adopt the idea of creation in the divine image in its universal sense in a manner that is more radical and far-reaching than that of the Bible itself; the term "son," however, is attributed specifically to Israel, and the two terms – "image" and "son" – are connected in an explicit manner.

The idea of creation in the image of God in its universal sense and its understanding in rabbinic literature – namely, that all Israel are sons of the Omnipresent – would also seem to relate (albeit indirectly) to the sages' political view. It is possible to connect the rejection of royal theology with these approaches as they are unable to exist together: if every human being is created in the image of God and all Israel are "sons of the Omnipresent," it is difficult to see how one can base political authority on the view that the king has a special relationship to God. This holds true, whether one is speaking of a divinization of the king, or of a more moderate version of sacral rule.[70] It is worthwhile in this context to examine the statement of Rabbi Meir towards the end of Tractate Avot:

67 What is surprising about Hillel's saying and numerous other sayings of this type is the attitude revealed toward the cult of the images of the emperor, at a time that numerous Talmudic sources – both tannaitic and amoraic – severely opposed it. See Herr, "Roman Rule," pp. 148–153, 159–161, and his discussion there.
68 See Knohl, *In Wake of the Messiah,* pp. 98–99.
69 See Lorberbaum, *Image of God,* Chapters 6–8.
70 But the possibilities of imagination and interpretation are unlimited. It is possible to conceive a structure of thought, which would integrate the idea that all human beings are in the divine image with the view that the king has a special, stronger relationship to God. Thus, for example, the structure of thought in early Christianity regarding the relationship between Jesus and all the believers (the Church): see Ephesians 4:10–24 and Colossians 1:15–20. And cf. Lorberbaum,

Rabbi Meir said: Whoever engages in Torah for its own sake merits many things. Moreover, he is deserving of the entire world – he is called a beloved friend; one who loves the Omnipresent, who loves people, who causes joy to the Omnipresent, who causes joy to people; he is robed in modesty and awe, and it enables him to be righteous, pious, upright and truthful; it distances him from sin and draws him close to merit. And people enjoy from him advice and counsel, understanding and might, as is said: "I have counsel and sound wisdom, I have understanding, I have strength" (Proverbs 8:14); and he is given kingship and dominion and the searching out of the law; and the secrets of Torah are revealed to him; and is like a constantly flowing spring and a river which does not cease.[71]

The sixth chapter of *Avot,* known as *Kinyan Torah* ("the Acquisition of Torah"), was not an original part of *Avot,* but was added at a later date.[72] Both in terms of content and style, this saying is unusual, not only for the Mishnah but also in terms of tannaitic literature generally. It is nevertheless possible that it (at least in part) originates from a tannaitic source, and possibly even from Rabbi Meir himself.

The above words, given in the name of Rabbi Meir, require extensive discussion, which we cannot undertake here. For our purposes, this saying is interesting because the totality of those qualities which, according to royal theology were attributed to the king, are here applied to the rabbinic sage. According to this saying, one who "engages in Torah for its own sake" is beloved by God and is like a companion to Him. Moreover, he mediates between the upper worlds and lower worlds ("who loves the Omnipresent, who loves people, who causes joy to the Omnipresent, who causes joy to people"). One who studies Torah acquires sublime qualities ("righteous, pious, upright and truthful"). Moreover, he is filled with counsel, sound wisdom, and understanding, which are a kind of

Image of God, Chapter 5.4 and 7.5; R. Jewett, *Paul's Anthropological Terms: A Study of their Use in Conflict Setting* (Leiden, 1971). Such a line of thought did not take shape, or, rather, was not perfected, in rabbinic literature, seemingly because of the centrality of the idea of creation in the divine image in its "democratic" version.

71   *Mishnah Avot* 6.1.

72   This chapter appears in full in *Seder Eliyahu Rabbah* (ed. Friedman, pp. 15–16) and in *Masekhet Kallah Rabbati,* Chapter 8. See M. Higger, "*Perek Kinyan Torah*" (in Hebrew), *Horev,* 3 (1936): 285–296; and see Albeck's edition of the Mishnah, *Seder Nezikin,* pp. 351, 381.

emanation of the divine wisdom. It should be noted that the proof text brought in support of this idea – "I have counsel and sound wisdom, I have understanding and strength" – appears in its original context in the Book of Proverbs as referring to wisdom, which is a kind of divine hypostasis.[73] Among all these qualities, it is stated that the sage is also given "kingship and dominion!" These attributes are clearly unusual and even surprising in this context. Their place among all the other "acquisitions" of the sage seems rooted in their relationship to a structure of thought whose source lies in royal theology. This saying thus transfers a structure of thought, which according to royal theology is attributed to the king, to the rabbinic sage.[74] As in the statements of Rabbi Hillel and Rabbi Akiva regarding the divine image, so too in the saying of their disciple Rabbi Meir (if it is indeed his), a kind of democratization of the approach of royal theology is implied – although in this case not to every human being as such but to one who "engages in Torah for its own sake."

The models for the shaping of monarchy available to the sages were, on the one hand, direct theocracy and, on the other, the limited understanding of monarchy of the Book of Deuteronomy. The sages preferred the latter model as it was consistent with their own view regarding the need for a strong and stable rule. One may also link to this argument the fact that the sages' interpretation of the divine image in Genesis 1 reduces the idea of man's domination (every man's!) over the world, connected in Genesis in a clear way with the idea of the creation in the divine image.

In Talmudic literature, emphasis is placed on the connection between the idea of the divine image and the multiplication of the human race, whereas in post-biblical Jewish literature – that is to say, in that Jewish literature that preceded the tannaitic – the situation is reversed: this literature does not relate extensively to the idea of creation in the divine image nor to the idea of propagation of the species, but, in contrast, emphasizes the mastery of man over creation.[75] It would appear that by

---

73   See D. Flusser and S. Safrai, "The Essenes' Doctrine of Hypostasis and Rabbi Meir," *Immanuel,* 14 (1982): 47–57.

74   See *Genesis Rabbah* 94 (ed. Theodore-Albeck, p. 1183): "Rabbi Akiva said in the name of Rabbi Judah bar Simon: Whoever is arrogant towards the king is as if he were arrogant towards a sage." I thank Dr. Vered Noam for drawing my attention to this saying.

75   This view is consistent with the tendency of the tannaim to diminish the idea of the universal political rule of Israel to the future, eschatological age. As Yaakov Blidstein has shown, this tendency tends to focus on describing political attainments in a more modest way: the end of subjugation to other nations and

diminishing the idea of human domination over the cosmos in Talmudic literature – specifically against the background of the ascent of creation in the divine image in this same literature – it emphasizes the importance and vitality that the sages attached to a strong and stable political order.

the restoration of sovereignty to the people of Israel dwelling in its land. Blidstein demonstrates that, in the tannaitic approach, the concept of redemption is completely lacking in the belief in the universal rule intended for the people of Israel. "The belief in the value of man as such," writes Blidstein, "is not easily compatible with an approach that sees the subjugation of [other] people as a component in the vision of redemption." See G. J. Blidstein, "Hast Thou Chosen Us to Rule? The Political Dimension of Israel's Election in the Sages' Literature" (in Hebrew), in S. Almog and M. Heyd (eds.), *Chosen People, Elect Nation and Universal Mission* (Jerusalem, 1991), pp. 99–120; at p. 119. In this context I should note that this point also reflects the distance between the tannaim's limited conception of kingship and royal theology, as one of the fundaments of royal theology is the all-inclusive rule of the king over the world. This motif also refers to the kings of Israel in the Bible, in those sources that reflect the idea of the king-god. See, for example, Ben Sira 17:1–12; Jubilees 2:14; and cf. Lorberbaum, *Image of God,* Chapter 8.1; J. Cohen, *"Be Fertile and Increase, Fill the Earth and Master It": The Ancient and Medieval Career of a Biblical Text* (Ithaca, NY, 1989), pp. 68–76.

FIVE

Echoes of Direct Theocracy and of Royal
Theology in the Aggadah

In the previous chapters of this book I have demonstrated that Talmudic
halakhah – as it appears in the Mishnah, the Tosefta, and in the Talmudic
discussions – adopts the approach of limited monarchy. I noted the
reasons for the adoption of this model and other contexts within which
this approach was integrated. I showed that the adoption of the model
of limited monarchy involved the rejection (at times explicit, at times
implicit) of the other two models; however, these models – direct theocracy
and royal theology – did not disappear from Talmudic literature. They
are alluded to, at times explicitly, in the Midrash and in other sources
already discussed above, and they are clearly expressed in the sources to
be discussed below.

In the previous chapter, I brought various sources emphasizing the
need for centralized rule in order to assure law and order. But one may
also find among the sages those sources that express an approach opposed
to monarchy and call for anarchy and, at times, for direct theocracy.
These sources, all of which are taken from the aggadah, express the
opposite approach to that emerging from the halakhic sources. Thus,
in *Deuteronomy Rabbah* one finds a series of midrashim reflecting this
mood:

1. "When you come into the land ..." [Leviticus 25:2]. The Rabbis
   said: Thus said the Holy One blessed be He to Israel: "My sons,
   thus I thought that you would be free from kingship, as is said, "a
   wild ass used to the wilderness" [Jeremiah 2:24]. Just as the wild
   ass grows up in the desert and has no fear of kings, so did I think
   that fear of kingship would not be upon you. But you did not
   think thus; rather, "in her heat sniffing the wind" [Jeremiah 2:24].
   And the wind refers to none other than kingship. From whence?
   As is said, "and behold, the four winds of heaven were stirring up
   the Great Sea" [Daniel 7:2]. The Holy One blessed be He said: If
   You think that I do not know that in the end you will abandon Me,
   know that I was already warned through Moses and said to him: as
   they shall ultimately seek a king of flesh and blood, let them take
   to reign a king from among themselves and not a foreign king.
   From whence? From what we have read regarding this matter,
   "and you shall say, 'I will put a king upon me,' etc."

2. Another word. "And you shall say, I will put a king upon me.'" Concerning this it is written, "that a godless man should not reign, that he should not ensnare the people" [Job 34:30]. R. Yohanan and Resh Lakish [interpreted this]. R. Yohanan said: If you have seen a godless and evil person who is the leader of the generation, it is better for that generation that they jump in the air and not make use of him. And this phrase, "that he should not ensnare the people" refers to naught but flying, as is said, "Does a bird fall in a snare on the earth when there is no trap for it?" [Amos 3:5].

3. Another word. "That a godless man should not reign" [Job 34:30]. Our Rabbis said: Once there were kings over Israel they began to subjugate them. The Holy One blessed be He said: Is it not you who abandoned Me and sought a king? That is, "I shall put a king upon me."

4. Another word, "I shall put a king over me." Concerning this it is written: "Put not your trust in nobles" [Psalms 146:3]. R. Simon said in the name of R. Joshua ben Levi: Whoever trusts in the Holy One blessed be He merits to be like Him, as is said, "Blessed is the man who trusts in the Lord" [Jeremiah 17:7]. But whoever trusts in idols shall be like them, as is said, "Those who make them shall be like them" [Psalms 115:8].

5. The Rabbis said: Whoever relies upon transient flesh and blood, even his *prostaya* [i.e. protector] is destroyed, as is said: "in a son of man, in whom there is no help" [Psalms 146:3]. What is written thereafter: "When his breath departs he returns to his earth" [Psalms 146:4]. The Holy One blessed be He said: And they know that flesh and blood is naught, and they leave aside My honor and say: "put a king over us." Why do you seek a king? By your lives, in the end you shall feel what happens to you beneath the hand of your king, as is said, "All their kings have fallen, and none of them calls upon Me" [Hosea 7:7].

6. Another word. "I shall put a king upon myself." Our Rabbis said: The Holy One blessed be He said: In this world you sought kings, and kings rose up and killed you by the sword. Saul caused them to fall at Mt. Gilboa, as is said, "and the men of Israel fled before the Philistines, and fell slain on Mount Gilboa" [1 Samuel 31:1]. David placed a plague among them, as is said: "So the Lord sent a pestilence upon Israel" [2 Samuel 24:15]. Ahab caused the rains to stop for them, as is said: "there shall be neither dew nor rain" [1 Kings 17:1]. Zedekiah caused the Temple to be destroyed. Once they saw what befell them from the hands of their kings,

they began to cry out: We do not want a king, we want our first king, as it is said, "for the Lord is our judge, the Lord is our lawgiver, the Lord is our king; He will save us" [Isaiah 33:22]. The Holy One blessed be He said to them: Thus shall I do. From whence? As is said, "And the Lord will be king over all the earth" [Zechariah 14:9].[1]

All these midrashim rely upon the language of the Bible in Deuteronomy, whose subject is Israel's initiative to establish a monarchy: "I shall place a king upon myself." Nearly all of the above passages express reservations about royal rule, against which they propose a decentralized political system in which the Holy One blessed be He rules directly over Israel – a kind of direct theocracy. These midrashim assemble a wide variety of arguments against royal rule and, in practice, against the establishment of any political system in which power and authority are given to mortal human beings. Like the biblical sources cited from Judges and Samuel, these passages express the view that human monarchy or political authority is tantamount to worshipping idols.

Section (1) in the extract above compares Israel to a "wild ass used to the wilderness," to an *arod* (a particular species of wild donkey) that "is not subject to the fear of kingship." God thought that Israel would be free of monarchy and the fear that it imposes. It would appear that this author's intention was that Israel would be run without any central government and would enjoy a direct connection to God; however, according to the spirit of this midrash, even God would not fulfill the function of a king, as He is not represented in the midrash as a substitute for "the fear of kingship." The form of rule implied by this midrash is an anarchic one, without any fear; however, Israel did not adjust to this political "framework" and did not agree to such "freedom" or "liberty" and, as an expression of their "flight from freedom," they sought a king. In the spirit of Samuel's words, the author represents the request for a king as an abandonment of God and even connects Israel's request with a longing to serve idols. This connection follows, among other things, from the condition that Israel may not place upon themselves a foreign king – a condition that implies the identification of monarchy with an alien cult. The opposition between this midrash and the sources discussed above (in Chapters 2.1–2 and 4.1) regarding the subject of monarchy is

---

1   *Deuteronomy Rabbah Shoftim* (ed. Lieberman, pp. 98–100; the division into numbered sections is mine). Compare *Deuteronomy Rabbah* (ed. Vilna), where the text is somewhat different, but not significantly so for our purposes.

evident: the above sources emphasize the need for a regime that imposes fear while the author here negates this need and even sees in the fear of flesh and blood a tendency toward idolatry. To use the terms of Isaiah Berlin, it would appear that this midrash connects the service of God with the optimal extension of negative freedom, specifically.

The midrash in Section (2) does not take exception to monarchy in a principled manner but merely warns against wicked and corrupt kings. However, the following homily, Section (3), identifies rulership in general and monarchy in particular with subjugation. As opposed to the view expressed above, and in the spirit of the midrash in Section (1), here too one finds a clear reservation regarding monarchy and the subjugation and oppression it represents. It would appear that this midrash also advocates an anarchic regime.

The midrash in Section (4) is seemingly unconnected to the political realm or to the issue of kingship, connected rather to the quality of human trust in God. According to R. Simon (in the name of R. Yehoshua ben Levi), the difference between one who serves the Almighty and one who serves idols is rooted in their belief in the power of the object of their worship. The expression, "Whoever trusts in the Holy One blessed be He" refers to one who fulfills the mitzvot because of his faith in God's power and His ability to help him at every moment, against which "whoever trusts in idols" is one who serves out of the belief that idols hold the power to help him in times of trouble and distress. "Whoever trusts in the Holy One blessed be He shall merit to be like Him" – that is, one who believes in God and serves Him enjoys His protection, and his sense of self-security is like the confidence that God has, who places His protection over him.[2] In contrast, one who places his trust in idols is lacking in protection, as the object of his faith and his worship is in vain and is empty or, in the language of the prophet Jeremiah, "and they went after worthlessness and became worthless" (Jeremiah 2:5).[3]

However, the context within which this midrash is incorporated, and the fact that it revolves around the verses, "I shall put a king on me" and "Put not your trust in nobles" also gives it a political meaning: the "idolatry" spoken of here is none other than the king of flesh and blood.

2   The term כיוצא בו ("similarly") in this midrash does not necessarily indicate a similarity between the Creator and the human beings who believe in Him, as it does in other places in the Midrash. See, for example, *Sifra, Behukotai* 3 (ed. Weiss, p. 111b); and the text proposed by S. Leiberman, *Sheki'in*, 2nd edn (Jerusalem, 1992), p. 14; and cf. Y. Lorberbaum, *The Image of God: Halakhah and Aggadah* (in Hebrew) (Jerusalem, 2004), Afterword.
3   Cf. 2 Kings 17:15.

As in the previous midrashim in this grouping, this midrash likewise expresses reservations regarding royal rule and, in practice, regarding human rule in general. According to this conjecture, this midrash, more than being concerned with the opposition between the sacred service of God and the service of idols, is concerned with the opposition between God's power and the nullity of a human leader, whose nothingness is like the nothingness of idols. Even if there is no explicit advocacy of direct theocracy in this midrash, it reflects a lack of trust in the ability of the political framework to provide man with security. Similar to this midrash is the following passage from *Midrash Taana'im* to Deuteronomy:

> "And I besought the Lord" [Deuteronomy 3:23]. R. Meir said: Once Israel knew that the Holy One blessed be He had said to Moses, "The time has come for you to depart this world," all of Israel gathered around him and said to him, "Our teacher Moses! When you were among us we all enjoyed it and thrust our burden upon you. Now, who shall stand up for us after you, and who will close our breaches, and to whom do you leave us?"
>
> He answered him and said: "Put not your trust in nobles" (Psalms 146:3). Before a person places his trust in flesh and blood and beseeches him to save him, let him first save himself from death. You should have no trust except in He who spoke and created the world, blessed be He, who lives and endures forever, as is said, "Trust in the Lord forever" (Isaiah 26:4). And it says, "Trust in Him at all times" (Psalms 62:9). Whether you are sinful or whether you are meritorious, "pour out your heart before him" (Psalms 62:9) in repentance.
>
> Immediately Israel answered him and said, "God is our shelter, Selah" (Psalms 62:9).[4]

While this midrash does not explicitly mention the subject of monarchy, it is nevertheless clear that its subject is the failure of mortal leaders. Because of his special relationship to God, Moses' leadership is understood by this midrash as the direct rule by God over His people. The proper replacement for Moses' leadership after his death is not another prophet like him – for "There has not arisen a prophet in Israel like Moses" (Deuteronomy 34:10) – but, rather, the leadership of He who spoke and the world came into being – i.e. of God Himself, Who in practice had led the people even during the lifetime of the prophet. However, even

---

4   *Midrash Tanna'im le-Devarim, Vaethanan*, 3.23 (ed. Hoffman, pp. 14–15).

here it is not direct and everyday rule being discussed but a solution for occasional crises, and only after Israel has poured out its heart before God. In other words, this midrash implies a lack of government – that is, a kind of anarchy.

Similar to the midrash in Section (4) and the above passage from *Midrash Tana'im,* in Section (5), the rabbis also criticize one who sets aside the honor of God and relies upon flesh and blood "who cannot save." One who relies upon human beings, the rabbis say, "his *prostaya* passes over" – that is, he has no protection.[5] According to these sages, man is a transient creature, and therefore the end of the mortal king is to fall and to fail.

The last passage, Section (6), expresses a similar outlook. To recall, according to the Book of Samuel, the elders of Israel sought a king who would "go out before us and fight our battles" (1 Samuel 8:20); however, against this request the sages state that his end will inevitably be one of defeat and failure. Those kings who ruled over Israel – Saul, David, Ahab, and Zedekiah – embarked on wars resulting in destruction, ruination, and death. According to this midrash, the failures of the kings necessarily follow from the military ethos rooted in the institution of the monarchy. Following this series of harsh failures, Israel will cry out and seek "our first king" – God Himself – and in the future He will answer them and reign over them directly. Analogous to this midrash is the following passage, from *Midrash Psalms*:

> "In You, O Lord, I seek refuge; may I never be put to shame" (Psalms 31:1). Thus is it said in Scripture: "Israel is saved by the Lord with everlasting salvation; you shall not be put to shame or confounded" (Isaiah 45:17) …
>
> Israel said before the Holy One blessed be He: Did you not already redeem us through Moses, and through Joshua, and through judges and kings? And yet now we are once again enslaved, and we are ashamed as if we had never been redeemed.
>
> The Holy One blessed be He answered them: Because your redemption was by means of flesh and blood, and your leaders were human beings, who today are here and tomorrow in the grave, therefore your redemption was a transient redemption. But in the future [I Myself shall redeem you]. And as I live and endure, I shall redeem you with a permanent and eternal redemption, as

---

5   *Prostaya* refers to protection over a person; see *Deuteronomy Rabbah* (ed. Lieberman, p. 99, n. 1).

is said, "Israel is saved by the Lord with everlasting salvation"
(Isaiah 45:17).[6]

This series of midrashim, which the editor of *Deuteronomy Rabbah* placed
adjacent to the verse that opens the Chapter of the King in Deuteronomy
– "I shall put a king upon me" – presents a sequence of arguments
against the institution of monarchy: that the human ideal is freedom,
meaning a life free of subjugation and particularly political subjugation;
that kings by nature are crooked and evil, and therefore oppress and
subjugate people; that one cannot rely upon a king of flesh and blood,
who is a transient, mortal creature; that the military ethos of monarchy
leads to death and destruction. Thus, this series of midrashim as a
whole expresses a viewpoint opposed to that of the Mishnah and the
other halakhic sources. If we relate to the former as the establishment
position of Talmudic literature, then this collection constitutes a kind of
subversive voice within the Talmudic literature.[7]

All of these passages are taken from those midrashic collections edited
fairly lately. Their late date may be felt, of course, from their language
and terminology. It is possible that the outlooks following from them are
also late; however, it may also be that they are simply late formulations of
earlier positions, which were widespread among the sages and competed
with those outlooks implicit in the earliest Talmudic sources, such as the
Mishnah, the halakhic tannaitic midrashim, and the *beraitot* found in the
Tosefta and in the two Talmuds.[8]

---

6   *Midrash Tehillim*, 31 (ed. Buber, p. 119a).

7   Close to this midrashic series is the version recited in the blessing of *Malkhuyot*
on Rosh Ha-Shanah: "to establish [or to correct] the world in the kingdom of
the Almighty, so that and all flesh shall call upon Your Name ... for the Kingship
is Yours, and forever You will rule in glory." Scholars think that this version was
fixed in the second century, that it expresses an anticipation of the coming
of the Kingdom of Heaven, and that it may express a protest against the cult
of the emperor. See Y. Heinemann, *Prayer in the Period of the Tanna'im and the
Amora'im* (in Hebrew) (Jerusalem, 1964), pp. 62, 173–174; M. D. Herr, "Roman
Rule in Tannaitic Literature (Its Image and Valuation)" (in Hebrew), doctoral
dissertation, Hebrew University of Jerusalem, 1970, p. 143. On the text of this
blessing, see Herr, "Roman Rule," n. 52. It is nevertheless difficult to determine
whether this prayer and other similar sayings (see, for example, *Sifrei Devarim*,
323 [ed. Finkelstein, p. 372]), which pose against one another the Kingdom of
Heaven and a kingdom of flesh and blood, indeed reflect a political approach
that rejects earthly rule – even of an Israelite king – preferring a direct theocracy,
or whether they merely express a commitment towards Heaven.

8   *Genesis Rabbah* 42 (ed. Theodor and Albeck, p. 419): "'At the Valley of Shaveh, that

Not only those sources calling for anarchic rule – that is, for direct theocracy – appear in aggadic literature. This literature also includes sources expressing a viewpoint related to royal theology. Thus, for example, in the statement of R. Yudan found in *Genesis Rabbah* – "Whoever behaves arrogantly towards the king, is as if he behaved arrogantly towards the *Shekhinah*"[9] – or in the following midrash:

1. "This month shall be for you" [Exodus 12:2]. Of this it is written, "The righteous shall flourish in his day and there will be much peace as far as the moon" (Psalms 72:7). Before the Holy One blessed be He took Israel out of Egypt, He hinted to them that the kingship would not come to them until thirty generations, as is said, "This month shall be for you the first of the months" (Exodus 12:2). The month is thirty days, and your kingship shall be for thirty generations. The moon begins to shine on the first of Nissan, and shines more and more until the fifteenth day, when its disk is full; and from the fifteenth day until the thirtieth day its light diminishes, and on the thirtieth it is not visible.

2. Thus Israel: there were fifteen generations from Abraham until Solomon. Abraham began to shine in the world, as it is said, "Who is this who shines from the east? Righteousness calls him at his feet" (Isaiah 41:2). Isaac came and shone, as is said, "light is sown for the righteous" (Psalms 97:11). Jacob came and added light, as is said, "and the light of Israel shall be like fire" (Isaiah 10:17). And thereafter came Judah, Peretz, Hezron, Ram, Aminadav, Nahshon, Boaz, Obed, Yishai and David. Once Solomon came, the disk of the moon was filled, as it is said, "And he placed Solomon upon the throne of the Lord as King" (1 Chronicles 29:23).

3. Is it possible for a man to sit upon the throne of the Holy One blessed be He, of whom it is said, "His throne was fiery flames" (Daniel 7:9)? Rather, just as the Holy One blessed be He rules from one end of the world to the other and rules over all the kings, as is said, "all the kings of the earth shall praise You, O Lord" (Psalms 138:4), so did Solomon's [reign] from one end of

is, the King's Valley' [Genesis 14:17]. R. Berachiah and R. Helbo in the name of R. Shmuel bar-Nahman said: That there all the nations were made equal, and they said to Abraham: Be king over us. He said to them: Let not the world lack its king and its God." Here too, in a passage taken from an extremely early midrash, there is implicit a view which sees the establishment of the king as a kind of separation from God, even if formulated in a more moderate manner.

9   *Genesis Rabbah* 94 (ed. Theodor and Albeck, p. 1183).

the earth to the other, as is said, "All the kings of the earth sought the presence of Solomon" (2 Chronicles 9:23); "Every one of them brought his gift" (2 Chronicles 9:23). Therefore it is said, "And Solomon sat upon the throne of the Lord as king." The Holy One blessed be He is clothed in glory and splendor and gives Solomon the glory of his kingship, as is said, "And He bestowed upon him royal majesty" (1 Chronicles 29:25). Concerning the throne of the Holy One blessed be He it is written, "As for the likeness of their faces, each had the face of a man, the face of a lion ..." (Ezekiel 1:10), and regarding Solomon it is written, "And on the panels that were set in the frames were lions, oxen and cherubim" (1 Kings 7:29), and another verse says, "they were made like the wheels of the Chariot" (1 Kings 7:33). No evil thing can touch the throne of the Holy One blessed be He, as is said, "Evil shall not dwell with you" (Psalms 5:5), and regarding Solomon it is written, "there is neither adversary nor misfortune" (1 Kings 5:18). The Holy One blessed be He made six heavens and he dwells in the seventh; and concerning the throne of Solomon it is written, "six steps to the throne" (1 Kings 10:19), and he sits upon the seventh step.

4. Behold, the disk of the moon was filled; and from there on in the kings progressively declined (1 Chronicles 3:10–16): Solomon's son Rehoboam, and Rehoboam's son Aviah, and his son Assa, Jehoshaphat, Jehoram, Ahaziahu, Joash, Amaziah, Uziah, Jotam, Ahaz, Hezekiah, Manasseh, Josiah, Jehoiakim. Once Zedekiah came, as is said, "And the eyes of Zedekiah were put out" (Jeremiah 39:7) – lacking in the light of the moon.

5. And all those years, even though Israel were sinning, the Patriarchs prayed on their behalf and made peace between Israel and the Omnipresent, as is said: "Let the mountains bear peace for the people" (Psalms 72:3), and the "hills" are none other than the Patriarchs, as is said: "Hear, O hills, the quarrel of the Lord" (Micah 6:2). And till when did the patriarchs pray on their behalf? Until Zedekiah lost his eyes and the Temple was destroyed, as is said, "and peace abound, till the moon be no more" (Psalms 72:7) – until thirty generations that Israel had kingship. From that hour until now, who makes peace on behalf of Israel? The Lord, as is said: "May the Lord lift up his face to you and give you peace" (Numbers 6:26).[10]

---

10   *Exodus Rabbah* 15.26 (ed. Vilna, pp. 31a–b; the division into numbered sections is mine).

This midrash too is evidently late. It is not attributed to any particular sage, and it may have been composed close to the time of editing of *Exodus Rabbah* in the Middle Ages.[11] Even though there is no proof that it represents an opinion that was widespread among the sages, it may echo earlier views that were pushed to the margins. The approach implied in this midrash regarding kingship contradicts the view that emerges from the earlier Talmudic sources discussed above, while also opposing the approach found in the later midrashim, brought above at the beginning of this chapter (i.e. from *Deuteronomy Rabbah, Midrash Tanna'im* to *Devarim,* and *Midrash Psalms*).

This midrash connects the myth of the waxing and waning of the moon with the establishment of monarchy in Israel.[12] This connection is also found in another Talmudic source: according to those things attributed to R. Judah the Prince, the renewal of the lunar month is marked by the proclamation, "David king of Israel lives and endures."[13] The author in *Exodus Rabbah* draws a parallel (and possibly also a causal relationship) between the cyclicity of the moon and the historical continuity of the development of monarchy in Israel. This development is embodied in the institution of the monarchy, and it attained its height in a king whose status, qualities, and power are described by terms taken from royal theology.[14]

The thirty days of the month are compared to thirty generations, the status of each generation measured by the status of the king who reigns therein. Just as the moon becomes progressively fuller from the

11   On *Exodus Rabbah* and its various parts, see L. Zunz, *Ha-Derashot be-Yisrael* (*Sermons in Judaism*) (in Hebrew), edited and completed by H. Albeck (Jerusalem, 1974) from the German: *Die Gottesdienstlichen Vortrage Der Juden Historisch Entwickelt,* p. 124; and see Albeck's comments on p. 125; and cf. the Introduction by A. Shinan to his edition of *Midrash Exodus Rabbah, Chapters 1–14* (Jerusalem, 1984), pp. 11–32. Our midrash belongs to what is known in research literature as *Exodus Rabbah II* (i.e. Chapters 15–52), which begins with the *petihtot* to Exodus 12:2, and which appears to be is earlier than *Exodus Rabbah* I (Chapters 1–14).

12   On the waxing and waning of the moon, see *Babylonian Hullin* 60b.

13   *Babylonian Rosh Hashana* 25a: "R. Hiyya saw that the moon was in the north on the twenty-ninth of the month, and send out a declaration: In the evening we need to sanctify it, and you are seen thus?! Go and cover yourself. Rabbi said to R. Hiyya: Go with a good eye and sanctify the moon, and he sent a sign: David king of Israel lives and endures." And cf. E. E. Urbach, *The Sages: Their Concepts and Beliefs* (in Hebrew) (Jerusalem, 1969), vol. I, pp. 678–679.

14   This source is also related to the messianic approach of R. Judah the Prince; see below, Chapter 6, n. 34. Here the messianic approach draws upon royal theology.

time of the New Moon, so from the beginning of the establishment of the monarchy and through the generations the king becomes progressively stronger and more powerful. On the fifteenth day of the month, the moon is at its fullest. Parallel to this, in the fifteenth generation, the generation of Solomon, monarchy reached its peak. From this point on, just as the moon gradually diminishes, so too does the status, moral level, and power of the kings gradually diminish until the thirtieth generation. Just as on the thirtieth day of the month the moon "becomes darkened" (i.e. disappears), so too "the king's eyes are darkened" and destruction and exile ensue. It would seem that, like the natural cyclicity of the moon, so, too, Israelite history is cyclical. The broad biblical plot – from the time of Abraham (the establishment of the people) until that of Zedekiah (Destruction of the Temple and the Babylonian Exile) – depicts a single historical cycle, which is perhaps instructive for what shall follow.

For our purposes, the reign of Solomon – the height of the biblical cycle – is emblematic of all the cycles in general. His reign is described in terms of royal theology: Solomon sits upon the throne of the Almighty (a motif we have already encountered in the passages from *Midrash Tanna'im* discussed earlier); he rules from one end of the world to the other; God's glory emanates upon him; and he is given gifts just like God.[15]

If we strip this midrash of its fantastical elements and separate it from its cyclical, mythical-cosmic foundations, it indeed encapsulates biblical history. In the final analysis, the approach regarding a divine king, or at the very least a sacral king, is described in the Bible as developing and strengthening until reaching the height of its splendor; from that point on, it declines and becomes gradually dimmer and diminished. One cannot compare the sacral monarchy of Saul with that of David, nor can the sacral status of David be compared with the quasi-divine standing of Solomon.[16]

---

15 *Hod* ("glory") is a widespread image used for describing God in Mesopotamian literature. Glory is what God emanates upon the king, which is His image and likeness. See M. Weinfeld, "God the Creator in Gen. I and in the Prophecy of Second Isaiah" (in Hebrew), *Tarbiz*, 37 (1967): 105–132; pp. 131–132. On the connection between glory and leadership, and between both and the light of the sun and of the moon, see *Babylonian Bava Batra* 75a: "Similarly you say, 'And you shall invest your glory [or: authority] upon him' (Numbers 27:20) – [of Your glory,] but not all Your glory. The elders of that generation said: The face of Moses was like the face of the sun; the face of Joshua was like the face of the moon."

16 We may also connect to these midrashim later midrashim that describe Moses in terms of a divine king. Thus, for example, *Pesikta de-Rav Kahana*, Addenda, Chapter 1 (ed. Mandelbaum, vol. II, p. 443): "'[Moses] the man of God' (Deuteronomy 33:1): a man – when he ascended on high; of God – when he descended below. 'When Aaron and all the people of Israel saw Moses [behold, the skin of his face

From the time of Solomon on, the Bible presents the history of a declining monarchy. In this respect, the biblical model of royal theology (even if

shone]' (Exodus 34:30)." Similarly in *Tanhuma, Va'era* 7 (ed. Buber, p. 11b): "Another thing. 'Who is this King of Glory?' [Psalms 24:10] Who is this king who shared His glory with those that fear him? 'The Lord of Hosts.' How so? A king of flesh and blood, one does not sit upon his throne; but the Holy One blessed be He placed Solomon upon his throne, as is said, 'and Solomon sat upon the throne of the Lord' (1 Chronicles 29:23). A king of flesh and blood, one does not ride upon his steed, but the Holy One blessed be He placed Elijah upon His steed. And what is the steed of the Holy One blessed be He? Storm and whirlwind, as is said, 'His way is in whirlwind and storm' (Nahum 1:3). A king of flesh and blood, one does not make use of his scepter, but Moses made use of the scepter of the Holy One blessed be He, as is said, 'And Moses took the rod of God in his hand' (Exodus 4:20). A king of flesh and blood, one does not wear his crown, but the Holy One blessed be He placed crowns upon the head of King Messiah, as is said, 'You set a crown of fine gold upon his head' (Psalms 21:4). A king of flesh and blood, one does not wear his garments. But Israel wore the garments of the Holy One blessed be He, which is glory (*oz*) as is said, 'Awake, awake, put on strength, O right arm of the Lord' (Isaiah 51:9). And he gave it to Israel, as is said, 'The Lord will give strength to His people,' etc. (Psalms 29:11). A king of flesh and blood, one does not call by his name, like Augustus, Caesar, Basilius; and if a man were to be called by one of these names, he would not live. You should know that a man calls his friend, Augustus so-and-so. But the Holy One blessed be He said to Moses: 'I have made you like Myself to Pharaoh. I am called God, and with that name I created the world, as is said, 'In the beginning God created the heavens and the earth' (Genesis 1:1). And I have made you, like Myself, a god to Pharaoh, as is said, 'See, I make you as God to Pharaoh' (Exodus 7:1) This is: 'Who is this king of glory' Who gave of His glory to those who fear Him." A parallel to this midrash in *Exodus Rabbah* is discussed above (near note 10); and cf. *Deuteronomy Rabbah* 11.3 (ed. Vilna, p. 118d): "'And this is the blessing' (Deuteronomy 33:1). This is what Scripture said: 'Many women have done valiantly, but you surpass them all' (Proverbs 31:29). What is meant by, 'you surpass them all'? This refers to Moses, who ascended more than any others. How so? Adam said to Moses: I am greater than you, for I was created in the image of the Holy One blessed be He. From whence? From what is said: 'And God created man in His image' (Genesis 1:27). Moses said to him: I ascended more than you. That honor which was given you was taken away from you, as is said, 'man cannot abide in honor' (Psalms 49:13). But I, the radiance of the face which was given me by the Holy One blessed be He, is with me. From whence? As is said, 'His eye was not dim, nor was his vigor abated' (Deuteronomy 34:7)." It would appear that the qualities attributed to Moses in these sources connect his special relationship to God with his political status as a leader. It should also be noted that in the latter midrash, the 'light of the face' is a substitute for the image of the original Adam. See W. Meeks, "Moses as God and King," in J. Neusner (ed.), *Religions in Antiquity* (Leiden, 1970), pp. 354–371.

it is essentially one of sacred monarchy) is not static, but dynamic. The midrash thus presents us with an interesting and possibly original version of royal theology, according to which one is speaking of a monarchy that develops and becomes stronger and thereafter declines and disintegrates.

There would thus seem to be a clear opposition between this midrash and that of Resh Lakish in *Babylonian Sanhedrin*, discussed above in Chapter 4.1. Resh Lakish criticizes the "hubris" embedded in royal theology, the most striking representative of which in the biblical Jewish tradition is Solomon. This midrash, in contrast, sees that model of kingship as the theological, political ideal towards which the historical process is striving, from which one progressively descends, only to ascend once again.

The midrashim cited in this chapter reflect the tension in Talmudic literature between the various divergent understandings of the monarchy and by extension of the ideal political order. Scholars have observed a certain tension, and even opposition, that exists at times between halakhah and aggadah.[17] It is nevertheless important to emphasize that the opposition presented here is not necessarily between halakhah and aggadah as literary genres; it is not between the ethical-religious plane and the halakhic-practical plane, nor between the ideational-conceptual plane and the earthly-concrete plane.[18] Rather, it is an opposition between different viewpoints regarding the monarchy and political organization. The one, which supports the approach of limited monarchy, emerges from the halakhic sources and is found in aggadic sources as well; the others, those of direct theocracy and of royal theology, emerge from aggadic material that have no halakhic applications in the Talmudic sources known to us. It may be that the latter outlooks had no halakhic applications because they were adopted by sages who were "aggadic teachers" alone, who did not even distinguish that their opinions were opposed to that view implied in the halakhic sources. Or, these approaches may reflect voices in the Talmudic literature that were reluctant to openly confront the established halakhah and therefore refrained from giving their views a halakhic expression. The latter approach seems more plausible if these were indeed late voices – of amoraim or preachers from a later period.

---

17   See Y. Frankel, "The Halakhah in Aggadic Narratives" (in Hebrew), in J. Sussman and D. Rosenthal (eds.), *Talmudic Studies* (Jerusalem, 1990), pp. 205–215; S. Safrai, "The Attitude of the Aggada to the Halacha" (in Hebrew), in A. Kasher and A. Oppenheimer (eds.), *Dor Le-Dor: From the End of Biblical Times Up to the Redaction of the Talmud – Studies in Honor of Joshua Efron* (Jerusalem, 1995), pp. 215–234.

18   Frankel and Safrai discuss this contrast in the studies mentioned in the previous note.

SIX

The Sages' Understanding of Monarchy in
Light of Their Own Political Situation

It is commonly thought that a text of a political nature – even one that
is theoretical and abstract – cannot be isolated from the sociopolitical
context within which it was written. Indeed, there are those who assert
that this holds true with regard to any text, not only political; be that as it
may, in the present context I shall limit myself to the assertion regarding
the context of a theoretical text with political subject matter. According
to this view, we cannot read the political theory in Plato's *Republic* without
some familiarity with the political milieu of fourth-century BCE Athens and
Plato's own place within that reality; likewise, a proper understanding of
Aristotle's political writings, including those laws that he proposed, requires
knowledge of the political context within which Aristotle presented his own
teaching to his students. The same holds true, if not more so, with regard
to Machiavelli's *The Prince,* which cannot be detached from the tumultuous
political circumstances in which its author was involved, or with regard to
Thomas Hobbes' *Leviathan* or Spinoza's *Theological-Political Tractate,* which
were similarly written under unstable political circumstances in which
their authors played an inseparable part.

It would appear that the Mishnah, the halakhic midrashim, and
the other Talmudic sources dealing with the subject of the king are
no exceptions to this rule. In the final analysis, the brief body of laws
appearing in *Mishnah Sanhedrin* and in parallel sources is a political text.
The Mishnah, with all of its orders and tractates, is not a theoretical but
a normative text (whose exact nature remains to be fully clarified) that
includes political components: its discussion of kingship is doubtless
one of them. My purpose in this book has been, among other things, to
uncover the political approach and principles underlying the handful
of laws in the Mishnah and in other Talmudic sources concerning the
subject of the king. Thus far, our discussion has been conducted to a large
extent in isolation from the sociopolitical context within which the sages
found themselves and has deliberately ignored the question: Do the laws
and decisions regarding monarchy, its status and prerogatives, reflect the
political longings and interests of the sages themselves as individuals, who
were not detached from the political reality of their time and place?

The sages did not live in an ivory tower; they had to deal with
different groups and elements in both Jewish and Gentile society of
their day. It is therefore interesting, and perhaps essential, to examine

their political views and the political principles embodied within their halakhic decisions against the background of these confrontations and conflicts. But before turning to present a number of thoughts on this question, I wish to articulate two interrelated reservations pertaining to the depiction of a broader picture of the sages' political outlook.

First, it is impossible to discuss the sociopolitical context of the sages' concept of the king without first undertaking an abstract explication of the concept of monarchy as implied by the laws of the king in Talmudic literature. Such a prior clarification was necessary, for if we had begun our examination of the political approach of the sages directly with its historical and sociopolitical context we would have found ourselves within a kind of hermeneutic closed circle, in which the context would have dictated the political approach, without that approach being examined in its own right and without fully clarifying the nature of that influence. The discussion presented thus far is therefore of great and independent value, even without discussing the sociopolitical context.

Second, as I understand it, the context and circumstances (social, political, economic, cultural, and others) alone do not dictate – certainly not in the strong (i.e. deterministic) sense – the decisions of human beings. In the final analysis, different individuals react in different ways to similar circumstances (or even to the same circumstance). In other words, as important as the explanatory power of "influences" may be, it is nevertheless only partial. Even if we take into account the totality of "influences" to which the spirit is exposed, in the final analysis the decisions and choices of human beings – including the fruits of their imagination and of their intellectual creativity – are the result of their free spirit (in the libertarian sense). I therefore believe that the study of "influences" is of only limited importance in understanding phenomena within the world of consciousness and thought, including political thinking.

We shall now return to the sages' political approaches and their historical context. What are the sociopolitical circumstances under which the sages acted and created? Who were the rivals, against whom their political approach was shaped?[1] The answers to these questions are subject to debate among historians. Until the last generation, the widespread approach among historians of the period of the Mishnah and

---

1   One must not confuse this question with the issue of the "significant other" of the sages in other contexts – for example, in theological polemics. Here it is possible to imagine many groups which are discussed in the research, such as Christians, Gnostics, pagans, and other sectarians. It seems to me that these groups are not significant to the present discussion, which is concerned with political rivals.

Talmud – particularly in wake of Gedaliah Alon – was that the sages, i.e. the tannaim, were the spiritual and political leaders of the Jewish people in Palestine (and possibly also throughout the Jewish Diaspora) following the destruction of the Temple and throughout the first centuries CE.[2] However, in recent decades, a number of scholars have questioned this approach; more than a few historians (particularly Americans) have negated this "Rabbinocentric" approach and have asserted that the tannaim were not the leaders of the Jewish community (or communities) in Palestine as a whole but, at most, led a certain community or social group, which was only one segment of the Jewish population of Palestine.[3] There are even those who assert that "The rabbis were but a small part of Jewish society, an insular group which produced an insular literature."[4]

Another topic subject to controversy among the historians – directly connected to the previous one – relates to the question of the political structure of Jewish society in Palestine following the Temple's destruction. Gedaliah Alon claims that the Jewish settlement during this period was led by two institutions: the *nasi*, or prince, and the Sanhedrin. According to this dual structure, the *nasi* was the only leader, his task passing from father to son (the dynasty traced itself back to Hillel the Elder and to the Davidic monarchic house).[5] The Sanhedrin, in addition to being a theoretical academic institution (*Bet Midrash*), was also a legislative body

2   See G. Alon, *History of the Jews in Palestine* (Tel Aviv, 1953), vol. I, pp. 101–193; and in his wake many others. Cf. H. Shapira, "The Court in Yavneh: Status, Authority and Functions" (in Hebrew), in Y. Habba and A. Radzyner (eds.), *Studies in Jewish Law: Judge and Judging* (Ramat-Gan, 2007), pp. 305–334. I thank Dr. Haim Shapira for making this article available to me prior to publication. The following description of the state of research is based upon his article.

3   See Lee I. Levine, *The Stature of the Sages in Palestine in the Talmudic Period* (in Hebrew) (Jerusalem, 1986), pp. 85–89, 130–132; S. J. Cohen, "The Rabbi in Second Century Jewish Society," in W. Horbury, W. E. Davies, and J. Sturdy (eds.), *The Cambridge History of Judaism III: The Early Roman Period* (Cambridge, 1999), p. 975; R. Kalman, *The Sage in Jewish Society in Late Antiquity* (London and New York, 1999); and cf. M. Goodman, *State and Society in Roman Galilee*, AD *132–212* (Totowa, NJ, 1983). For a survey of this dispute, see I. Gafni, "'A Generation of Scholarship on Eretz Israel in the Talmudic Era: Achievement and Reconsideration" (in Hebrew), *Cathedra,* 100 (2001): 199–226; and see also S. Schwartz, "Historiography of the Jews in the Talmudic Period (70–640)," in M. Goodman et al. (eds.), *The Oxford Handbook of Jewish Studies* (Oxford, 2002), pp. 79–114.

4   See Cohen, "The Rabbi in Second Century Jewish Society," p. 975.

5   *Palestinian Ta'anit* 4.2 (68a); *Genesis Rabbah* 98.8 (ed. Theodor and Albeck, 1259). On this attribution, see L. I. Levine, "The Period of R. Judah Ha-Nasi" (in Hebrew),

and the highest court, which decided on matters of jurisprudence and law brought before it.[6]

This approach, adopted by the majority of those historians who were Alon's contemporaries, was challenged in the mid-1980s by Lee I. Levine, who argued that, at least subsequent to the Bar Kokhba Revolt (132–135 CE), the Sanhedrin did not exist at all and that thereafter (perhaps as part of its results), the Jewish community was led by the *nasi* alone.[7] The *Bet ha-Midrash* or *Bet Ha-Vaad* where the sages gathered did not bear any judiciary or legislative authority; these prerogatives were in the hands of the *nasi*. Levine bases his claim on the Talmudic sources, where he finds no indication of the Sanhedrin's existence following the Bar Kokhba Rebellion. These sources indicate the existence of study institutions alone.[8]

Against Levine's claim – that the Sanhedrin did not exist following the Bar Kokhba Revolt – David Goodblatt argues that it ceased to exist already during the period of Yavneh. Goodblatt's historical thesis is extensive and all-encompassing: the leadership of the Jewish community during the Second Temple period and that of the Mishnah and the Talmud was based upon the monarchic principle, and throughout this lengthy period Jewish society was led by a single leader: during the period of the Temple, a king or high priest; and after the Destruction, the *nasi*.[9] According to Goodblatt, the monarchic principle was dominant during Yavneh period as well. There was no Sanhedrin then nor any other [central] judicial institution, and the *nasi* alone led the Jewish

in Z. Baras, S. Safrai, Y. Zafrir, and M. Stern (eds.), *Eretz Yisrael from the Destruction of the Second Temple until the Muslim Conquest*, vol. I: *Political, Social and Cultural History* (Jerusalem, 1982), at p. 117; and see the references and bibliography there, n. 120.

6   Alon, *History of the Jews*, pp. 136, 195.

7   Levine does not take a stand regarding the existence of the Sanhedrin during the Yavneh period.

8   Levine, *Stature of the Sages*, pp. 47–52.

9   This thesis is connected with Goodblatt's claim regarding the lack of separation between the kingship and the priesthood during the Second Temple period. See above, Chapter 2.6, and the notes there. It should be mentioned that during the Second Temple period Jewish society was led by priests (Simon, Yohanan, Judah) who refrained from assuming the royal crown. The first priest-leader to attribute to himself the title of king (evidently under Hellenistic influence) was Judah Aristobulus. The combination of these two offices reached its peak in the days of Yannai. See above, Chapter 2, n. 119, and the references to the writings of Josephus, *Jewish Antiquities*, trans. R. Marcus et al., 9 vols., Cambridge, Mass., 1963, n. 129.

community.[10] An advisory council may have operated alongside him, but it was not independent. The yeshivas and the *Beit ha-Vaad* of the sages, mentioned in the Talmudic sources, were academic institutions without any sociopolitical standing.[11]

As mentioned, the issue of the political structure of Jewish society – centering around the question of the existence, power, and authority of the Sanhedrin – has been discussed by scholars in relation to the status of the sages in Palestinian Jewish society following the Destruction. The reason for this is quite clear: the sages were identified with the High Court, the Sanhedrin, and the existence and extent of authority of this institution bore direct implications on the question of their own sociopolitical standards. It is no coincidence that Gedaliah Alon – who portrayed the sages as the leaders of the people – argued for the existence of an (authoritative) Sanhedrin in those days, whereas Levine and Goodblatt – who downplayed the image of the sages as political leaders – negated the existence (and, *ipso facto,* the authority) of this institution in their day. It is nevertheless important to note that it is possible (and perhaps even desirable) to separate these two questions, as the sages may have fulfilled a leadership function even if the Sanhedrin did not exist in their day, and even if their leadership was given no formal expression in the sources.[12]

Who then was the political rival of the sages? In light of the brief survey presented here, one may suggest several mutually exclusive answers to this question. According to Gedaliah Alon and those of his school, it would appear that the political rivals of the sages did not come from within Jewish society, which willingly accepted their authority and that

10   In the wake of other scholars, Goodblatt thinks that even during the time of the Temple the Sanhedrin did not exist as a political institution with autonomous authority, operating in an established manner over a period of time. See D. Goodblatt, *The Monarchic Principle: Studies in Jewish Self-Government in Antiquity* (Tübingen, 1994), pp. 77–130, and his summary there, pp. 128–130; and cf. J. Efron, "The Great Sanhedrin in Vision and Reality," in his *Studies in the Hasmonean Period* (Leiden, 1987), pp. 238–287; and cf. E. R. Sanders, *Judaism, Practice and Belief, 63* BCE*–66* CE (Philadelphia, Pa., 1992), pp. 472–488.

11   See Goodblatt, *The Monarchic Principle.* For a critique of his approach, see Shapira, "The Court in Yavneh."

12   Levine writes as follows: "The sages as a group enjoyed recognition as spiritual figures in Israelite society but did not have any official political standing ... In order to fully evaluate the communal activity of the sages and the source of their political–social authority within the Israelite society, one needs to examine the task of the *Nasi* in this respect and the relation of the sages to the institution of the *Nasi.*" See Levine, *The Stature of the Sages,* p. 89.

of the *nasi*. Even though one may conjecture that the sages had certain rivals from within (see below), it is reasonable to assume that their main opponents came from without. The first factor that comes to mind is, of course, Rome, which the sages refer to as "the evil kingdom." According to this suggestion, the sages' political approach implied confrontation and struggle with the Roman system of rule and with the emperor who stood at its head. Indeed, the Roman emperorship may be considered the "significant other" in each of the descriptions surveyed above regarding the political structure of Jewish society during the first centuries CE. In the final analysis, the Roman Empire was *the* political power throughout the geographical region in which the sages were active. Any political theory or structure of thought created during this period and within this region cannot ignore the Roman Empire, nor the nature of the rule that it embodied. Nevertheless, according to Alon's approach, reducing the importance of internal rivals further intensifies the importance of the external rival.

Alon thought that the sages had another internal rival as well: namely, the *nasi*. There is no reason to assume that friendly relations always prevailed between the *nasi* and the sages.[13] The Talmudic sources themselves testify to the tension between them – as, for example, in the story of the deposition of Rabban Gamaliel.[14] According to Goodblatt's thesis, the *nasi* was the rival of the sages. In light of the plausible assumption that the sages did not fully accept his single-handed rule, one must read the tannaitic sources regarding the king (and especially his limitations) against the background of the political status of the *nasi*. I will elaborate upon this point presently.

But these are not all of the possible options. If we adopt the extreme view according to which the sages were a marginal group in Jewish society, they may have had other political rivals among the leaders of the communities in Palestine, who were not subject to the sages or to the

---

13   See R. Kimelman, "R. Yohanan and the Status of the Rabbinate" (in Hebrew), *Shenaton ha-Mishpat ha-Ivri*, 9–10 (1982–1983): 329–358.

14   *Palestinian Berakhot* 4.1 (7d); *Babylonian Berakhot* 27b–28a; and cf. H. Shapira, "The Deposition of Rabban Gamaliel: Between History and Legend" (in Hebrew), *Zion*, 64 (1999): 5–38. Shapira shows that the reliable historical basis of this story is the outbreak against Rabban Gamaliel and the interruption of the yeshiva. However, the story of his removal from the office of *nasi* is a literary legend without historical basis. In any event, this story indicates the real tension between the sages and the *nasi*. On the relations between the sages and the *nasi* in the third century CE, see Levine, *Stature of the Sages*, pp. 90–109.

way of life that they attempted to impose.[15] This possibility exists even
if we adopt a more moderate view, according to which the sages were
the leaders of a certain segment of the Jewish public, possibly even of
a significant portion thereof, but not of all of it. Rivalry with the urban
aristocracy, with the oligarchic class that did not submit to the authority of
the sages, may even have existed according to historians such as Levine,
who support an intermediate position, according to which the sages
enjoyed a certain position of leadership within Jewish society – though
not an exclusive one, and generally speaking not in official positions.
In this context one must also take into account the tension and rivalry
that evidently existed between the sages and the priestly families, who
were apparently the outstanding oligarchy within Jewish society, not only
during the Second Temple period but even after its destruction.[16]

I do not have the tools to decide among the different theories
regarding the status of the sages in Jewish society in Palestine after the
destruction during the first two centuries CE. In what follows I shall present
several thoughts relating to the different descriptions proposed by the
historians (at least their majority). Most of these claims have already been
mentioned in the above discussion; however, their examination within
the historical context proposed here may shed fresh light upon them.

As already hinted above, it is clear that the sages identified
themselves, among all the sources of authority in the political structure
proposed in *Mishnah Sanhedrin* (and in parallel tannaitic sources), with
the Sanhedrin. The relationship between the sages and the Sanhedrin
is called for because of the close connection to the halakhic tradition
– of the sages, on the one hand, and of the Sanhedrin (as depicted by
the sages) on the other. As far as we know, this relationship did not exist
during that same period between other social groups and the Sanhedrin
– at least insofar as that body is described by the sages. In other words,
had the Sanhedrin been established during that same period, almost
certainly (again, according to the sages' view) its members would have

---

15 We learn of these social groups, among other things, from archeological findings
    and from sources that are not part of rabbinic literature such as *Sefer ha-Razim* and
    the various parts of the Hekhalot literature. It is also possible to infer information
    from the Talmudic literature itself: see Levine, *Stature of the Sages*, p. 65 n. 3; see
    also pp. 65–89, and especially his discussion of the *Am ha-aretz*, pp. 75–79.

16 See Alon, *History of the Jews*, p. 14; and especially R. Kimelman, "The Conflict
    Between the Priestly Oligarchy and the Sages During the Talmudic Period (An
    Explication of *Jerusalem Shabbat* 12.3 [13c]=*Horayot* 3 [48c])" (in Hebrew), *Zion*,
    48 (1983): 135–147.

been numbered among the sages, as they alone had the training and knowledge required for this task.

It therefore follows, from numerous tannaitic sources, that the sages saw themselves as potential members of the Sanhedrin. Thus, for example, at the end of Chapter 1 of Tractate *Makkot:* "R. Tarfon and R. Akiva said: Had we been in the Sanhedrin, no person would ever have been executed." Everyone agrees that the Sanhedrin did not exist at the time of R. Tarfon and R. Akiva; hence, the phrase "had we been in the Sanhedrin" does not express frustration that the Sanhedrin was dominated by another social group and that the sages had no place therein; rather, the language of the Mishnah makes it clear that the institution did not exist at that time. This wording also implies that, had the Sanhedrin been in existence, "we" (i.e. R. Tarfon and R. Akiva) would have been members thereof, and that then, when discussing capital cases, "no person would ever have been executed."[17] Moreover, in the Mishnah and the *Tosefta* the Sanhedrin is described as if organized along the lines of the study house of the sages. Thus, in *Tosefta Sanhedrin* we read the following:

> The Sanhedrin sat in a semi-circle [half of a threshing floor] so that they could see one another. The *Nasi* sat in the center and the elders sat to his right and his left.
>
> R. Eleazar b. Zaddok said: When Rabban Gamaliel sat in Yavneh, father and another person sat at his right and the elders at his left. And for what reason does one sit with an elder at his right? Because of the honor of the elder.
>
> Three rows of sages sat before them: the greatest ones[18] in the first row, those of second [rank] in the second row, and those of third [rank] in the third. From there on there was no protocol, but whoever preceded his fellow within four ells got to sit [first].[19]

Louis Ginsberg and J. N. Epstein conjectured that the order of seating in the Sanhedrin as described here reflects the order of seating in the Palestinian *Bet Midrash* or yeshivot.[20] Haim Shapira, who studied the

---

17 On the substance of this claim, see Y. Lorberbaum, *The Image of God: Halakhah and Aggadah* (Jerusalem, 2004), Chapter 7.

18 Thus in MS. Vienna and in MS Arfort: הגדול.

19 *Tosefta Sanhedrin* 8.1–2 (ed. Zuckermandel, p. 427); and compare *Mishnah Sanhedrin* 4.3–4. The reading has been corrected at the suggestion of H. Shapira, "Beit ha-Midrash (The House of Study) During the Late Second Temple Period and the Age of the Mishnah: Institutional and Ideological Aspects" (in Hebrew), doctoral dissertation, Hebrew University of Jerusalem, 2002, p. 184.

20 L. Ginsberg, *Perushim ve-Hiddushim be-Yerushalmi*, 4 vols. (New York, 1941–1961),

institutional and ideational contents of the *Bet Midrash* at the end of the Second Temple period and during the Mishnaic period, questions this conjecture, asking, is the description of the Sanhedrin in the *Tosefta* (and in the Mishnah) a reliable description, by whose inspiration the sages determined the order of seating in their own institutions – or does it perhaps have no historical basis, rather only reflecting the order of seating in the rabbinic *Bet Midrash* after the destruction?[21] Whatever the answer to this question, one cannot deny that these sources indicate a profound relationship, if not total identification, between the sages and the institution of the Sanhedrin – whether the post-destruction *Bet Midrash* was modeled after the Sanhedrin, or whether (and perhaps even more so!) the description given here is fictitious.[22] In either case, the manner of seating in the Study House is, according to tannaitic sources, based on the model of the Sanhedrin. Due to these considerations and these sources (of which there are numerous examples in Talmudic literature), the assumption that the sages had a close relationship to the Sanhedrin is common to all of those descriptions proposed by historians regarding the Sanhedrin and the status of sages in Jewish society in the Land of Israel.

If we examine the structure of political thought expressed in the tannaitic sources in light of these assumptions, based on a perception of the sages as political people struggling for their status and power, and for the implementation (both in the life of the individual and the community) of the world view and way of life in which they believed, then the following points emerge: first, it is interesting to note that the dominant opinion among the sages was that the appointment of a king was a mitzvah; second, the self-consciousness of the sages as potential members of the Sanhedrin indicates, on the one hand, those prerogatives from which they detached themselves and, on the other, the tasks that they appropriate for themselves. The sages did not explicitly see themselves as leaders, nor did they see the king as coming from among their ranks, as the

---

vol. III, p. 189; J. N. Epstein, *Studies in Talmudic Literature and Semitic Languages* (in Hebrew), ed. E. Z. Melamed (Jerusalem, 1984), vol. I, p. 129; Shapira, "The Study House."

21 Shapira, "The Study House," pp. 184–192. The Sanhedrin depicted here is evidently that of seventy-one and not of twenty-three members. See Shapira's discussion, p. 187.

22 This assertion is correct even if there are a number of differences between the pattern of the Bet Midrash and the nature of the seating in the Sanhedrin, as testified by the sages themselves. See, for example, the words of R. Eleazar b. R. Zaddok in the above *Tosefta* passage; and see Shapira, "The Study House."

king is not a sage. The functions that they appropriate for themselves are, rather, the operation of the judicial system, legislation, and supervision of the activities of the king, even regarding those matters that explicitly fall under the aegis of his authority – namely, foreign relations and security. Before turning to a more detailed discussion of these points, I shall note here that they are interesting and significant in terms of all, or at least the majority, of the historical descriptions proposed above.

Regarding the first point – that the majority of the sages thought that the appointment of the king was a mitzvah – we saw in the above discussion that this position is far from the literal meaning of the text. To recall, the central normative Torah text regarding this matter – namely, the Chapter of the King in the Book of Deuteronomy – only states that it is permitted to appoint a king, not that one is obligated to do so. Moreover, the impression gained from the Torah is that the appointment of a king is a kind of necessary evil and that a system without a king would be preferable.[23] From the viewpoint of Scripture, hence, there was no normative pressure on the sages to state an obligation to establish a monarchic system. Hence, the position of the sages was based, among other things, on a conservative approach regarding the need for a strong and stable central regime that would impose law and order. For this reason, they even extended the authority of the king relative to the limitations placed on him in Deuteronomy. This conclusion is interesting, specifically, because the sages did not see themselves as fulfilling royal functions. As we stated, the sages identified themselves with the Sanhedrin – and it was clear that the king did not come from their ranks. The direct and everyday handling of the ongoing running of matters of society and state were therefore given over by the sages to a different political authority.[24]

It is quite possible that this approach reflects the sages' acceptance or reconciliation with the authority of the *nasi* (and possibly even the acceptance of his status from the outset). As I noted earlier, most historians think that the institution of the *nasi* was the senior (some think the only) political office in Jewish society at the time of the sages and that from a certain point in time onwards the *nasi* was also recognized by the Roman authorities. There are those who think that the Romans already

---

23   See above, Chapter 1.3 and 2.1.
24   It would appear that this approach was the dominant one among the tannaim. A real change may have occurred in the days of the amora R. Yohanan. Reuven Kimelman thinks that R. Yohanan attempted to create a rabbinic type who would be similar to the Roman jurist (*juris prudens*). See Kimelman, "Rabbi Yohanan and the Status of the Rabbinate," especially p. 339.

acknowledged the political authority of the *nasi* during the period of Rabban Gamaliel in Yavneh, while others date the Roman recognition later, to the time of R. Judah the Prince.[25] Historians likewise disagree regarding the question of when use was first made of the term *nasi*: was it already current during the period of the Temple and throughout the period of the Mishnah, or only thereafter?[26] For our purposes, the issue of the use of this title is of secondary importance, as it would appear that even if Rabban Gamaliel (for example) was not called *nasi*, he was the recognized political leader of the Jewish community in Palestine and was in many respects a political rival of the sages and therefore a focus of their attention.

At least in the linguistic sense, the sages identified the *nasi* with the monarchy. Thus, for example, in *Mishnah Horayot* 3.3: "Who is the *Nasi*? He is the king, as is said, 'doing any one of all the things which the Lord his God has commanded' (Leviticus 4:22). The *Nasi* – who has none above him except for the Lord his God." And in *Tosefta Horayot* 2.2: "Who is the *Nasi*? The prince of Israel, and not the prince of [one of] the tribes."[27] Maimonides summarizes these laws as follows:

25 Gedaliah Alon thinks that Rabban Gamaliel was recognized as *nasi* by the Roman government; see Alon, *History of the Jews,* pp. 71–78. David Goodblatt thinks that he was even appointed by the Romans: see David Goodblatt, "The Origins of Roman Recognition of the Palestinian Patriarchate" (in Hebrew), *Studies in the History of the Jewish People and the Land of Israel* (in Hebrew) (Haifa, 1978), vol. IV, pp. 89–102. Cf. Levine, "The Period of R. Judah Ha-Nasi," pp. 102–104. As against that, Martin Goodman thinks that Rabban Gamaliel did not enjoy any sort of recognition on the part of the Roman government; see Goodman, *State and Society,* pp. 111–118.

26 See H. Mantel, *Studies in the History of the Sanhedrin* (Hebrew) (Tel Aviv, 1961), pp. 3–63. Mantel thinks that the use of this title was early. In contrast, Goodblatt thinks that Rabban Gamaliel was not referred to as *nasi* and that the title only came into use after the Second Rebellion; see David Goodblatt, "The Title '*Nasi*' and the Ideological Background of the Second Revolt" (in Hebrew), in A. Oppenheim and U. Rappaport, *The Bar-Kokhva Revolt: A New Approach* (Jerusalem, 1984), pp. 113–132. For further bibliography on this matter, see Shapira, "The Deposition of Rabban Gamaliel," p. 5, n. 1.

27 *Tosefta Horayot* 2.2 (ed. Zuckermandel, p. 475). It should be noted that the identity between the title *nasi* and the king already appears in the book of Ezekiel. "And my servant, David, shall be prince (*Nasi*) among them" (Ezekiel 34:24); "And David my servant shall be their prince (*Nasi*) forever" (Ezekiel 37:25). See Goodblatt, "The Title of *Nasi*," p. 116. Goodblatt argues there that there is no echo of these verses in rabbinic literature.

> Who is the *Nasi* referred to in the Torah? This is the king, who
> is not subject to the authority of any person in Israel, and above
> him there is naught in his kingdom save the Lord his God – this,
> whether he was from the Davidic house or from any of the other
> tribes of Israel. And if there were numerous kings, and none of
> them is subordinate to his fellow, each one of them brings a goat
> for [in the event of] inadvertent transgression.[28]

It should be noted that, according to Maimonides, the king is one "who
is not subject to the authority of any person in Israel," and, as G. J.
Blidstein emphasizes, an Israelite leader would be considered, according
to Maimonides, as the "king of Israel" even if he is subjected to foreign
political forces; his status as a king is rooted in his dominion over his
brethren.[29] Evidently, Maimonides had in mind the Israelite kings of the
Second Temple period and possibly also the princes during the period
following the destruction, who were subject to the Roman emperor. It
seems to me that even though the Mishnah is rather vague on this point,
Maimonides' words express his intentions.

The Babylonian tradition (*Babylonian Horayot* 11b) relates that, when
R. Judah Ha-Nasi was deliberating the question whether the laws relating to
the goat brought as an offering to atone for an inadvertent transgression of
the *nasi* (Leviticus 4:22–26) applied to himself, he addressed this question
to R. Hiyya, who answered him in the negative.[30] The *sugya* records two
versions of the answer given by R. Hiyya. In one version, R. Judah Ha-Nasi
did not enjoy the status of *nasi* with regard to bringing a sacrifice because
he was not the highest political authority: he was subordinate to the
Exilarch, and, as mentioned, the *nasi* "has no one above him except for the
Lord his God." According to the other version brought in the *sugya*, Rabbi
was not a *nasi* for purposes of the sacrifice because, unlike the Exilarch in
Babylon, he had no coercive power over others ("staff") but only legislative
or instructional power ("lawmaker").[31]

---

28   Rambam, *Hilkhot Shegagot* 15.6; and see G. J. Blidstein, *Political Concepts in
     Maimonidean Halakha* (in Hebrew) (Ramat-Gan, 2001), p. 38.

29   See Blidstein, *Political Principles*.

30   See n. 34 below.

31   See *Babylonian Horayot* 11b: "Rabbi asked Rabbi Hiyya: One such as myself, what
     would be my standing with regard to the goat [i.e. would I be required to bring a
     sacrificial goat in the event of error]? He said to him: Behold, you have a rival in
     Babylonia [i.e. the Exilarch, who is your equal in stature]. He answered him: the
     kings of Israel and the Davidic kings, these bring for themselves and these bring

This issue raises a number of historical questions regarding the subjugation of the *nasi* in the Land of Israel (during the period of Rabbi) to the Exilarch in Babylon. There are those who think that it is late and does not reflect the balance of political power between R. Judah Ha-Nasi and the Exilarch.[32] I will not discuss this question here but will simply comment that, if there is any historical truth to this tradition in *Babylonian Horhayot,* it reflects the sages' uncertainty regarding the political stature of the *nasi* in relation to the status of the king. But even though the question raised in this *sugya* is one of halakhic-academic interest – and is without any practical significance, as the Temple was already destroyed – it nevertheless alludes to political contexts. It is clear that Rabbi's question is not an innocent one; he implies therein his wish to be considered as a *nasi*-king.[33] Moreover, it follows from the Talmudic sources that there were those who related to R. Judah ha-Nasi as a messiah and that this was likewise his own self-understanding.[34] R. Hiyya denies his status as king, and it would seem that, beneath the surface of the discussion in this *sugya* (in both versions), presented as an halakhic-academic discussion, lies great political tension between the *nasi* and the sages.

for themselves. He said to him: In their case, neither of them was subjugated to the other. But here – we are subject to them. Rav Safra taught as follows. Rabbi asked Rabbi Hiyya: One such as myself, what would be my standing with regard to the goat? He answered him: There, *shevet* [i.e. a scepter – that is, there was rule that has authority], here, *mehokek* [i.e. a law maker; that is, you have no real power]. And they taught, 'The scepter (*shevet*) shall not depart from Judah' [Genesis 49:10] – this refers to the Exilarch in Babylonia, who rules over Israel with a scepter, 'nor the ruler's staff (*mehokek)* from between his feet' – these are the descendants of Hillel who teach Torah to Israel in public." And cf. *Babylonian Sanhedrin* 5a, where a *beraita* appears on the verse "the scepter shall not depart" followed by an anonymous discussion, from which it also follows that the Land of Israel is subjugated to the Exilarch in Babylonia. And cf. *Genesis Rabbah* 97 (ed. Theodor and Albeck, p. 1219). On the *sugya* in *Babylonian Horayot,* see O. Meir, *Rabbi Judah the Patriarch: Palestinian and Babylonian Portraits of a Leader* (in Hebrew) (Tel Aviv, 1999), pp. 30–31; and on the entire subject see Goodblatt, *The Monarchic Principle,* pp. 157–160.

32   For a survey of the various opinions, see Goodblatt, *The Monarchic Principle;* Levine, "The Period of Rabbi Judah Ha-Nasi." On the halakhic implications of this statement, see, for example, Maimonides, *Mishnah Commentary, Bekhorot* 4.4 (ed. Kapah, pp. 161–163).

33   Meir, *Rabbi Judah the Patriarch,* p. 91.

34   See, for example, *Palestinian Shabbat* 16.1 (15c): "Rabbi and R. Hiyya Rabbah and R. Ishmael and R. Yossi were sitting and expounding the Scroll of Lamentations on the eve of Tisha b'Av which fell on the Sabbath from the afternoon on. And there

But whatever the exact status of the *nasi* might be, it is clear that, even if this political office was not precisely in the image of the monarchy, it was understood at the time, both by the public and by the sages, as a political office of the highest order. In light of all this, the political view implied by the discussion in *Mishnah Sanhedrin* of the power and authority relations between the king and the Sanhedrin would also seem to reflect the tension between the sages and the house of the *nasi*. Indeed, historians have noted the rise and fall in the status of the *nasi* in relation to the sages. Thus, for example, Reuven Kimelman has noted a consistent polemic between R. Yochanan and Resh Lakish regarding the status of the house of the *nasi* in relation to that of the sages.[35]

If our assumption is correct, the picture that emerges from *Mishnah Sanhedrin* regarding the king implies that, while the sages left the everyday governing of the people to the *nasi*, they assumed extensive authority, particularly in relation to the legal system and to decisions in halakhic matters. In this context I should note that, as editor of the Mishnah, R. Judah ha-Nasi played down the image of the king and specifically

remained one alphabet [i.e. one chapter – i.e. to study]. They said, 'Tomorrow we shall come and finish it.' As Rabbi was returning to his home, he stumbled and hurt his finger and said of himself, 'Many are the pangs of the wicked' [Psalms 32:10]. Rabbi Hiyya said to him: It is on our account that this befell you, as is said, 'The breath of our nostrils, the Lord's anointed, was taken because of our corruption' [Lamentations 4:20]." And cf. *Babylonian Rosh Hashana* 25a, where R. Hiyya states that he had sanctified the new moon as an agent of Rabbi Judah and said in relation to him: "David, king of Israel lives and endures." Rabbi's self-image as redeemer and messiah follows likewise from the following passage in *Palestinian Ta'anit* 4.7 (69b): "Rabbi sought to uproot [i.e. abolish] Tisha b'Av and was not allowed to do so"; cf. *Babylonian Megillah* 5a. R. Judah's wish to abolish the fast of Tisha b'Av was evidently based on the view that in his time Israel would be redeemed and he would be the redeemer. See E. E. Urbach, *The Sages: Their Concepts and Beliefs* (Jerusalem, 1969), vol. I, pp. 678–679; but cf. Levine, "The Period of Rabbi Judah Ha-Nasi," p. 117, where he states that R. Judah's desire to abolish the fast of Tisha b'Av was rooted in his intention to remove sources of tension between Jews and Romans. But Levine also thinks that Rabbi had messianic ambitions; see Levine, "The Period of Rabbi Judah Ha-Nasi." There are other scholars who think that this story has no historical basis and that one cannot infer from it that Rabbi considered himself the Messiah. See Y. Frankel, *The Ways of Aggadah and Midrash* (in Hebrew) (Givatayim, 1991), pp. 250–251; cf. Goodblatt, *The Monarchic Principle*, pp. 160–161, and further bibliography mentioned there; and see Meir, *Rabbi Judah the Patriarch*, pp. 77, 357–358 n. 20.

35   See Kimelman, "R. Yohanan and the Status of the Rabbinate" and "The Conflict Between the Priestly Oligarchy and the Sages."

emphasized the power of the sages. This finding is interesting in light of Lee Levine's claim that "R. Judah ha-Nasi did not know any competition or challenge to his leadership in the religious-spiritual realm (the dual functions of Head of the Court and *Hakham,* which existed prior to his time, had disappeared by his day)."[36] This distinction is sharpened in light of the fact that at the time of R. Judah the claim was first introduced that Hillel, whose offspring were R. Judah ha-Nasi and his father and sons, the *nesi'im,* traced his ancestry back to the Davidic line – a claim connected with Rabbi's self-image as Messiah.[37]

It is possible that the view of the appointment of the king as a mitzvah – a move that removed the sages from everyday leadership – also reflects their own ambivalent attitude towards political involvement: on the one hand, they are profoundly aware of the importance of such activity, as well as of its far-reaching implications; on the other hand, they do not attribute to political life as such any real value, certainly not on the transcendent level. Unlike the Greek political ideal, as explicitly embodied in Plato's *Republic* (and to a certain extent also in the ethical and political writings of Aristotle), and particularly as opposed to the Roman republicans, the sages do not see political activity as the supreme good incumbent upon the best members of society to realize. They do not think that the highest human ideal is for the sage to return to the cave and to lead the ignorant masses. The sages were of course involved in matters of state and society but, unlike the Platonic approach, do not perceive these matters as the pinnacle (or result) of their realization of the theoretical-contemplative ideal: i.e. the study of Torah.[38]

Thus, the sages left the leadership and management of the ongoing matters of the kingdom in the king's hands; however, in their view, the power of the king is itself limited, and the main source of the limitations placed on the king lies in the authority given to the Sanhedrin (that

36 See Levine, "The Period of Rabbi Judah the Prince," p. 115; for more on the relations between Rabbi and the sages, see pp. 115–118.

37 On the relating of Rabbi to the Davidic dynasty, see *Palestinian Ta'anit* 4.2 (68a); *Genesis Rabbah* 98.8 (ed. Theodor and Albeck, p. 1259); and see Levine, "The Period of Rabbi Judah Ha-Nasi." On Rabbi's self-understanding as Messiah, see n. 34 above.

38 *Sifrei Devarim* 41 (ed. Finkelstein, p. 85): "And Rabbi Tarfon and Rabbi Akiva and Rabbi Yossi the Galilean were sitting [...] in Lod. This question was asked before them: Which is greater: study or deeds? Rabbi Tarfon answered: Deeds are greater. Rabbi Akiva said: Study is greater. All of them answered together: Study is greater, for study leads to deeds." However, it seems that this dispute pertains to the relation between study and the performance of *mitzvot* and not to the relation between study and political activity.

is, to the sages themselves, according to their view). The Sanhedrin is responsible for the judicial system and, to a large extent, also serves as the legislative body, as it has the highest authority to interpret the Torah. The Sanhedrin is likewise charged with the administrative aspects of the judicial system (i.e. appointment of the "small" Sanhedrin of twenty-three, the expansion of the Temple courtyards and the limits of the city of Jerusalem, etc.), and it also oversees the king's policy in his conduct of foreign and security matters – at least with regard to waging optional wars. The sages do not assume any task in the area of cult and Temple; however, the king is also separated from these areas, under the aegis of the priests, headed by the High Priest.[39]

The political structure that emerges from the Mishnah may also be seen as a critique of the political-theological rule of the emperors. As mentioned earlier, imperial rule was based on the divinity of the emperor, his cult, and on that of his statues. Attribution of a divine dimension (exclusively) to the king is inconsistent with the democratization of the idea of creation of human beings in the divine image, which was adopted and developed by the sages.[40] The removal of any sacral dimension from the Israelite king implies the reservations held by the sages regarding the cult of the emperor and its political implications. Moreover, one may read the limitations on the king that appear in the Mishnah – particularly limitations on the part of the Sanhedrin – as a criticism of the centralized approach widespread in Rome, which placed unlimited political authority in the hands of the emperor without any restraining elements or political institutions to serve as a brake on his power and balance it.

In my opinion, *Tractate Sanhedrin* to a large degree challenges the assumption (or explanation) that the sages were a marginal group within Jewish society without any standing or position of leadership. In this tractate, the sages deal with the creation of a political system or the shaping of a regime that is not isolated from the social and political environment within which they lived. *Mishnah Sanhedrin* clearly involves a utopian dimension too, as it was created and written after the destruction of the Temple at a time when Israel did not enjoy political independence and all the institutions discussed in this tractate – the priesthood, the

---

39   This follows from the structure of the first chapters of *Tractate Sanhedrin*, which separate between the courts (including the Great Court, i.e. the Sanhedrin) and the high priest (beginning of Chapter 2) and the king (end of Chapter 2). Nevertheless, the sages also supervise the priesthood and the high priest; see, for example, *Mishnah Yoma*, Chapter 1.

40   See above, Chapter 4.2.

king, the Sanhedrin, and apparently also the lower courts – were not in fact operative.[41] This utopian dimension is reflected in the "capital laws" with which the main bulk of the tractate deals (from the middle of Chapter 4 until the end of the tractate, as well as its continuation in *Tosefta Makkot*).[42] It is nevertheless difficult to accept the assumption that such a work was the result of a marginal group that did not enjoy status or social standing and that was lacking in any leadership status. While the impression that emerges from *Tractate Sanhedrin* is of a utopian text, it is a utopia that implies the longing of its authors and of the halakhists – who had political authority and responsibility in actuality – for other times, in which these prerogatives would mature into real political institutions and political power. The assumption that *Tractate Sanhedrin* was created, authored and edited by a small, marginal, and eccentric social group, whose creation and activity were totally lacking any influence or echo within the public, requires us to assume that we are dealing with a text that is a wild and unrealistic fantasy of its authors.[43]

41   I tend to accept the position of those historians who think that the Sanhedrin did not exist following the Destruction of the Temple; even if a court existed that was staffed by the sages, its authority was greatly restricted in comparison to those of the Sanhedrin as depicted in *Tractate Sanhedrin* and they have nothing in common but the name. Shapira ("The Study House") noted that the term "Sanhedrin" is not used at all in reference to the court that acted (if indeed it did) in Yavneh.

42   On the utopian dimension of the capital laws in *Tractate Sanhedrin,* see Lorberbaum, *The Image of God,* Chapter 7.

43   This claim is to a large extent true also with regard to the Mishnah as a whole but is particularly striking (for obvious reasons) in relation to *Mishnah Sanhedrin.* See A. Schremer, "Seclusion and Exclusion: The Rhetoric of Separation in Qumranic and Tannaitic Literature," in S. J. Fraade, A. Shemesh, and R. A. Clements (eds.), *Rabbinic Perspectives: Rabbinic Literature and the Dead Sea Scrolls – Proceedings of the Eighth International Symposium of the Orient Center for the Study of the Dead Sea Scrolls and Associated Literature, January 7–9, 2003* (Leiden and Boston, Mass., 2006), pp. 127–145. Through comparison of the separatist discourse of the Qumran sect and the sectarian discourse of the sages, Schremer notes a fundamental literary difference: the members of the sect describe themselves as having separated themselves from the general community of Israel (thus, for example, in a famous passage in the scroll, *Mikzat Ma'aseh ha-Torah*), whereas the sages during the period of the tannaim and amoraim view themselves as having forcefully rejected the heretics or sectarians from the people of Israel. This distinction is based upon a simple principle, according to which the stronger party rejects the weak and deviant, whereas the weaker party separates and distinguishes itself from the stronger majority. Here, too, one may of course argue that the sectarian discourse of the sages is a kind of fantasy of political power that has no basis in reality.

While such a conclusion regarding the work of the sages is clearly not impossible, in the absence of concrete evidence to support this theory there is no reason to adopt it; indeed, *Tractate Sanhedrin* and the tone that emerges from it mitigate against adopting such a view. While it is impossible to conclude from this tractate exactly the political and social standing of the sages, and it is clearly impossible to conclude from it that the Sanhedrin operated during the period of the sages, or that they led Jewish society in any exclusive manner, nevertheless, this document may indicate to us that the sages, at least in their own self-understanding, were not a marginal group in Jewish society of their time and place. One cannot dismiss this consciousness of self when we set about to discuss the question of the status of the sages in Jewish society of their time, and particularly when dealing with their political views.[44]

And, indeed, there were those scholars who claimed that the sectarian discourse of the sages (like the discussion of heresy among the early Church fathers) was intended primarily to build the social power of the sages and to strengthen their standing as a political "center," and that therefore one ought not to attribute to it any descriptive dimension. In the view of these scholars, the sectarian discourse does not reflect a historical reality. See D. Boyarin, *Border Lines: The Partition of Judaeo-Christianity* (Philadelphia, Pa., 2003), pp. 50–51. Schremer rightly criticizes this view. In the absence of concrete historical evidence and findings, the claim of "building" – which removes any descriptive dimension from these texts – is no less "naive" and dogmatic than that reading that accepts the supposedly historical descriptions in the Mishnah and Talmud in a literal sense. So too regarding our subject: in the absence of any opposite evidence, the claim that one is only speaking here of an attempt of the sages to build their political power – for which reason one cannot derive any historical conclusion from these sources – seems to me dogmatic and ideologically tendentious and therefore unlikely. It is important to emphasize that it is not my intention to derive from *Mishnah Sanhedrin* any historical conclusion apart from the conjecture that the authors of this tractate were not a minor group that lived on the margins of Jewish society during the first centuries after the destruction.

44 In this context, one must take into account that, throughout the length of the Talmudic literature, the sober recognition by the sages of the political "weakness" of God (the "Jewish" God) as opposed to the power of Rome stands out. This idea is embodied, among other things, in the idea of the exile of the *Shekhinah*. See S. Spiegel, *The Fathers of Piyyut: Texts and Studies Toward a History of the Piyyut in Eretz Yisrael* (in Hebrew) (Jerusalem and New York, 1996), pp. 308–368.

Bibliography

Sources

Classic Rabbinic Sources

Mishnah
Shisha Sidrei Mishnah, with commentary and additional notes by H. Albeck, vocalized by H. Yalon, 6 vols., based on MS. Kaufmann A50 (Jerusalem, 1953).

Palestinian Talmud
Talmud Yerushalmi, according to MS. Or. 4720 (Scal. 3) of the Leiden University Library with Restorations and Corrections, ed. J. Sussmann, the Academy of the Hebrew Language (Jerusalem, 2001).

Babylonian Talmud
Talmud Bavli, 20 vols., standard editions.

Tosefta
Tosefta: Sedarim Zera'im, Mo'ed ve-Nashim, u-masekhtot Bava Kamma, Bava Metzi'a u-Bava Batra, ed. S. Lieberman (New York 1955–1988).
Other tractates, ed. M. S. Zuckermandel (Jerusalem, 1970) (Hebrew).
Cf. below: Lieberman, *Tosefta ke-feshuta.*

Tannaitic Midrashim

Midrash Tannaim
Midrash Tannaim 'al Sefer Devarim, ed. D. Z. Hoffmann (Berlin, 1908–1909).

Mekhilta de-Rabbi Ishmael
Mekhilta de-Rabbi Yishmael, ed. H. S. Horovitz and L. A. Rabin (Frankfurt, 1931).
Mekilta de-Rabbi Ishmael, ed. J. Lauterbach, 3 vols., with English translation (Philadelphia, Pa., 1949).

Mekhilta de-Rashbi
Mekhilta de-Rabbi Shimon bar Jochai, eds. J. N. Epstein and E. Z. Melamed (Jerusalem, 1955).

Sifra
Sifra de-Bei Rav, ed. A. M. Weiss (Vienna, 1862).

Sifrei Bamidbar
Sifrei al Sefer Bamidbar (Siphre ad numeros adjecto), ed. H. S. Horovitz (Leipzig, 1917).

Sifrei Devarim
Sifrei Devarim (Sifrei on Deuteronomy), ed. L. Finkelstein (New York, 1969). Cf. below, Kahana, *Sifrei Zuta le-Devarim.*

Sifrei Zuta
See below, "Studies": Kahana, *Sifrei Zuta le-Devarim.*

Other Midrashim

Avot de-Rabbi Nathan
Aboth De Rabbi Nathan, ed. S. Schechter (New York, 1967).

Deuteronomy Rabbah
Midrash Devarim Rabbah, ed. S. Lieberman, 3rd edition with additional notes and corrections (Jerusalem, 1974).

Exodus Rabbah
Midrash Shemot Rabbah, Chapters 1–14, ed. A. Shinan (Jerusalem and Tel Aviv, 1984).

Genesis Rabbah
Midrash Bereshit Rabbah, ed. J. Theodor and H. Albeck (Jerusalem, 1965).

Leviticus Rabbah
Midrash Vayiqra Rabbah, ed. M. Margulies (Jerusalem, 1953–1958) (Hebrew).

Midrash Hagadol
Midrash Haggadol on the Pentateuch: Genesis, ed. M. Margulies (Jerusalem, 1947). Exodus, ed. M. Margulies (Jerusalem, 1956). Leviticus, A. Steinsalz (Jerusalem, 1976). Numbers, Z. M. Rabinowitz (Jerusalem, 1967). Deuteronomy, S. Fisch (Jerusalem, 1972).

Midrash Psalms
Midrash Tehillim (Shoher Tov), ed. S. Buber (Vilna, 1895).

Midrash Shmuel
Midrash Samuela, ed. S. Buber (Vilna, 1925).

Midrash Tanhuma
Midrasch Tanchuma, ed. S. Buber (Vilna, 1885)

Midrash Teman
Midrash Teman, ed. S. Lieberman, 2nd edn (Jerusalem, 1992).

Pesikta de-Rav Kahana
Pesikta de-Rav Kahana, ed. B. Mandelbaum (New York, 1962).

Seder Eliyahu Zuta
Seder Eliyahu Zuta, ed. M. Friedman (Vienna, 1904).

Dead Sea Scrolls, Apocrypha and Pseudepigraphica and Related Literature

Book of Jubilees
Sefer ha-Yovlim, in *Ha-Sefarim ha-Hitzoni'im* (*The Apocrypha*), ed. A. Kahana (Jerusalem, 1970), vol. I, pp. 216–313.

Dead Sea Scrolls
Vermes, G., *The Complete Dead Sea Scrolls in English* (London, 1998).

Josephus' Antiquities
Josephus, *Jewish Antiquities,* trans. R. Marcus and H. St. J. Thackeray, 9 vols., Cambridge, Mass., 1963.

Philo
Philo of Alexandria Writings, ed. F. H. Colson and G. H. Whitaker, *The Works of Philo* (Cambridge, Mass. and London, 1929–1953).

The Temple Scroll
Megillat ha-Miqdash, ed. Y. Yadin (Jerusalem, 1977).
Megillat ha-Miqdash, ed. E. Qimron (Jerusalem, 1996).

Medieval Jewish Texts

Akedat Yitzhak
Yitzhak Arama, *Akedat Yitzhak, Vayikra* (Pressburg, 1849).

Maimonides' Guide for the Perplexed
Sefer Moreh Nevukhim le-Rabbenu Moshe ben Maimon, trans. Shmuel b. Yehudah Ibn Tibbon, ed. J. Ibn Shmuel (Jerusalem, 1982).

Maimonides' Mishnah Commentary
Mishnah 'im Perush Rabbenu Moshe ben Maimon, trans. J. Kapah (Jerusalem, 1965).

Maimonides' Mishneh Torah
Mishneh Torah, hi ha-Yad ha-Hazakah shel Rabbi Moshe Ben Maimon, standard editions (Hebrew).

Nahmanides' Torah Commentary
Perush ha-Ramban 'al ha-Torah (*Commentary on the Torah by R. Moshe b. Nahman*), ed. C. B. Chavel, 2 vols. (Jerusalem, 1962).

She'iltot

Sheiltot, ed. S. C. Mirsky, 5 vols. (Jerusalem, 1960–1977).

Studies

Albeck H., *Mavo la-Mishnah* (*Introduction to the Mishna*) (Jerusalem, 1979).

Alon, G., *Toldot ha-Yehudim be-Eretz Yisrael be-tequfat ha-Mishnah veha-Talmud* (*History of the Jews in Palestine*) (Tel Aviv, 1953).

——— *Mehqarim be-Toldot Yisrael* (*Studies in Jewish History: In the Time of the Second Temple the Mishna and the Talmud*), 2 vols. (Tel Aviv, 1967–1970).

Amit, Y., "The 'Men of Israel' and Gideon's Refusal to Reign" (in Hebrew), *Shenaton: An Annual for Biblical and Ancient Near Eastern Studies,* 11 (1997): 25–31.

——— *The Book of Judges: The Art of Editing* (Leiden, 1999).

Aptowitzer, V., "The Heavenly Temple in the Aggadah" (in Hebrew), *Tarbiz,* 2 (1931): 137–153, 257–287.

Atlas, S., "The King Does Not Judge and Is Not Judged" (in Hebrew), in his *Paths in Hebrew Law* (New York, 1970), pp. 156–206.

Bacher, B. Z., *Aggadot ha-Tannaim* (Berlin, 1922).

Barzilay, Y., "'The Law of the King' in the Temple Scroll: Its Original Characteristics and Later Redaction" (in Hebrew), *Tarbiz,* 72 (2003): 59–84.

Ben-Shalom, I., *Beit Shammai u-ma'avaq ha-Qana'im neged Romi* (*The School of Shammai and the Zealots' Struggle Against Rome*) (Jerusalem, 1993).

Berlin, I., "Two Concepts of Liberty," in his *Four Essays on Liberty* (Oxford, 1969), pp. 118–172.

Berman, H. J., *Law and Revolution: The Formation of the Western Legal Tradition* (Cambridge, Mass., 1983).

Biton, G., "On the Meaning of the Root *ml'k*" (in Hebrew), *Beit Miqra,* 96 (1984): 85–87.

Blidstein, G. J., "The Monarchic Imperative in Rabbinic Perspective," *AJS Review,* 7–8 (1982–1983): 15–39.

——— "'The Israeli Legal System as Viewed by Contemporary Halakhic Authorities" (in Hebrew), *Dinei Yisrael,* 13–14 (1986–1988): 21–42.

——— "Hast Thou Chosen Us to Rule? The Political Dimension of Israel's Election in the Sages' Literature" (in Hebrew), in S. Almog and M. Heyd (eds.), *Ra'ayon ha-Behirah be-Yisrael uva-'Amim* (*Chosen People Elect Nation and Universal Mission*) (Jerusalem, 1991), pp. 99–120.

———— *'Eqronot medini'in be-mishnat ha-Rambam* (*Political Concepts in Maimonidean Halakha*) (Ramat-Gan, 2001).

Boyarin, D., *Border Lines: The Partition of Judaeo-Christianity* (Philadelphia, Pa., 2003).

Buber, M., *The Kingship of God,* trans. R. Scheimann (New York, 1967).

Cogan, M. and Tadmor, H., *II Kings* (New York, 1988).

Cohen, J., *"Be Fertile and Increase, Fill the Earth and Master It": The Ancient and Medieval Career of a Biblical Text* (Ithaca, NY, 1989).

Cohen, S. A., *The Three Crowns: Structures of Communal Politics in Early Rabbinic Jewry* (Cambridge, 1990).

Cohen S. J., "The Rabbi in Second-Century Jewish Society," in W. Horbury, W. D. Davies, and J. Sturdy (eds.), *The Cambridge History of Judaism,* vol. III: *The Early Roman Period* (Cambridge, 1999), pp. 922–990.

Daube, D., *Ancient Hebrew Fables* (Oxford, 1973).

De Vaux, R., *Ancient Israel: Its Life and Institutions,* 2 vols. (London 1961).

Driver, S. R., *Deuteronomy* (Edinburgh, 1901).

Efron, J., *Studies in the Hasmonean Period* (Leiden, 1987).

Elat, M., *Shmuel ve-kinun ha-melukhah be-Yisrael* (*Samuel and the Foundation of Kingship in Ancient Israel*) (Jerusalem, 1998).

Elbaum, J. R., "Eleazar Hamodai and R. Joshua on the Amalek Pericope" (in Hebrew), in I. Ben-Ami and J. Dan J. (eds.), *Studies in Aggadah and Jewish Folklore,* 7 (1983): 99–116.

Eliade, M., *The Myth of the Eternal Return,* trans. W. R. Trask (New York, 1954).

———— "Hieros Gamos," in his *Encyclopedia of Religion* (London and New York, 1987), vol. VI, pp. 317–321.

———— "Myth and Ritual," in his *Encyclopedia of Religion* (London and New York, 1987), vol. X, pp. 282–285.

Epstein, J. N., *Mevo'ot le-Sifrut ha-Tanna'im* (*Introductions to Tannaitic Literature*) (Jerusalem, 1957).

———— *Mehqarim be-Sifrut ha-Talmud uve-leshonot Shemi'im* (*Studies in Talmudic Literature and Semitic Languages*), ed. E. Z. Melamed (Jerusalem, 1991).

———— *Mavo le-nusah ha-Mishnah,* 3rd edn (*Introduction to the Mishnaic Text*) (Jerusalem, 2000).

Fishwick, D., *The Imperial Cult in the Latin West* (Leiden, 1987), vol. I, p. 1.

Flusser, D. and Safrai, S., "The Essenes' Doctrine of Hypostasis and Rabbi Meir," *Immanuel,* 14 (1982): 47–57.

Fraade, S. T., "The Torah of the King (Deuteronomy 17:14–20) in the Temple Scroll and Early Rabbinic Law," in J. R. Davila (ed.), *The Dead Sea Scrolls as Background to Postbiblical Judaism and Early Christianity:*

Papers from an International Conference at St. Andrews in 2001 (Leiden, 2003), pp. 25–60.

Frankel, Y., "The Halakhah in Aggadic Narratives" (in Hebrew), in J. Sussman and D. Rosenthal (eds.), *Talmudic Studies* (Jerusalem, 1990), pp. 205–215.

—— *Darkei ha-Aggadah veha-Midrash* (*The Ways of Aggadah and Midrash*) (Givatayim, 1991).

Frankfort, H., *Kingship and the Gods: A Study of Ancient Near Eastern Religion as the Integration of Society and Nature* (Chicago, Ill., 1971).

Freeman, G. M., *The Heavenly Kingdom: Aspects of Political Thought in Talmud and Midrash* (Lanham, Md., 1986).

Gafni, I. M., "Yeshiva and Metivta" (in Hebrew), *Zion*, 43 (1978): 12–37.

—— "A Generation of Scholarship on Eretz Israel in the Talmudic Era: Achievement and Reconsideration" (in Hebrew), *Cathedra*, 100 (2001): 199–226.

Galinsky, K., *Augustan Culture: An Interpretive Introduction* (Princeton, NJ, 1996).

Garsiel, M., "The Dispute Between Samuel and the People" (in Hebrew), *Beit Miqra*, 87 (1981): 324–343.

German, G., *Melekh Yisrael: Ribbonut l'dorot ber'i ha-Halakhah* (*Kingship in Israel: The Halachic View of Sovereignty through History*) (B'nei-Berak, 2003).

Ginzberg, L., *Perushim ve-Hiddushm be-Yerushalmi* (*A Commentary on the Palestinian Talmud: A Study of the Development of the Halakah and Haggadah in Palestine and Babylonia*) (New York, 1941–1961).

Goldin J., *Hillel the Elder: The Emergence of Classical Judaism* (New York, 1956).

Goodblatt, D., "The Origins of Roman Recognition of the Palestinian Patriarchate" (in Hebrew), in *Studies in the History of the Jewish People and the Land of Israel* (Haifa, 1978), vol. IV, pp. 89–102.

—— "The Title *Nasi* and the Ideological Background of the Second Revolt" (in Hebrew), in A. Oppenheimer and U. Rappaport (eds.), *The Bar-Kokhva Revolt: A New Approach* (Jerusalem, 1984), pp. 113–132.

—— *The Monarchic Principle: Studies in Jewish Self-Government in Antiquity* (Tübingen, 1994).

—— "The Union of Priesthood and Kingship in Second Temple Judea" (in Hebrew), *Cathedra*, 102 (2001): 7–28.

Goodman, M., *State and Society in Roman Galilee, AD 132–212* (Totowa, NJ, 1983).

Goshen-Gottstein, A., "God and Israel as Father and Son in Tannaitic Literature" (in Hebrew), doctoral dissertation, Hebrew University of Jerusalem, 1987.

Halbertal, M., *Mahpekhot Parshaniyot be-hithavutan* (*Interpretative Revolutions in the Making: Values as Interpretative Considerations in Midrashei Halakhah*) (Jerusalem, 1997).

—— "God's Kingship," in M. Walzer, Menachem Lorberbaum, Noam J. Zohar, and Yair Lorberbaum (eds.), *The Jewish Political Tradition*, vol. I: *Authority* (New Haven, Conn., 2000), pp. 128–132.

Halevi, E. E., "The Authority of Kingship" (in Hebrew), *Tarbiz*, 38 (1969): 225–230.

Harvey, Z., "Anarchy and Theocracy in Martin Buber's Philosophy" (in Hebrew), in A. Kasher and M. Halamish (eds.), *Israelite Philosophy* (Tel Aviv, 1983), pp. 9–19.

Hassid, A., "Ethical Compromise: Two Justifications" (in Hebrew), *Iyyun*, 50 (2001): 107–130.

Heinemann, J., *ha-Tefillah be-tequfat ha-Tanna'im veha-Amoraim* (*Prayer in the Period of the Tanna'im and the Amora'im: Its Nature and Its Patterns*) (Jerusalem, 1966).

Hendel, R. S., "The Social Origins of the Aniconic Tradition in Early Israel," *The Catholic Biblical Quarterly*, 50 (1988): 365–382.

Henshke, D., "When is the Time of Hakhel?" (in Hebrew), *Tarbiz*, 61 (1992): 177–194.

—— "How 'the King's Portion?' On Methods of Editing the Mishna," (in Hebrew), *Sidra*, 16 (2000): 21–32.

Herr, M. D., "Roman Rule in Tannaitic Literature (Its Image and Valuation)" (in Hebrew), doctoral dissertation, Hebrew University of Jerusalem, 1970.

Higger, M., "*Perek Kinyan Torah*" (in Hebrew), *Horev*, 2 (1936): 285–296.

Idel, M., *Kabbalah: New Perspectives* (New Haven, Conn., 1988).

—— *Messianic Mystics* (New Haven, Conn., 1998).

Japhet, S., *The Ideology of the Book of Chronicles and its Place in Biblical Thought* (Frankfurt, 1969).

Jewett, R., *Paul's Anthropological Terms: A Study of Their Use in Conflict Setting* (Leiden, 1971).

Kahana, M. I., *Otzar Kitvei ha-Yad shel Midreshei ha-Halakah: Shihzur ha-'otaqim ve-tiuram* (*Manuscripts of the Halakhic Midrashim an Annotated Catalogue*) (Jerusalem 1995).

—— *Ha-Mekhiltot le-Parashat 'Amaleq* (*The Two Mekhiltot on the Amalek Portion: The Originality of the Version of the Mekhila D'Rabbi Ishma'el with Respect to the Mekhilta of Rabbi Shim'on ben Yohai*) (Jerusalem, 1999).

—— *Sifrei Zuta la-Devarim, muva'ot mi-midrash tanna'i hadash* (*Sifre Zuta on Deuteronomy: Citations from a New Tannaitic Midrash*) (Jerusalem, 2002).

Kalmin, R., *The Sage in Jewish Society in Late Antiquity* (London and New York, 1999).

Kantorowicz, E. H., *The King's Two Bodies: A Study in Mediaeval Political Theology* (Princeton, NJ, 1957).

Kasher, A., "Introduction: The Causal and Circumstantial Background of the War of the Jews Against the Romans" (in Hebrew), in A. Kasher (ed.), *The Great Rebellion: The Reasons and Circumstances for its Outbreak* (Jerusalem, 1983), pp. 9–90.

Kaufmann, Y., *Toldot ha-Emunah ha-Yisraelit* (*The Religion of Israel: From Its Beginnings to the Babylonian Exile*), 8 vols. (Jerusalem, 1960).

———— *Sefer Shoftim* (*The Book of Judges*) (Jerusalem, 1962).

Kfir, Z., "King Yannai and Shimon ben Shetah: An Amoraic Legend in Historical Disguise" (in Hebrew), *Tura*, 3 (1994): 85–97.

Kimelman, R., "The Conflict Between R. Yohanan and Resh Laqish on the Supremacy of the Patriarchate," in *Proceedings of the Seventh World Congress of Jewish Studies: Studies in the Talmud, Halachah and Midrash* (Jerusalem, 1981), pp. 1–20.

———— "R. Yohanan and the Status of the Rabbinate" (in Hebrew), *Shenaton ha-Mishpat ha-Ivri*, 9–10 (1982–1983): 329–358.

———— "The Conflict Between the Priestly Oligarchy and the Sages in the Talmudic Period (An Explication of PT Shabbat 12:3, 13c = Horayot 3:5, 48c)" (in Hebrew), *Zion*, 48 (1983): 135–148.

———— "Laws of War and Its Limitations" (in Hebrew), in I. Gafni and A. Ravitzky (eds.), *The Sanctity of Life and Martyrdom* (Jerusalem, 1993), pp. 233–254.

Kister, M., "Metamorphoses of Aggadic Traditions" (in Hebrew), *Tarbiz*, 60 (1991): 179–224.

———— *'Iyyunim be-Avot de-Rabbi Natan: Nosah 'Arikhah u-Parshanut* (*Studies in Avot de-Rabbi Nathan: Text, Redaction and Interpretation*) (Jerusalem, 1998).

Knohl, I., *The Sanctuary of Silence: The Priestly Torah and the Holiness School* (Minneapolis, Minn.: Fortress Press, 1995).

———— *Be-'Iqvot ha-Mashiah* (*In Wake of the Messiah*) (Jerusalem, 2000).

———— *The Divine Symphony: The Bible's Many Voices* (Philadelphia, Pa., 2003).

Levine, L. I., "The Period of R. Judah Ha-Nasi" (in Hebrew), in Z. Baras, S. Safrai, Y. Zafrir, and M. Stern (eds.), *Eretz Yisrael from the Destruction of the Second Temple until the Muslim Conquest*, vol. I: *Political, Social and Cultural History* (Jerusalem, 1982), pp. 93–118.

———— *Ma'amad ha-Hakhamim be-Eretz Yisrael be-tequfat ha-Talmud* (*The Stature of the Sages in Palestine in the Talmudic Period*) (Jerusalem, 1986).

Levinson, B. M., *Deutoronomy and the Hermeneutics of Legal Innovation* (Oxford, 1998).

—— "The Reconceptualization of Kingship in Deuteronomy and the Deuteronomistic History's Transformation of Torah," *Vetus Testamentum*, 61 (2001): 511–534.

Licht, J., "The Kingdom of God" (in Hebrew), *Encyclopaedia Biblica* (Jerusalem, 1963), vol. IV, p. 1121.

Lieberman, S., *Hellenism in Jewish Palestine* (New York, 1950).

—— *Tosefta Ki-fshutah: Zera'im-Nashim* (Jerusalem 1962).

—— *Greek in Jewish Palestine*, 2nd edn (New York, 1965).

—— "Some Aspects of After Life in Early Rabbinic Literature," in *Harry Austryn Wolfson Jubilee Volume* (Jerusalem, 1965), vol. I, pp. 495–532.

—— *Sheki'in*, 2nd edn (Jerusalem, 1992).

Liebes, Y., "De Natura Dei," in his *Studies in Jewish Myth and Jewish Messianism* (Albany, NY, 1993), pp. 55–61.

Liver J., *Toldot Beit David* (*The House of David: From the Fall of the Kingdom of Judah to the Fall of the Second Commonwealth and After*) (Jerusalem, 1959).

—— "Anointing" (in Hebrew), in *Encyclopedia Biblica* (Jerusalem, 1968), vol. V, pp. 526–531.

—— "King, Kingship" (in Hebrew), in *Encyclopedia Biblica* (Jerusalem, 1968), vol. IV, pp. 1083–1088.

Loewenstamm, S. E., "Man as Image and Son of God" (in Hebrew), *Tarbiz*, 27 (1957): 1–2.

Lorberbaum, M., *Politics and the Limits of Law: Secularizing the Political in Medieval Jewish Thought* (Palo Alto, Calif., 2001).

Lorberbaum, Y., "The Image of God in Rabbinic Literature: Maimonides and Nahmanides" (in Hebrew), doctoral dissertation, Hebrew University of Jerusalem, 1997.

—— "Murder, Capital Punishment and Imago Dei" (Man as the Image of God in Early Rabbinic Literature), *Pelilim*, 7 (1998): 223–272.

—— "'The Doctrine of Corporeality of God Did Not Occur Even for a Single Day to the Sages, May Their Memory Be Blessed' (*The Guide of the Perplexed*, vol. I, p. 46): Anthropomorphism in Early Rabbinic Literature – A Critical Review of Scholarly Research" (in Hebrew), *Mad'ei ha-Yahadut*, 40 (2000): 3–54.

—— *Tzelem Elohim: Halakhah va-Aggadah* (*The Image of God: Halakhah and Aggadah*) (Jerusalem, 2004).

Mantel, H., *Mehqarim be-Toldot ha-Sanhedrin* (*Studies in the History of the Sanhedrin*) (Tel Aviv, 1961).

McCarter, P. K., *I–II Samuel* (Garden City, NY, 1985).

Meeks, W., "Moses as God and King," in J. Neusner (ed.), *Religions in Antiquity* (Leiden, 1970), pp. 354–371.

Meir, O., *Rabbi Yehudah ha-Nasi: Diyuqno shel Manhig be-mesorot Eretz Yisrael u-Bavel (Rabbi Judah the Patriarch: Palestinian and Babylonian Portraits of a Leader)* (Tel Aviv, 1999).

Mettinger, T. N. D., *King and Messiah: The Civil and Sacral Legitimation of the Israelite Kings* (Lund, 1976).

Morag, S., "On Horn, On Salvation and on the Horn of Salvation" (in Hebrew), in his *Studies on Biblical Hebrew* (Jerusalem, 1995), pp. 218–224.

Mowinkel, S., *The Psalms in Israel's Worship*, trans. D. R. Ap-Thomas (Oxford, 1967).

Naveh, J., "Marginalia on the Inscriptions from Dan and Ekron" (in Hebrew), *Eretz-Israel*, 26 (1999): 119–122.

———— "Epigraphic Miscellanea," *Israel Exploration Journal*, 52 (2002): 240–253.

Ne'eman, N., *He-'Avar ha-mekhonen et ha-hoveh (The Past that Shapes the Present: The Creation of Biblical Historiography in the Late First Temple Period and After the Downfall)* (Jerusalem, 2002).

Neusner, J., *Rabbinic Political Theory* (Chicago, Ill., 1991).

Noth, M., "God, King and Nation," in his *The Laws in the Pentateuch and other Essays*, trans. D. R. Ap-Thomas (Edinburgh, 1966), pp. 152–175.

Price, S. F. R., *Rituals and Power: The Roman Imperial Cult in Asia Minor* (Cambridge, 1984).

Rofé, A., "Qumran Paraphrases, the Greek Deuteronomy and the Late History of the Biblical *Nasi*," *Textus*, 14 (1988): 169–173.

Roth, S., *Halakhah and Politics: The Jewish Idea of the State* (New York, 1988).

Safrai, S., "The Attitude of the Aggada to the Halacha" (in Hebrew), in A. Kasher and A. Oppenheimer (eds.), *Dor Le-Dor* (Jerusalem, 1995), pp. 215–234.

Sanders, E. R., *Judaism, Practice and Belief, 63 BCE–66 CE* (Philadelphia, Pa., 1992).

Schechter, S., "*Mekhilta Le-Devarim, Parashat Re'eh*" (in Hebrew), in M. Brann and J. Elbogen, *Festschrift zu Israel Lewy's Siebzigstem Geburtstag* (Breslau, 1911), pp. 187–192.

Schiffman, L. H., *Halakhah, Halikhah u-Meshihiyut be-Kat Midbar Yehudah (Law, Custom and Messianism in the Dead Sea Sect)* (Jerusalem, 1993).

Schneider, M., "*Joseph and Osnat* and Early Jewish Mysticism" (in Hebrew), *Kabbalah*, 3 (1998): 303–344.

Schremer, A., *Zakhar u-Neqevah Bera'am: Nisuin be-shilhei Bayit Sheni uve-tequfat ha-Mishnah veha-Talmud* (*Male and Female He Created Them: Jewish Marriage in the Late Second Temple, Mishnah and Talmud Periods*) (Jerusalem, 2003).

––––––– "Eschatology, Violence and Suicide: An Early Rabbinic Theme and its Influence in the Middle Ages," in A. Amanat and J. J. Collins (eds.), *Apocalypse and Violence* (New Haven, Conn., 2004), pp. 19–43.

––––––– "Seclusion and Exclusion: The Rhetoric of Separation in Qumran and Tannaitic Literature," in S. J. Fraade, A. Shemesh, and R. A. Clements (eds.), *Rabbinic Perspectives: Rabbinic Literature and the Dead Sea Scrolls: Proceedings of the Eighth International Symposium of the Orion Center for the Study of the Dead Sea Scrolls and Associated Literature, January 7–9, 2003* (Leiden, 2006), pp. 127–145.

Schwartz, D. R., *Agrippas ha-Rishon: Melekh Yehudah ha-Aharon* (*Agrippa I: The Last King of Judaea*) (Jerusalem, 1987).

––––––– "On Pharisaic Opposition to the Hasmonean Monarchy," in his *Studies in the Jewish Background of Christianity* (Tübingen, 1992), pp. 44–56.

––––––– "Priesthood and Monarchy in the Hasmonean Period," in his *Studies in the Jewish Background of Christianity* (Tübingen, 1992), pp. 44–56.

Schwartz, S., "Historiography of the Jews in the Talmudic Period (70–640)," in M. Goodman, Jeremy Cohen, and David Sorkin (eds.), *The Oxford Handbook of Jewish Studies* (Oxford, 2002), pp. 79–114.

Seeligmann, I. L., "From Historical Reality to a Historiosophic Approach in the Bible" (in Hebrew), *Peraqim*, 2 (1971): 273–313.

Segal, R. A. (ed.), *The Myth and Ritual Theory: An Anthology* (Oxford, 1998).

Shapira, H., "The Deposition of Rabban Gamaliel: Between History and Legend" (in Hebrew), *Zion*, 64 (1999): 5–38.

––––––– "*Beit ha-Midrash* (the House of Study) during the Late Second Temple Period and the Age of the Mishnah: Institutional and Ideological Aspects" (in Hebrew), doctoral dissertation, Hebrew University of Jerusalem, 2001.

––––––– "The Court in Yavneh: Status, Authority and Functions" (in Hebrew), in Y. Habba and A. Radzyner (eds.), *Studies in Jewish Law: Judge and Judging* (Ramat Gan, 2007), pp. 305–334.

––––––– "The Debate Over Compromise and the Goals of the Judicial Process," *Dinei Yisrael*, 26 (2009): 183–228.

––––––– "'For the Judgment is God's': On the Relation Between God and Human Judgment in Jewish Legal Tradition," *Bar-Ilan Law Review*, 26 (2009): 51–89.

Sicker, M., *The Judaic State: A Study in Rabbinic Political Theory* (New York, 1988).

Silver, A., "Kingship and Political Agency," in M. Walzer, Menachem Lorberbaum, Noam J. Zohar, and Yair Lorberbaum (eds.), *The Jewish Political Tradition* (New Haven, Conn., 2000), pp. 122–126.

Smith, M., "The Image of God: Notes on the Hellenization of Judaism with Especial Reference to Goodenough's Work on Jewish Symbols," *The John Ryland Library*, 40 (1958): 473–512.

Sokoloff, M., *A Dictionary of Jewish Babylonian Aramaic* (Ramat Gan, 2002).

Spiegel, S., *Avot ha-Piyyut: Meqorot u-Mehqarim le-toldot ha-piyyut be-Eretz Yisrael* (*The Fathers of Piyyut: Texts and Studies toward a History of the Piyyut in Eretz Yisrael*) (Jerusalem and New York, 1996).

Stern, D., *Ha-Mashal ba-Midrash: Sipporet u-farshanut be-Sifrut Hazal* (*Parables in Midrash: Narrative and Exegesis in Rabbinic Literature*) (Tel Aviv, 1995).

Stern, M., *Greek and Latin Authors on Jews and Judaism*, 3 vols. (Jerusalem, 1974).

——— "The Reign of Herod and the Herodian Dynasty," in S. Safrai and M. Stern (eds.), *The Jewish People in the First Century* (Assen, 1974), pp. 216–283.

Sussman, J., "Tradition of Learning and Tradition of Versions of the Jerusalem Talmud: To Clarify the Versions of the *Yerushalmi Shekalim*" (in Hebrew), in *Studies in Talmudic Literature: Study Day in Honor of the 80th Birthday of Saul Lieberman* (Jerusalem, 1983), pp. 12–76.

Talmon, S., "The Law of the King" (in Hebrew), in *Sefer Biram* (Jerusalem, 1956), pp. 45–56.

Taylor, L. R., *The Divinity of the Roman Emperor* (Middletown Conn., 1931).

Trifon, D., "A Mishnah Fragment as Evidence of the Status of King Agrippa 2" (in Hebrew), *Cathedra*, 53 (1989): 27–48.

Uffenheimer, B., *Ha-Nevu'ah ha-Qedumah be-Yisrael* (*Ancient Prophecy in Israel*) (Jerusalem, 1984).

Urbach, E. E., *The Sages Their Concepts and Beliefs* (Jerusalem, 1969).

——— *Ha-Halakah: Meqoroteha u-hitpathutah* (*The Halakhah: Its Sources and Development*) (Givataim, 1986).

——— "Laws of Idolatry in the Archaeological and Historical Reality of the Second and Third Centuries" (in Hebrew), in his *From the World of the Sages: Collected Studies* (Jerusalem, 1988), pp. 125–178.

——— "The Biblical Monarchy as Viewed by the Sages" (in Hebrew), in A. Rofé and Y. Zakovitch (eds.), *Isaac Leo Seeligmann Volume: Essays on the Bible and the Ancient World* (Jerusalem, 1983), pp. 439–451.

Also available as E. E. Urbach, *The World of the Sages: Collected Studies* (Jerusalem, 2002), pp. 363–375.

Versnel, H. S., *Transition and Reversal in Myth and Ritual* (Leiden, 1993).

Walzer, M., Lorberbaum, M., Zohar, N. J. and Lorberbaum, Y. (eds.), *The Jewish Political Tradition* (New Haven, Conn., 2000).

Weber, M., *On Charisma and Institution Building: Selected Papers,* ed. S. N. Eisenstadt (Chicago, Ill., 1968).

Weinfeld, M., "God the Creator in Gen. I and in the Prophecy of Second Isaiah" (in Hebrew), *Tarbiz,* 37 (1967): 105–132.

———— "The Covenant of Grant in the OT," *Journal of the American Oriental Society,* 90 (1970): 184–203.

———— *Social Justice in Ancient Israel and in the Ancient Near East* (Jerusalem and Minneapolis, Minn., 1995).

Weisman, Z., *Moshi'im u-Nevi'im: shnei panim shel ha-kharizma ba-Miqra. (Saviours and Prophets: Two Aspects of Biblical Charisma)* (Tel Aviv, 2003).

Weiss, Z., "The Jews of Ancient Palestine and the Roman Games: Rabbinic Dicta vs. Communal Practice" (in Hebrew), *Zion,* 66 (2001): 427–450.

Westermann, C., *Genesis 1–11: A Continental Commentary,* trans. J. J. Scullion (Minneapolis, Minn., 1992).

Winter, I. J., "Idols of the King: Royal Images as Recipient of Ritual Action in Ancient Mesopotamia," *Journal of Ritual Studies,* 6 (1992): 13–42.

Wise, M. O., *A Critical Study of the Temple Scroll From Qumran Cave 11* (Chicago, Ill., 1990).

Wolfson, H. A., *Philo,* rev. edn (Cambridge, Mass., 1962).

Zanker, P., *The Power of Images in the Age of Augustus* (Ann Arbor, Mich., 1990).

Ziegler, I., *Die Königsgleichnisse des Midrasch* (Breslau, 1903).

Zunz, L., *Ha-Derashot be-Yisrael (Sermons in Judaism),* edited and completed by H. Albeck (Jerusalem, 1974).

Index of Sources

Aggadic Midrashim

Babylonian Talmud

Index of Names